Language and Philosophy

Language
AND
Philosophy
STUDIES IN METHOD

MAX BLACK
Professor of Philosophy, Cornell University

Cornell University Press

ITHACA, NEW YORK, 1949

Printed in the United States of America

The inconveniences of living in a country so densely populated with demons, vampires, spirits, ghouls, dragons, omens, forces and influences, both good and bad, as our own unapproachably favoured empire is, cannot be evaded from one end of life to the other.

—*Kai Lung's Golden Hours*

Preface

THESE essays are intended to show how linguistic considerations are relevant to some philosophical problems. Those recommending such an approach still disagree too much about principles and methods for any systematic philosophy of language to have much hope of general acceptance. So I have tried mainly to *use* ideas about language to clarify philosophical problems. I hope also to have shown how some influential doctrines about language need improvement. Serious criticism may be taken as sufficient compliment; and it seemed unnecessary to eulogize those from whom I had so much to learn. Examples for the pillory, if I had wanted them, could have been found more readily in the works of inferior writers.

All but two of these essays (III and X) have been previously published. Misprints and minor inaccuracies of phrasing have been corrected, but no substantial changes have been made. Some answers to criticism are assembled in the section "Additional Notes and References" at the end of the book.

I wish to express my warm thanks to Mr. Paul Ziff who helped with the Index and the proofs.

Permission to reprint some of these essays was kindly granted by the editors of *Philosophy and Phenomenological Research*, *Philosophy of Science*, *Analysis*, *Aristotelian Society Proceedings*, *Philosophical Review*, and *Journal of Philosophy;* by Professor P. A. Schilpp for The Library of Living Philosophers; and by Count Alfred Korzybski for the Institute of General Semantics. To all of these and to the authors and publishers of works from which short quotations have been used I am grateful.

MAX BLACK

Ithaca, New York
April, 1949

Contents

CONTENTS

CONTENTS

Language and Philosophy

I

Linguistic Method
in Philosophy

I. INTRODUCTION

N THIS ESSAY I shall illustrate and explain a method having wide application to philosophical problems, especially to those connected with certain famous sceptical paradoxes. After centuries of discussion, philosophers are still embarrassed by the resurgence of doubts about free will, the reality of time, the existence of other minds and the external world, the possibility of knowledge about the future or matters of fact; and any method which promises to give a satisfactory and permanent answer to such sceptical questionings deserves careful examination.

Linguistic analysis in philosophy can be illustrated by any of the problems mentioned; I shall begin by showing its application to problems arising from the so-called "incommunicability of content." A contemporary version of this sceptical doctrine (quoted from Professor C. I. Lewis' *Mind and the World Order*) will first be shown to generate a peculiar type of *reductio ad absurdum*. In identifying and criticizing the trains of thought leading to so paradoxical a conclusion, I shall hope to make clear the nature of the method employed.

2. AN ILLUSTRATIVE SCEPTICAL PARADOX

The following passage from Professor Lewis' *Mind and the World Order*[1] is a clear formulation of an influential and widely maintained position.

Lewis says:

"Suppose it should be a fact that I should get the sensation you signalize by saying 'red' whenever I look at what you call 'green' and vice versa. Suppose that in the matter of immediate sense qualities my whole spectrum should be exactly the reverse of yours. Suppose even that what are for you sensations of pitch, mediated by the ear, were identical with my feelings of color-quality mediated by the eye. Since no one can look directly into another's mind, and the immediate feeling of red or the middle C can never be conveyed, how

---

[1] New York, 1929, p. 75.

[3]

should we find out if such personal peculiarities should exist? We could never discover them so long as they did not impair the power to discriminate and relate as others do."

Every philosopher knows how exceedingly plausible such arguments as these can appear, and not merely to the professional; the man in the street or the student in the classroom finds them equally persuasive and incredible. It is characteristic of such sceptical arguments, as Hume remarked in a similar connection, that they produce no conviction and yet seem to admit of no refutation. Perhaps nobody, whether professional philosopher or "plain man," really believes that his associates may be having auditory sensations through the eyes; yet, in the light of the sceptical considerations advanced, it seems impossible that any evidence could refute such a possibility. (For are we not always supplied with the mere outward symptoms of the other person's unknown and for ever unknowable inner condition?)

Before criticizing the thesis of incommunicability of content, let us make sure that we understand exactly what is being *asserted*.

Lewis has told us, in effect, that another person never succeeds in conveying all that he intends to say; for he means to refer to the felt and enjoyed *content* of his experiences, while we are able to apprehend only their *relational structure*. Let us pause therefore to consider another, more familiar, type of situation in which a speaker's words may convey partial and fragmentary information concerning his intended meaning.

Let it be supposed that some Latin American, lately arrived from Venezuela, is giving a report on political conditions in his native land; and that his account is enlivened by constant references to the intrigues and struggles of the so-called "Greens" and "Yellows." Our Venezuelan friend, we may further suppose, is acquainted with members of the Green and Yellow parties; he has encountered specimens of the denotation of each of these terms. We, his hearers, having never visited Venezuela, are, however, unacquainted with any individuals who are "Greens" or "Yellows"; the two

[4]

terms accordingly mean less to us than to the man who uses them. To be more precise, "Greens" means to us exactly the same as "members of some Venezuelan political party, we don't know which"; and "Yellows" exactly the same as "members of some other Venezuelan political party, we don't know which." More concisely, the two terms have, *for us*, connotation but no denotation; while for the Venezuelan they have both connotation and denotation.

This situation is, in some respects, very similar to that depicted in Lewis' account. When any man uses the words "green" or "yellow," the words are understood by him to refer to certain experiences to which he has direct access. But we, the hearers, are barred from visiting the country of his mind; nor could we ever find conveyance to transport us into that permanently inaccessible region. The word "green," in the mouth of our interlocutor, denotes some distinctive "feelings of color-quality" (to use Lewis' language); to us, who cannot "look directly into his mind," it can, at best, connote "some experiential quality, we don't know which."

It may be useful to summarize the situation in another way by saying that words such as "green" and "yellow," according to Lewis' account, are *constants* for a speaker who uses them, but mere variables to his hearers. In place of "green" and "yellow" he might with equal significance (though at the cost of some practical inconvenience) use "X" and "Y." And he would still be understood quite as well, provided it was clear that his "X" and "Y" connoted some unknown *experiential quality*. Should less than this be conveyed, communication would be impossible. If "X" and "Y" stood not for some unknown experiential quality but rather for something whose generic nature was *completely* unknown, we should be quite at a loss to decipher the speaker's intention. For a speaker to be understood, even on Lewis' interpretation, his symbols must communicate at least the generic nature of their referents. X and Y therefore must be partially known, though also partially unknown. They mean some unknown *experiential quality*, not something completely unknown.

[5]

Now we can see an important difference between the inability of a speaker to make us acquainted with the felt quality of his experiences and the inability of a foreigner to acquaint us with the denotation of *his* terms. We were able to understand part of what was said by the Venezuelan because, and only because, we *were* familiar with specimens of the denotation of *some* of the terms he was using; we knew that the "Yellows" were "members of some political party," and these terms, "members," "political," "party," were for us constants, not variables. The variables used by our Venezuelan friend were understood because they came to us in a setting of constants. His terms had connotation *for us* because they connoted general characteristics exemplified in *our* experience. And if this were not the case, his remarks would be gibberish. If *all* his symbols were variables, our condition in regard to them would be that of Alice trying to interpret the Jabberwocky poem. ("Somehow it seems to fill my head with ideas —only I don't exactly know what they are.")

And now we come to the decisive point. On Lewis' showing, we ought to find every utterance of *every* speaker as baffling as Jabberwocky. For the very same considerations which inculcate scepticism concerning the individual *qualia* of another person's experiences ought to raise insuperable doubts concerning the character of the classes to which they belong. If we cannot be sure that another person means by "red" or "middle C" the same as ourselves, we have no better grounds for believing that such relatively general terms as "sensations," "sense-quality," or "feeling" mean the same to hearer and speaker. We cannot even be sure that the names of colors and tastes apply at all to sensory experience rather than to some features of, say, logical deduction.

An easy way to make this clear is to adapt the language of the original quotation in some such fashion as this:

"Suppose that what for you are sensations, mediated by the senses, are for Lewis thoughts, mediated by the mind. Since no one can look directly into Lewis' mind, except Lewis himself, how should the rest of us ever find out that what for us is a bitter taste is not for him awareness of the inconsistency of a proposition?"

The argument works just as well; and not only in this case, but also in that of every term that Lewis or anybody else uses, whether empirical or logical. For the central tenet of Lewis' scepticism is that congruity of linguistic behavior is no guarantee of identity of the enjoyed qualities of experience. But what other grounds do we have for *any* knowledge about the contents of another person's mind? The question is rhetorical: on Lewis' view, "sensation" and "experience," "structure" and "identity," and *all* the words a sceptic uses, ought to be constants for him, variables for us. If we find Lewis' argument persuasive, we ought, in order to be consistent, to recognize that all *his own* sentences can mean nothing more to us than "Some unknown X stands in some unknown relation Y to some unknown Z." And if a phrase like this, riddled with variables, still fills our head with ideas—though we "don't exactly know what they are"—it is only because we allow ourselves still to use the *definite* term "relation." Strictly speaking, even this word is a variable when used by Lewis, and all his utterances are mere collocations of completely indefinite symbols.

On Lewis' view indeed, we ought to be in no position to understand *any* of his own statements. And if this is so, his view involves a very peculiar type of *reductio ad absurdum*. For if his thesis were true, it would be *meaningless* to us; therefore we cannot be expected to understand it; therefore we cannot be expected to believe it. (The form of this *reductio* is, of course, somewhat different from the more familiar type of argument in which some proposition is shown to entail its own falsity.)

To state the situation more bluntly: only the sceptic can ever know what he means by his sceptical assertions; and he can never tell us.

Conversely, if we *can* understand him and his contention *is* meaningful, then his thesis is untrue. (We may compare a type of dialogue familiar to those who know young children:

[7]

"Say elephant." "Can't." "Can't say what?" "Can't say elephant!")

3. TRANSITION TO SOLIPSISM

It is easy to slide from belief in incommunicability of content to solipsism and behaviorism. And these other versions of scepticism present, more strikingly, certain features of the sceptical position needing emphasis.

The transition to solipsism is a very natural one. The ground for maintaining that the felt quality of another's experiences is forever beyond our ken is the fact that we must rely upon external observations of his actions and speech. Since we cannot "look directly" into another's mind, the concordance of his words with our own is no evidence for identity of experiential quality.

Now, by the same token, there is, from this standpoint, no evidence at all even for the *existence* of another person's experiences. So long as he says "red" when I say "red" and "green" when I do (and so on for all words), how am I to know that he sees or smells or hears or indeed experiences *anything?* Since *all* the observable criteria are the same whether other people do or do not have experiences, how could we ever discriminate between the two possibilities? Perhaps all other people are, after all, no more than elaborate but unfeeling machines.

This solipsistic position is arrived at by the same kind of considerations and has the same degree of plausibility as the scepticism we originally considered.

The point now to be emphasized is that the *philosophical* doubt concerning the possibility of knowing another person's experiences is easily confused with a different kind of doubt arising in a *practical* context.

Everybody is familiar with a kind of doubt which can arise concerning the credibility of a witness or the genuineness of apparent manifestations of emotion. We may reasonably doubt whether an actor portraying King Lear really feels the bitterness of man's ingratitude every night punctually at nine.

[8]

And the fact that he displays familiar symptoms of consterna-
tion and grief may leave us puzzled. But this is a practical
difficulty which we know very well how to resolve by conversation with the actor, inspection of his private diary, and
so on. That the *philosophical* doubt is of a different type is
made clear by the fact that *no* testimony of the actor, oral or
written, has the least tendency to establish the condition of his
state of mind, or the existence in him of any feelings whatsoever. For the interpretation of the actor's testimony would be
based upon concordance of his linguistic behavior with our
own. And we saw that, according to the sceptic, such concordance is *no* evidence for the character of the actor's inner
experience.

At times it does seem as if the philosopher who is worried
about the existence of other minds is trying to solve a *practical*
difficulty; that he is really in search of some more efficient lie
detector or some other contrivance for overcoming hypocrisy
and the chronic deceitfulness of man.

Yet every *practical* device for facilitating communication between persons is irrelevant to the extreme forms of philosophical scepticism. Imagine the most fantastic contraption for
ensuring access to another person's experiences—a super
electron microscope for detecting the cerebral concomitants
of his utterances, or a Wellsian telepathic inductance coil for
producing simultaneous sensations of identical quality. Even
so, the sceptic would be not a jot nearer to "looking directly"
into another's mind. For he would still be having *his own* experience, whether of seeing gray matter in the microscope, or
feeling a stabbing pain whenever *you* sat on a pin. The sceptical doubt about the existence of other minds (in the extreme
form here considered) is not a practical difficulty and cannot
be resolved by the practical procedures of the witness box
or the laboratory.

4. ARGUMENT FROM ANALOGY

The distinction made between empirical and philosophical
difficulties will prepare us to understand why argument from

[9]

analogy is worthless as a means of refuting scepticism about the existence of other minds. This is not the usual view. On the contrary, it is generally said that we do believe that other minds exist on analogical grounds. When I see a pin stuck into *my* body, I experience a pain; hence when I see a pin stuck into *your* body, I argue *by analogy* that *you* are feeling a pain. And this hypothesis is confirmed by your testimony and subsequent behavior.

This account of the matter is indeed a description of how we may resolve the practical or empirical question whether another person is feeling pain. But the type of pain to which the sceptic refers is, as we saw, logically independent of all outward symptoms. The sceptic says that the screams of the wounded soldier are compatible *either* with his being in pain *or* with his being in the condition of exquisite enjoyment *or* even with the absence in him of any feelings whatsoever. Thus the very observations which we should use in an *empirical* study of pain are, on the sceptic's own account, quite worthless as evidence. For all the evidence, however fortified by further observation, is as compatible with the contradiction of the proposition to be proved as with that proposition itself.

Consider how analogy is used in a genuinely scientific or empirical inquiry. If we know that a certain species of fish carry an electric charge, we may reasonably conclude, with some degree of probability, that another closely related species will also bear an electric charge. But this conclusion will need to be strengthened by observing a representative selection of the second species of fish. For if the two species are alike in some respects, they also differ in others—else there would be nothing to prove—and some risk is always involved in neglecting the *dis*analogy between the things compared.

Suppose, now, the scientist were to be told that the question to be determined was the presence in the second species of fish of a kind of electricity which could never be detected by any observations or the application of any experimental procedures. How much weight would he *then* attach to any argument from analogy? Surely none at all, for the kind of electricity whose presence is to be established is by hypothesis utterly unlike anything with which he has had dealings; and he is told in advance that all conceivable observation would be equally compatible either with its presence or with its absence. In such a case the scientist would throw up his hands in incomprehension and despair.

For this reason we can hardly make much headway against scepticism by using Professor Moore's celebrated defense of common sense. We might adapt his way of talking and say as emphatically as we please: "How absurd it would be (and how callous too) to suggest that we did not know that a man whose leg was being amputated without an anaesthetic was in pain. And how still more absurd to suggest that *for all the appearances show* he might actually enjoy the experience!"

This is excellent argument at the common-sense level. But to the sceptic it is as irrelevant as Dr. Johnson trying to refute Berkeley by striking his foot against a stone. The sceptic would grant the absurdity of buying only *one* glove at a time, on the ground that the second hand might not exist, or of refusing to administer ether on the ground that the patient might not really be in pain. He did not need Moore to teach him how to behave in these practical contexts. But since the sceptic still insists that all the appearances are compatible with the sceptical thesis, we are back to the starting point. It was Moore's great merit to bring vividly to our attention the difference between an empirical and a philosophical issue, between a proof that would satisfy a selective service board and one that would convince Spinoza. But this doesn't solve the philosophical difficulty.

It is just because the philosopher secretly believes all the time that other people really do have feelings, while also believing that he has no grounds for such a belief, that the paradox persists. Nor does it help much to show, as was done earlier in this essay, that the sceptical thesis leads to absurdity. For it is the sign of a paradox that it leads by what seems irreproachable reasoning to an absurd result; and a paradox is not resolved until we understand why the reasoning is

[11]

wrong. Let us make a fresh start and examine closely the reasoning by which the sceptic reaches his conclusions.

5. LINGUISTIC ANALYSIS OF THE SCEPTICAL ARGUMENTS

Belief in incommunicability of content, and the solipsism to which it leads, may be reached in many ways. One train of thought I want to examine more closely arises from reflection upon abnormality of vision (or other sense experiences) and the difficulty of its detection. (It is a special form of the argument from illusion.)

A characteristic soliloquy by a sceptic might take this form:

"We all know about color blindness; and experts tell us that adults who are color-blind very often escape detection. A man who is color-blind shows great skill in hiding his abnormality by noticing differences in texture, slight defects in material, and other minute details commonly overlooked. Therefore anybody—even my best friend—might be color-blind, for all I know. An expert psychologist might find out the truth by inventing artificial and complex situations. But even *his* tests might not serve, and a sufficiently ingenious man might still be able to conceal his abnormality. Why should there not be a type of color blindness too subtle for *any* psychologist *ever* to discover? A man *might* agree with other people's behavior in *every* respect and so elude *every* test that could be applied. How could we ever know? Perhaps everybody is like this? And if I cannot be sure that my friend is not color blind, how can I be sure of *anything* about his experiences, or those of anybody else?"

From this point on, the argument takes a course with which we are now familiar: Since everybody might be color-blind in a way which no tests could reveal, it is impossible to be sure they are not. And exactly the same type of argument can of course be applied just as well to any other sense quality. We can never be sure that others do not smell when we see, or think when we feel, never be sure that they think or feel at all.

What has happened in the course of this imaginary, but

[12]

quite characteristic, line of thought? The central point to emphasize is that the criteria of application of the term "color blindness" used by the speaker *have gradually shifted* in the course of the argument. At the outset, the color blindness to which reference is made was the kind studied by psychologists. This type of color blindness is important in certain practical contexts (say that of the selection of engine drivers) and is recognizable in such situations by the application of well-known tests. *This* kind of color blindness is *defined* in terms of capacity to satisfy the tests.

The claim that this type of color blindness is so defined does not imply that the term "color blindness" has a single, authoritative, and explicit verbal definition. For some restricted purposes the term may be introduced into discourse by this kind of definition—a formal explanation of its meaning—but for ordinary purposes no precise statement of this kind is available. The claim that "color blindness," in the sense in which it is ordinarily used, is *defined* by its tests, does not assert that the tests are definite and precise. What is meant is that the use of the term is learned by taking note of the *kind* of thing which is evidence for that term's exemplification. We teach a child or a foreigner the *meaning* of the word "color blindness" by showing him situations in which the use of the term would be appropriate. We say, in effect, "this is a case of undoubted color blindness" and "that is a case of undoubted normality of color vision" and "that, again, is a borderline case." When the child or the foreigner has learned to describe these various situations as we do, we say he has learned to use the word. It would therefore be stupid to ask "Why should these vague tests be relevant to color blindness?"—just as stupid as asking "Why should pigs be called 'pigs'?" It is a *fact* that we do use the noise "pigs" to refer to porcine quadrupeds; it is a *fact* that the word "color blindness" is normally used to refer to a condition revealed by vaguely demarcated tests.

Nevertheless the sceptic is dissatisfied with the common usage of the vague term and would remain dissatisfied with every more precise substitute which the psychologist might

[13]

invent. If we could fully understand the source of this dissatisfaction, we should be near to a solution of the sceptical paradoxes.

What worries the philosophical sceptic so much is that the ordinary tests of color blindness, from a certain standpoint, appear so *arbitrary*.

This arbitrariness can be made clear by thinking about cases of borderline successes in passing the tests. A man who passes the tests now in vogue among psychologists might conceivably fail if the tests were made only *slightly* harder; and this hypothetical case does not seem to differ *in principle* from that of a man, who, failing to pass the current tests, would be *called* "color-blind." The two cases are different, of course, for one man passes and the other fails the present tests of abnormality; but the difference seems so slight that we can hardly help regarding it as unimportant. We feel a strong inclination (once we get into this way of thinking) to say that the term "color blindness" *ought* to be applied also to the case of a man who would fail at the slightly harder level.

If the tests *are* slightly modified, however, in the way the sceptic wishes, exactly the same objections could be brought against the new tests. And it is obvious that the same would be true of *every* definition of "color blindness" by means of a finite number of tests. No matter *what* tests were proposed, we could always imagine a man who just *barely managed* to pass them and always feel the same inclination to say his case did not differ *in principle* from that of his more successful competitors.

We are thereby driven to use "color blindness" in what I shall call a *limiting sense* (to be opposed to the *practical senses* of color blindness which are useful to the ordinary man or the psychologist). What especially characterizes the limiting sense of color blindness is the possibility of making such statements as that "there might be a case of 'color blindness' (in this limiting sense) which *no* tests could reveal."[2]

Similarly a sceptic may say: "You cannot be sure of the

[2] The meaning of "limiting sense" is explained later in this essay.

result of tomorrow's elections, even if the Gallup Poll does give an overwhelming majority for the Democrats. Even if all the voters told you their intentions in advance, you could not be sure, for they might change their minds. Evidence about the future can never be perfect."

Or he may say, following an ancient theological pattern: "A man's soul is clearly not the same as his body. He can lose both legs without loss of consciousness, and the same might conceivably be true of the loss of any limb or bodily organ. Now imagine a man to lose the whole of his body. What is *then* left, what could not conceivably be felt or touched or communicated with, is what I call the soul."

All three of these examples involve the introduction of limiting senses of crucial terms. And to all of them one appropriate reply would be "I fail to understand what you mean." If the sceptic uses "color blindness" initially in the way we commonly do (i.e., if we understand him at the outset), he is talking about the kind of thing revealed by *some* test however complicated. If he continues to mean even a part of this, to talk of a color blindness which is *in principle* not to be revealed is to contradict himself: it is to say that his limiting kind of color blindness both does and does not satisfy tests. And if he means something different by "color blindness" *in his sense*, then all we can say is that we fail to understand either the denotation or the connotation of his term: his statements contain semantic hiatuses.

Similar comment applies to the other two examples: *perfect* evidence for tomorrow's election results is a self-contradictory notion, if evidence still means what it usually means; but if it means something else, the onus is upon the sceptic to explain what it *does* mean. The notion of an invisible man is intelligible, as is that of an odorless and intangible man, but the notion of a soul with whom no communication could *in principle* be established is either self-contradictory or unintelligible. We can, by some stretch of the imagination, understand a Cheshire cat leaving only its grin behind; but a cat sans whiskers, sans body, sans grin, sans *everything*—everything

[15]

that might somehow, sometime, be detected—is a mere nothing.

To drive home the futility of these linguistic proceedings, let us consider how a limiting sense of a term would be introduced into a language. We saw a little while ago how the meaning of the term "color blindness" (in its familiar practical use) is made plain to a child or foreigner. He is shown cases where the term does apply, cases where it does not apply, and cases where its application is "doubtful" or "indeterminate." And it was a very important part of this learning procedure that cases of applicability were *contrasted* with cases of nonapplicability. We learn what "color blindness" means by getting to know what would be evidence for its *presence* and what would be evidence for its *absence*. Exactly the same is true of all terms applying to items or aspects of experience. We learn to use the word "knowledge" by contrasting cases of knowledge with cases of doubt and knowledge to the contrary; we learn to use "red" by learning the difference between cases of things being colored red, and their being colored green or some other color; we understand the word "variable" when we can distinguish a symbol which is a variable from one which is a constant, and so on.

Now suppose that, after a child had learned to use a term in this familiar way, the sceptic were to try to introduce to him a *limiting* sense of the term. Obviously the sceptic cannot produce *specimens:* for it is part of his contention that no specimens of the applications of terms in *his* senses can ever be encountered; the best he can do is to say something like this: "You have learned that there is a whole series of harder and harder tests of color blindness and corresponding *degrees* of that abnormality. Now imagine a color blindness *just like the kind with which you are already familiar*, but satisfying *none* of this series of tests—a color blindness infinitely hard to detect."

Or he says "You know what is meant by saying that this evidence for the result of tomorrow's election is stronger than that; you know how to arrange evidence about the character of the future in a series of steadily increasing probability. Now

[16]

imagine evidence *just like the kind you already know* but so strong that its probability could not be increased—infinitely probable evidence. That is what I call *real* evidence about the future."

Or he says, "Imagine a man to lose his body; what remains unaffected by injury, death, or decay is what I call the real, the essential man."

If we try to obey such linguistic instructions as these, we are bound to get into insuperable difficulties. It is as if we were told that a physical object were not really small unless it did not exist at all; or that an egg was not really cooked until it was boiled an infinite length of time. The new instructions in the limiting use of the terms conflict with the older explanations for the practical use of the homonyms.

It should, by now, be clear why a limiting sense of color blindness (or any other term) could never be explained or conveyed to another person. Yet it is just such limiting senses that the sceptic needs if he is to have anything of philosophical importance to say. For any practical doubt about the determination of color blindness in the practical sense could be resolved by practical procedures. (The sceptic is not concerned with the uncertainty of stock markets, the efficiency of psychometrists, or the difficulty of being in the right place to observe an eclipse.)

The label of "*limiting* sense" has been deliberately used to suggest an analogy with the process of "proceeding to the limit" which occurs in mathematics. It is of course a mathematical commonplace that assertions which are true of every member of a converging sequence of quantities may cease to hold where limiting values are inserted. (Thus every member of an infinite sequence may be greater than zero while the limiting value of the sequence is *equal* to zero.) And mathematicians are constantly on guard against the dangers of extrapolating their definitions to apply to limiting cases.

A simple mathematical example of the illegitimate introduction of limiting senses would arise if we were to talk about the *terminal digit of an infinite decimal*.

To talk in this way is to *assume* that the new phrase has

[17]

denotation, and in this instance the assumption is unjustified. Every finite (or terminating) decimal has of course a final digit. But to ask the value of *the* terminal digit of an infinite decimal is to do one of two things: *either* to imply that an infinite decimal has a final digit (a self-contradiction) *or* to introduce a *new but undefined and unexplained* locution.

It may be objected that the extrapolation of meanings is a procedure very characteristic of mathematics and the empirical sciences. And so it is; the history of mathematics and empirical science is full of fumbling attempts to introduce new terms. But these historical instances (of the first introduction of such terms as "infinitesimal," "infinite sum," "irrational number," "potential energy," "quasi-species," and the like) differ in an important respect from the philosophical transformations of common language. The mathematician or scientist introduces new terms to permit him to describe newly discovered relationships (homologous to those already in his possession). The first descriptions introduced may be confused and Pickwickian distortions of older terms, *but the new technical terms eventually receive an intelligible and self-consistent definition.*

The sceptic's attempt to introduce new terms is different. *He* has made no startling or unexpected discoveries about other minds, the future, or the external world; he is no fine connoisseur of evidence, prognostication, or moral judgment. He knows just what any other man knows, but insists on describing that knowledge differently. His alteration of common language is pointless because it serves no purpose at all except that of confusion of thought.

I have been trying to hold distinct two different ways in which pointless alteration of language can happen. When a term is used in a limiting sense in such a way that part of the original meaning is retained, it is *self-contradictory;* when continuity with the original meaning is severed, so that no clue is left to the intended meaning of the term in its new usage, it may be said to be used *vacuously*. Our criticism of the sceptical argument can now be summarized by saying that it involves the use of crucial terms in senses which are either vacuous or self-contradictory.

It has been urged that the philosopher is driven into the extremes of irrefutable scepticism by a search for distinctions *of principle* arising from dissatisfaction with the vagueness and continuity of application of ordinary language. The sceptic does succeed in the end in making a distinction of principle; but the principle is that involved in the distinction between a term having some meaning, though vague and fluctuating, and another incapable of exemplification because it is vacuous or self-contradictory by definition. The presence of such terms renders the sceptical objections in a very important respect meaningless; that Lewis' procedure entailed the meaninglessness of its own formulation is now seen to be no accident of his exposition, but rather a necessary consequence of what he set out to do.

All the examples so far used illustrate transition to limiting vacuity or self-contradiction. In other cases where linguistic considerations of the type which I have been presenting are relevant, a different though related pattern of thought may be observed.

This may be shown by considering one plausible retort to the above arguments against scepticism with respect to the existence of other minds. The sceptic might well object to the accusation that his use of "color blindness" or the more inclusive term "experience" is vacuous. For, he might say, *he himself* has actual experience of sense qualities, an experience *not identical* with its outward manifestations. Since "experience" means, for him, something *over and above* the tests, the term is *not* vacuous.

With part of this objection there is no need to disagree. It may be granted that a pain is not the *same* as its manifestations. But since the assertion has a deceptive appearance of being empirical it might be better to rephrase it in some such form as "we do not mean by 'pain' the same as 'manifestations of pain'; the 'manifestations' are symptoms of or evidence *for* the pain; they are not identical with the pain."

[19]

But though this is granted, the conclusion desired by the sceptic does not follow. And here again the procedure recommended is a careful consideration of how the sceptic could explain or introduce that sense of experience in which it refers to something accessible to him alone.

Once again we should begin by considering carefully how we learn to understand and above all to *contrast* such phrases as "*my* experience," "*your* experience," and "*his* experience" in practical contexts. There are familiar and common usages of these related expressions, and to understand them is to know the empirical tests which would be relevant to their exemplification. About these terms, in their familiar uses in practical contexts, there is no mystery and no *philosophical* problem.

Next we imagine the sceptic trying to explain what he means by an experience accessible to him alone. We may perhaps suppose him to be making an empirical assertion—implying perhaps that he himself is maladroit in speech and gestures. No, we are told, the difficulty is not of that practical order at all. Indeed, he assures us (for we remember that he is committed to the extremities of scepticism), this experience of which he speaks has *no* connection with its outward manifestations. Indeed it is a kind of accident that his experiences are accompanied by those outward symptoms. In some other possible world, he might have laughed where he now cries; in still another, feelings, even the strongest, might never be displayed at all. Nothing that we see or hear or touch is evidence *at all* for the personal and "private" sense qualities he is designating.

If he does say all this, we ought to reply that we *literally fail to understand what he means.* He doesn't mean what we *normally* mean by another person's experience, for the character of such experience we *can* infer from observations. But what else he means has not been made clear; the term "private experience" (experience in principle inaccessible to observation) is vacuous.

This case differs from that of "color blindness" (discussed

earlier) in the absence of any progression to the limit. The root of the trouble in this and some other versions of solipsism or idealism seems to be in the determination to apply a term *universally*, so that *every* item of knowledge shall be called a case of *my* knowledge or experience.

The explanations so far given are unlikely to convince a *genuine* sceptic; for he still has many lines of defense. He might perhaps retort that it is *we* who are stretching the common and familiar use of the term "meaning"; that he himself very well understands what he is talking about; that we must have understood him or else have had nothing to which to object; and that it is absurd to suggest that a man like Hume might have talked nonsense without knowing it!

Our response to this counterattack will be the same as that already sufficiently illustrated. We must try to get our sceptic to reflect upon the ways in which he now uses "meaning," to consider the tests he would be prepared to accept as constitutive of its application, and especially to examine the ways in which his tests differ from those already current.

The linguistic analysis is here more difficult in proportion to the notorious ambiguity of the central term "meaning." And we must not suppose that the simple critical considerations previously presented will serve without modification. The prevalence of linguistic confusions of the type I have been discussing is evidence of the difficulty of the critical enterprise here recommended. A full examination of the puzzles connected with solipsism alone would demand thorough discussion of a whole group of cross-related terms (especially the epistemological ones, "possibility," "knowledge," and so on).

Experience in the criticism of such puzzles suggests that the sceptical difficulty does in many cases arise from the surreptitious introduction of vacuous or self-contradictory terminology. Where the cases differ is in the great variety of routes by which competent and determined thinkers are led into making such terminological changes.

The method here recommended would be effective to the degree that it was able to take account of such individual differences. To say "it is all a matter of words" is too easy to be rewarding. What should be done is to show in detail exactly what it is that makes such formulas as "Everything is really mind," or "A proposition is nothing but its method of verification," or "Truth is only practical usefulness," or "Ethical judgments are mere exclamations" so perennially attractive (though not to all philosophers at once).

At some point in these wider explorations, we could make good use of a general description of those features of language which are of special relevance to philosophical puzzles.

The last point to be made concerns the *type* of evidence which could be produced in defense of the procedures here recommended. All that needs to be said at present is that the evidence is no more esoteric or otherwise mysterious than that employed in any empirical enterprise. We are, it is true, not offering direct evidence for or against the sceptic's position (except in a preliminary stage of the proceedings). But we do invite him to reflect conscientiously and persistently upon the meanings of the terms he is using. Evidence for the meaning of terms is obtained by the makers of dictionaries in perfectly familiar ways; the case of individual and variant or fluctuating meanings is more difficult of resolution, but the difficulty is a *practical* one. When we are engaged in clarifying genuine philosophical difficulties, the author of the paradox may be the best judge of the success with which his linguistic and epistemological intentions are made plain to him. But the methods he uses in detecting his own meanings are the ordinary empirical ones which can in principle be employed by any lexicographer, or translator, or linguist.

Philosophical clarification of meaning is, on this view, as practical as slum clearance and as empirical as medicine.

II

Vagueness:
An Exercise in
Logical Analysis

Vagueness and accuracy are important notions, which it is very necessary to understand—BERTRAND RUSSELL

The notation, however, is what we lack, and the verdict of the mere feeling is liable to fluctuate.—HENRY JAMES

I. INTRODUCTION

T IS A PARADOX, whose importance familiarity fails to diminish, that the most highly developed and useful scientific theories are ostensibly expressed in terms of objects never encountered in experience. The line traced by a draftsman, no matter how accurate, is seen beneath the microscope as a kind of corrugated trench, far removed from the ideal line of pure geometry. And the "point-planet" of astronomy, the "perfect gas" of thermodynamics, or the "pure species" of genetics are equally remote from exact realization. Indeed the unintelligibility at the atomic or subatomic level of the notion of a rigidly demarcated boundary shows that such objects not merely are not but could not be encountered. While the mathematician constructs a theory in terms of "perfect" objects, the experimental scientist observes objects of which the properties demanded by theory are and can, in the very nature of measurement, be only approximately true. As Duhem remarks, mathematical deduction is not useful to the physicist if interpreted rigorously. It is necessary to know that its validity is unaltered when the premise and conclusion are only "approximately true."[1] But the indeterminacy thus introduced, it is necessary to add in criticism, will invalidate the deduction unless the permissible limits of variation are specified. To do so, however, replaces the original mathematical deduction by a more complicated mathematical

---

[1] P. M. M. Duhem: "Une deduction mathématique n'est pas utile au physicien tant qu'elle se borne à affirmer que telle proposition, rigoureusement vraie, a pour conséquence l'exactitude de telle autre proposition. Pour être utile au physicien, il lui faut encore prouver que la seconde proposition rest à peu près exacte lorsque la première est seulement à peu près vraie" (*La Thèorie Physique* [Paris, 1906], p. 231).

[25]

theory in respect of whose interpretation the same problem arises, and whose exact nature is in any case unknown.

This lack of exact correlation between a scientific theory and its empirical interpretation can be blamed either upon the world or upon the theory. We can regard the shape of an orange or a tennis ball as imperfect copies of an ideal form of which perfect knowledge is to be had in pure geometry, or we can regard the geometry of spheres as a simplified and imperfect version of the spatial relations between the members of a certain class of physical objects.[2] On either view there remains a gap between scientific theory and its application which ought to be, but is not, bridged. To say that all language (symbolism, or thought) is vague is a favorite method for evading the problems involved and lack of analysis has the disadvantage of tempting even the most eminent thinkers into the appearance of absurdity. Duhem claims that "for the strict logician," a physical law is neither true nor false.[3] For Einstein mathematics is either uncertain or inapplicable,[4] and Russell cheerfully sacrifices logic as well.[5]

[2] Plato: "Those who study geometry and calculation . . . use the visible squares and figures, and make their arguments about them, though they are not thinking about them, but about those things of which the visible are images. Their arguments concern the real square and a real diagonal, not the diagonal which they draw, and so with everything. The actual things which they model and draw . . . they now use as images in their turn, seeking to see those very realities which cannot be seen except by the understanding" (*Republic*, 510; Lindsay's translation).

[3] "*Toute loi physique est une loi approchée; par conséquent, pour le strict logicien, elle ne peut être, ni vraie, ni fausse*" (*op. cit.*, p. 280).

[4] "*Insofern sich die Sätze der Mathematik auf die Wirklichkeit beziehen sind sie nicht sicher, und insofern sie sicher sind, beziehen Sie sich nicht auf die Wirklichkeit*" (*Geometrie und Erfahrung* [Berlin, 1921], p. 3).

[5] "All traditional logic habitually assumes that precise symbols are being employed. It is therefore not applicable to this terrestrial life, but only to an imagined celestial existence" ("Vagueness," *Australasian Journal of Philosophy*, 1 [1923]: 88). In this paper Russell contends that "all language is more or less vague." Again the "law of Excluded Middle is true when precise symbols are employed, but it is not true when symbols are vague, as, in fact, all symbols are" (*ibid.*, p. 85).

The aim of this essay is to avoid such wholesale destruction of the formal sciences by supplying in greater detail than has hitherto been attempted an analysis and symbolism for the "vagueness" or "lack of precision" of a language.

We shall not assume that "laws" of logic or mathematics prescribe modes of existence to which intelligible discourse must necessarily conform. It will be argued, on the contrary, that deviations from the logical or mathematical standards of precision are all pervasive in symbolism; that to label them as subjective aberrations sets an impassable gulf between formal laws and experience and leaves the *usefulness* of the formal sciences an insoluble mystery. And it is the purpose of the constructive part of the essay to indicate in outline an appropriate symbolism for vagueness by means of which deviations from a standard can be absorbed by a reinterpretation of the same standards in such a way that the laws of logic in their usual absolutistic interpretation appear as a point of departure for more elaborate laws of which they now appear as special or limiting cases. The method yields a process by which deviations, when recognized as such, can be absorbed into the formal system. At every stage the mathematics we already employ will provide the material for the increasing accuracy of the next stage.

It is one of the essay's main contentions that with the provision of an adequate symbolism the need is removed for regarding vagueness as a defect of language. The ideal standard of precision which those have in mind who use vagueness as a term of reproach, when it is not a shifting standard of a relatively less vague symbol, is the standard of scientific precision. But the indeterminacy which is characteristic of vagueness is present also in all scientific measurement. "There is no experimental method of assigning numerals in a manner which is free from error. If we limit ourselves strictly to experimental facts we recognize that there is no such thing as true measurement, and therefore no such thing as an error involved in a

[27]

departure from it."[6] Vagueness is a feature of scientific as of other discourse.

The impressionist painting of a London street in a fog is not a vague representation of what the artist sees, since his skill largely consists in the accuracy with which the visual impression is transcribed. But the picture is called vague in relation to a hypothetical laboratory record of the wave lengths and positions of the various objects in the street, while it is forgotten that that record, in supplying additional detail, obliterates just those large-scale relations in which the artist or another observer may be interested. This essay is designed to show that while the vague symbol has a part to play in language which cannot be equally well performed by more accurate symbols from another level (wave lengths as a substitute for names of colors), the transition to levels of higher accuracy can always in principle be made.

2. SUMMARY OF THE ARGUMENT

The process of logical analysis of a language can be regarded as the exhibition of a set of conventions for the use of symbols, abstracted from the regularity of linguistic habits in some postulated speech community, and proceeding by a series of successive approximations involving the use of "simplified" or "model" entities.

The vagueness of symbols in any such abstract system is a symptom of the degree of deviation of the "model" language from the empirically discoverable linguistic habits in the corresponding speech community.

A typical example of vagueness is described. A symbol's vagueness is held to consist in the existence of objects concerning which it is intrinsically impossible to say either that the symbol in question does, or does not, apply. The set of all objects about which a decision as to the symbol's application is intrinsically impossible is defined as the "fringe" of the symbol's field of application. It is claimed that all symbols

[6] N. R. Campbell, *An Account of the Principles of Measurement and Calculation* (New York, 1928), p. 131.

whose application involves the recognition of sensible qualities are vague, and a typical case is constructed for convenience
of reference. Vagueness is distinguished from generality and
from ambiguity. The former is constituted by the application
of a symbol to a multiplicity of objects in the field of reference,
the latter by the association of a finite number of alternative
meanings having the same phonetic form; but it is characteristic of the vague symbol that there are no alternative symbols
in the language, and its vagueness is a feature of the boundary
of its extension and is not constituted by the extension itself.
Russell's definition of vagueness (in a paper to which frequent
reference is made) as constituted by a one-many relation between symbolizing and symbolized systems is held to confuse
vagueness with generality.

The assumption of the existence of a well-defined set of
objects to which the application of a vague symbol is doubtful
is shown to be inconsistent with the usual meaning of negation, and the conclusion is shown to follow whether the number of individuals in the field of reference is finite or infinite.
But it is shown that there is no good reason to regard the
defining characteristic of vagueness as "subjective." The
crude notion of the "fringe" is therefore replaced by a statistical analysis of the frequency of deviations from strict uniformity by the "users" of a vague symbol. In this, the most
important section of the essay, it is found possible to define
the notion of a consistency profile or, its equivalent, a consistency function, corresponding to each vague symbol and
thus to classify, or even, theoretically, to measure, degrees
of vagueness.

The definition of consistency profile is based on the existence of "a group of users of a language" whose linguistic
habits are sufficiently stable and intercorrelated to permit of
limiting assertions concerning frequencies of deviations from
a standard. The definition of the users of a symbol is shown
to be another aspect of the definition of the symbol itself, and
the relation between the two processes is illustrated by analogy
with the definition of a biological species. An experiment is

[29]

described whose results illustrate the construction of a consistency profile, and the analysis is extended to the consideration of logical relations between vague symbols.

3. VAGUENESS DESCRIBED

The vagueness of a term is shown by producing "borderline cases," i.e., individuals to which it seems impossible either to apply or not to apply the term. Thus a word's vagueness is usually indicated, more or less explicitly, by some statement that situations are conceivable in which its application is "doubtful" or "ill-defined," in which "nobody would know how to use it," or in which it is "impossible" either to assert or deny its application.

Peirce's definition[7] is admirably clear: "A proposition[8] is vague when there are possible states of things concerning which it is *intrinsically uncertain* whether, had they been contemplated by the speaker, he would have regarded them as excluded or allowed by the proposition. By intrinsically uncertain we mean not uncertain in consequence of any ignorance of the interpreter, but because the speaker's habits of language were indeterminate."[9] An example will now be discussed in more detail.

Let us consider the word *chair*, say. On reflection, one is impressed by the extraordinary variety of objects to which the same name is applied: "Think of arm chairs and reading chairs and dining-room chairs, and kitchen chairs, chairs that

[7] Baldwin's *Dictionary of Philosophy and Psychology*, 2 (1902): 748.

[8] In this essay reference will always be made to the vagueness of a word or symbol, but no important difference is involved in speaking of a proposition's vagueness. The proposition can be regarded as a complex symbol and its vagueness defined in terms of that of its constituents, or vice versa.

[9] In the remainder of the passage Peirce explains that by an indeterminacy of habits he means the hypothetical variation by the speaker in the application of the proposition, "so that one day he would regard the proposition as excluding, another as admitting, those states of things." But the knowledge of such variation could only be "*deduced* from a perfect knowledge of his state of mind; for it is precisely because these questions never did, or did not frequently, present themselves, that his habit remained indeterminate."

pass into benches, chairs that cross the boundary and become settees, dentist's chairs, thrones, opera stalls, seats of all sorts, those miraculous fungoid growths that cumber the floor of the arts and crafts exhibitions, and you will perceive what a lax bundle in fact is this simple straightforward term. In co-operation with an intelligent joiner I would undertake to defeat any definition of chair or chairishness that you gave me."[10]

It is important in such a case that the variety of application to objects differing in size, shape, and material should not be confused with the vagueness of the word. The variety of application no doubt arises from the fact that chairs are defined by the need to be satisfied. "Every common noun, every concept is essentially merely an affective grouping. In a plurality of objects, differing from the point of view of perception even very widely from one another, we discover the same capacity to satisfy some given affectivity, some given need or desire of ours, and through this capacity we reduce this very plurality to a unity."[11] Being "a separate seat for one," as the dictionary puts it, is compatible with much variation in form and material.

But in speaking of the vagueness of the word chair, attention is directed only to the fact that objects can be presented whose membership in the class of chairs is incurably "uncertain" or "doubtful." It is the indeterminacy of the usage, not its extension, which is important for the purpose of the argument. The finite area of the field of application of the word is a sign of its *generality*, while its vagueness is indicated by the finite area and lack of specification of its boundary.[12]

[10] H. G. Wells, *First and Last Things* (London, 1908), p. 16.

[11] E. Rignano, *Psychology of Reasoning* (New York, 1923), p. 109.

[12] Cf. B. A. W. Russell: "A vague word is not to be identified with a general word" (*Analysis of Mind* [London, 1921], p. 184). He adds, however, "that in practice the distinction is apt to be blurred" and blurs it himself in saying "a memory is vague when it is appropriate to *many* occurrences" (*op. cit.* p. 182). This confusion between generality and vagueness invalidates his neat definition, "the fact that meaning is a one-many relation is the precise statement of the fact that all language is more or less vague" ("Vagueness," p. 89).

[31]

It is because *small* variations in character are unimportant to success in serving the purpose of being "a separate seat for one" that it is possible, by successive small variations in any respect, ultimately to produce "borderline cases." The cumulative action of such variation in producing large additive effects is at the root of the felt inability either to withhold or to apply a general term to the unusual and the extreme case.

One can imagine an exhibition in some unlikely museum of applied logic of a series of "chairs" differing in quality by least noticeable amounts.[13] At one end of a long line, containing perhaps thousands of exhibits, might be a Chippendale chair: at the other, a small nondescript lump of wood. Any "normal"[14] observer inspecting the series finds extreme difficulty in "drawing the line" between chair and not-chair. Indeed the demand to perform this operation is felt to be inappropriate *in principle: "chair* is not the kind of word which admits of this sharp distinction" is the kind of reply which is made "and if it were, if we were forbidden to use it for any object which varied in the slightest way from the limiting term, it would not be as useful to us as it is." This is the sensible attitude, but it raises difficulties for logic.

In order to circumvent these difficulties, we shall make use of the fact that the uncertainty of a single normal observer, or the variation in the decisions made by a number of such observers, either of which can be taken as the definition of vagueness, is a matter of degree, varying quantitatively,

---

The confusion may ultimately be traced to a certain uneasy nominalism in Russell's philosophy which tends to treat generality and vagueness indifferently as imperfections of symbolism in relation to the attempt to describe a universe composed exclusively of absolutely specific or atomic facts.

[13] The variation of this amount with the choice of the observer, and with conditions affecting the same observer, strengthens the subsequent argument by introducing further indeterminacy into the operation of "drawing the line."

[14] This is, in part, a definition of the "normal" observer; we shall reject the testimony of an observer who claimed to have discovered *the* point at which the division was to be made. Cf. section 7, pp. 49-51, for a fuller discussion of this point.

though not regularly, with the position of an object in the series. At the extremities of the series little or no uncertainty is felt, but the observer grows increasingly doubtful when the borderline cases in the center are approached; "everybody" agrees that the Chippendale chair *is* a chair, "nobody" wants to sit upon, still less to call a chair, a shapeless lump of wood, but in intermediate cases personal uncertainty is a reflection of objective lack of agreement.

We have used alternative but correlated definitions of vagueness in order not to prejudice the issue whether vagueness is subjective or objective.[15] On the one hand we can use an observer's feelings or report of his feelings; on the other, the set of divisions made by a set of independent observers who are given sufficient inducement to make a unique division in the series irrespective of their feelings of uncertainty.[16]

The vagueness of the word *chair* is typical of all terms whose application involves the use of the senses. In all such cases "borderline cases" or "doubtful objects" are easily found to which we are unable to say either that the class name does or does not apply. The case of a color name, whose relative simplicity is unobscured by the variation in application of such "artificial" names as chairs, is specially striking. If a series of colored cards of uniform saturation and intensity are arranged according to shades ranging by least perceptible differences from reds through oranges to yellows, the "uncertainty" which is typical of vagueness is at once demonstrated. "The changes of color in the spectrum are throughout so continuous that *it is not possible to find the exact point at which the changes of direction begin.*"[17] It would be easy, but uninstruc-

[15] See section 5, pp. 39-42.

[16] Cf. the experiment described in Appendix 1 when the subject agrees beforehand to make a unique division, the "inducement" being desire to keep his word, or curiosity, or some other motive.

[17] G. F. Stout, *Manual of Psychology* (London, 1898–99), p. 160. This manner of phrasing the situation suggests, of course, that the fault is in the language or in imperfect perception: there *is* an "exact point" where the transition occurs, but we are unable to find it.

[33]

tive, to multiply examples. Reserving the terms of logic and mathematics for separate consideration,[18] we can say that all "material" terms, all whose application requires the recognition of the presence of sensible qualities, are vague in the sense described.

4. LOCATION OF THE FRINGE

The quantitative variation in the degree of uncertainty felt by a typical observer, or the equivalent variation in the divisions made by a number of observers, will be used later as the basis of a method for symbolizing vagueness. But before doing this it is necessary to dispose of a plausible but mistaken view which seeks to solve the problem of borderline cases by allocating them to a region of "doubtful application," a kind of no man's land lying between the regions where a term applies and does not apply. For even if it is granted that all material terms are vague in the sense described it might still be said that the existence of borderline cases is unimportant. Such cases occur so infrequently, it might be argued, that consideration can always be restricted to objects concerning which the "doubt" does not arise. To such objects difficulties concerning the indeterminacy of the boundary will not be relevant; for these cases will remain unproblematic whichever separation is made in the field of application, and since we do not choose to argue about borderline cases no difficulty remains.

An objection of this sort misses the point: we do not claim to have discovered a serious practical difficulty but are trying to achieve the accommodation of an unduly simple conception of logic to the undoubted practical efficacy of formally invalid classificatory procedure. The presupposition of the existence of a class of "doubtful" objects will involve the assumption either of an exact boundary or of a doubtful region (of the second order)[19] between the fringe and the class of unproblematic objects.

[18] See Appendix 2, pp. 54–58.

[19] Russell assumes an infinite series of doubtful regions, each fringe having

Either assumption will be shown to be incompatible with the usual definition of negation and thus indirectly incompatible with the strict application of logical principles. The exposition will be simplified by using a set of symbols to illustrate the features of vagueness described in the last section. Let L then, be a typical example of a vague symbol. It has been seen that the vagueness of L consists in the impossibility of applying L to certain numbers of a series. Let the series S, say, be linear and composed of a finite number,[20] ten say, of terms x, let the rank of each term in the series be used as its name (so that the constant values of the variable x are the integers one to ten inclusive). Finally let the region of "doubtful application" or "fringe" be supposed to consist of the terms whose numbers are five and six respectively. There is, of course, no special significance in the choice of the numbers, ten, five, six, which are taken simply for the convenience of having definite numbers to which to refer.

In the usual notation of the propositional calculus "Lx" will mean L *applies to* x and "$\sim Lx$" will mean L *does not apply to* x or Lx *is false* (synonymous expressions).

Suppose now that $L1$, $L2$, $L3$, $L4$ are true, while $L5$ and $L6$ are "doubtful." It can only follow that to assert Lx of any x is positively to exclude it only from the range 7 to 10, since we cannot be sure, when Lx is asserted, that x does not perhaps occur in the range 5, 6. Thus to assert Lx is tantamount to confining x to the range 1 to 6.

Having obtained this result, it is easy to construct a similar argument in respect of $\sim Lx$. The assertion of $\sim Lx$ can, no more than the assertion of Lx, positively exclude x from the fringe 5, 6. It follows that to assert $\sim Lx$ is tantamount to excluding x from the range 1 to 4 and confining it to the range 5 to 10.

In short, inability to find a logical interpretation of doubtful assertions in terms of the two truth values, truth and false-

---

a fringe of higher order at its boundary, but he does not pursue the consequences of this assumption.

[20] The hypothesis of an infinite series is considered later in this section.

hood, forces us to admit that the ranges of application of Lx, 1 to 6, and of $\sim Lx$, 5 to 10, overlap in the fringe, 5, 6.

On the other hand, the statement $\sim Lx$ is, by definition of the logical operation of negation, true only when Lx is false, and false only when Lx is true. If, as we have assumed, asserting Lx confines x to the range 1 to 6, Lx is false only when x belongs to the range 7 to 10. Thus in contradiction to our previous result that $\sim Lx$ is true when and only when x belongs to the range 5 to 10, $\sim Lx$ should be true when and only when x belongs to the range 7 to 10. The formal properties of logical negation are incompatible with an interpretation which allows the domain and the complementary domain of a propositional function to overlap.

We can clinch the argument by attempting to translate the definition of L's vagueness, in some such form as *there is at least one term to which neither L nor its contradictory applies*, into the symbolism of the propositional calculus. Translating the italicized phrase in the last sentence gives

$$(\exists x)\ \{\sim L(x)\cdot \sim (\sim L(x))\}$$

which is at once transformed, by the rule of double negation, into

$$(\exists x)\ \{\sim L(x)\cdot L(x)\}$$

which is a contradiction. Such a contradiction is only to be evaded by denying the equivalence of $\sim(\sim L(x))$ and $L(x)$, i.e., by refusing to identify the operation $\sim$ when prefixed to a vague symbol with the ordinary operation of negation. This point of view will be incomplete and unplausible unless it is possible to define the new sense of $\sim$, i.e., to give the rules according to which the sign is to be used.

The situation is in some ways comparable to the reinterpretation of negation in mathematics arising from the criticisms of the Intuitionist school of philosophers of mathematics. Refusal to accept a theorem and its contradictory as exclusive alternatives forces the Intuitionists to construct a logical calculus, in which ordinary negation is eliminated, its function being taken by a new notion differing in its formal properties.[21] Whereas, however, the Intuitionists, setting out from a fairly well-defined criterion of constructibility are able to invent an appropriate calculus, our present investigation is still in the more rudimentary stage of knowing simply that "the notation is what we lack" and "the verdict of the mere feeling" is liable not merely to fluctuate but to lead to contradictions.

This part of the discussion should be completed by showing that we are bound to reach the same overlapping of domains and hence the same contradiction, if we were to allow the fringe to be itself bounded by a fringe of higher order, and that in turn by another and so on *ad infinitum*.[22]

It will be sufficient to consider the case of a linear continuum, e.g., the set of all geometrical points from a point a upon a straight line to a point b on the same straight line. If there is a series of fringes each limited by a subsidiary fringe (all composed of points between a and b) there must be two points c and d, which may be identical with a and b respectively, beyond which *no* fringe extends. If we choose c and d to be as close together as possible,[23] the assertion of Lx will assign x to the interval a to d, and the assertion of $\sim Lx$ to the interval c to b, these ranges overlapping as in the argument for the finite case. In either case, whether the number of terms in the field of reference is finite or infinite, denial of the existence of a unique boundary between the domains of Lx and $\sim Lx$ leads to contradiction. Thus it is impossible to accept Russell's suggestion that the fringe itself is ill-defined.[24] Ill-defined can only mean undefined—there is no place for a *tertium quid* in traditional logic. But an undefined fringe means

[21] Cf. M. Black, "The Claims of Intuitionism," *The Philosopher* 14 (1936): 89–97.

[22] This is Russell's assumption in the paper to which reference has already been made.

[23] The argument would need trivial adjustments if the field of reference, while having an infinite number of terms, did not constitute a continuum.

[24] *Op. cit.*, p. 88.

absence of all specification of boundary between the fields of application of a term and its contradictory—and this is in flagrant contradiction with the facts of the ordinary use of language. *Red* and *yellow* are used as distinct, not identical, symbols in a way which is not seriously affected by the existence of continuous gradations between the two colors.

On the other hand, the awkwardness of assuming a well-defined boundary to the fringe is shown clearly in the classical paradox of the heap, sometimes attributed to Zeno.[25] The argument is paraphrased by Adamson[26] in this way. "A measure of corn when thrown out makes a sound. Each grain and each smallest part of a grain must therefore have made a sound, yet no sound is made by a single grain." What is essentially the same argument sometimes appears in modern dress as the paradox of the bald man. Plucking a single hair from a man's head cannot make him bald if he is not so before. But the plucking of all his hair will make him bald, and this can be accomplished by the successive pluckings of single hairs.

Both forms of the paradox are associated with the emergence of qualities as a result of successive small alterations in respect of some other (quantitative) characteristic, none of which, except the last, produce *any* change in quality. The repugnance felt towards this type of discontinuity may be merely a prejudice, but it seems to be more; and I am unaware of any satisfactory discussion of it. So long as this type of argument is held to apply to a few vague terms the matter is not serious, but if we admit *all* terms are vague its application will invalidate any deductive argument into which it is inserted and is as awkward for logic as the notorious mathematical antinomies are for mathematics.

The difficulty is serious enough. If we are right in our claim that all material terms are vague, the formal apparatus of logic (and indirectly of mathematics, though this has not been shown) seems to break down. We are unable even to

[25] G. Burnet, *Greek Philosophy* (London, 1914), pp. 114, 115.
[26] R. Adamson, *Development of Greek Philosophy* (London, 1908), p. 38.

assume that Lx is incompatible with $\sim Lx$, without the assurance that x is not in the fringe, and we are unable to say when the fringe begins and ends. The attempt to assert that x does not belong to L's fringe, say $A(``Lx")$ leads us into an infinite regress

$$A\{`A(`Lx')\}, \ A\{`A\{`A(`Lx')\}\}, \text{ etc.}$$

and does not evade the difficulty. To say, as Russell does, "All traditional logic habitually assumes that precise symbols are being employed. It is therefore not applicable to this terrestrial life, but only to an imagined celestial existence"[27] is to abandon "traditional logic." If we can "imagine" precise symbols we can construct them—and if "*all* symbols are vague" we cannot even imagine precise ones.[28]

5. IS VAGUENESS SUBJECTIVE?

Subjective is here taken to mean whatever belongs to the processes of cognition, feeling, or willing as distinct from whatever belongs to the notion of their object.[29] Suppose an observer O, in the presence of an environment E, utters a set of words S. We shall say that a feature of S is subjective or objective according as the fact that that feature occurred in the situation which consisted of O's enunciating S is evidence for a fact about O or a fact about E respectively. Thus suppose S was uttered in an unusually loud voice; the intensity of the sounds occurring is, in the English language,[30] evidence of O's state of mind (e.g., that he is angry) but not evidence about the ostensible subject matter of his report.[31] Thus the intensity of the sounds in S is a subjective feature. Again if a sufferer from delirium tremens says, "There is a pink lizard

---

[27] *Op. cit.*, p. 88.

[28] Cf. section 9 where Russell's argument on this point is further discussed.

[29] Cf. article on "Objective," Baldwin's *Dictionary of Philosophy and Psychology* 2: 192.

[30] The qualification is necessary because some languages such as Chinese use differences of pitch as significant linguistic elements.

[31] Since O's state of mind may depend upon his environment, evidence about O's state of mind, may of course, *indirectly* yield evidence also about E.

[39]

over there," we are able to deduce only that he is *seeing* a pink lizard (a fact about O), not that there *is* a pink lizard over there (a fact about E). Thus the occurrence of the terms *pink* and *lizard* in his statement are subjective features.

The distinction between subjective and objective features of an utterance is therefore closely connected with the distinction between psychological and physical data, and the title of this section can be rephrased as follows: Are the defining phenomena of vagueness, i.e., the variations in the position of the boundary chosen by various observers (or the same observer at various times), facts about human behavior (psychological or sociological data) or facts about the physical world?

The question is best answered by comparison with the corresponding deviation from strict regularities of scientific instruments. For there is no essential difference in this context between the human reporter and the scientific instrument. We can regard the observer as an instrument for making divisions in a series of objects; the report of his feelings can then be likened to the oscillation of an instrument in a range where direct measurement is difficult.

(Conversely, the scientific instrument always needs a human observer before its readings can be incorporated into the scientific record, so that in a sense the instrument is merely a prolongation and reinforcement of the scientists' sense organs.) What is needed is a description of the circumstances in which a variation of the readings supplied by an instrument reporting the character of an object E is ascribed (a) to an "error" of the instrument, or (b) to a change in E. The cases (a) and (b) correspond to the variations in the reading, being, in the terminology of this section, "subjective" and "objective," respectively.

It is clear that the use of a single instrument I, measuring some physical magnitude of an object E and yielding (as all scientific instruments do) various readings on various occasions, is not sufficient for choice between cases (a) and (b) of the last paragraphs. For a character which is present in all

[40]

measurement cannot serve as a criterion for discriminating between two types of measurement. The method actually used by scientists is of course to keep E and the whole of its environment except I unchanged[32] while using other instruments I', I'', etc. in order to perform the same readings. If the variations in the readings are systematic, i.e., if they conform to a law which is confirmed by all the instruments, the variation is ascribed to a change in E. If, for example, the length of a body is recorded at intervals of a second as alternately one inch and two inches by every instrument, the systematic variation would be interpreted as a periodic alteration in the body's length. In mathematical terminology, the necessary and sufficient condition for variations in the readings of an instrument to be regarded as indication of changes (objective patterns) in the object measured is that the law connecting such variations should be invariant with respect to replacement of the measuring instrument by another of a certain set of instruments. Conversely, if the variations are not connected by an invariant law, they are ascribed to changes in the instrument (subjective factors). This assumption is strengthened if a law can be discovered connecting the variations with the internal structure of the instrument, for such a law allows prediction of the nature and amount of the variations irrespective of the nature of E. But in default of such a law the variations may simply be called "random," the essential being that the variations are invariant.

It is for such reasons that in physics gross deviations in measurements of position are ascribed to defects of the measuring instruments, while the joint indeterminacy of position and momentum of quantum mechanics, is regarded as objective.

Are the variations in the boundary decisions made by various members of a set of observers analogous to the errors of a scientific instrument or to the variations in the readings of an instrument in accordance with objective variations in the situation measured? We have assumed that the variations are

[32] In practice this can never be completely successful.

not purely random and that the variant decisions exhibit some statistical regularity. If this is a justified assumption (and without it we are unable to account for the success with which vague symbols are used), vagueness is clearly an objective feature of the series to which the vague symbol is applied.[33] And it will be shown in the next section how the vagueness of the symbolism can be made explicit in a way which ordinary language fails to do[34] and be made in this way to serve as an adequate model of those relations in the field of application from which it arises.

6. DEFINITION OF THE CONSISTENCY PROFILE

We propose to replace the crude and untenable distinction between fringe and region of certain application by a quantitative differentiation, admitting of degrees and correlated with the indeterminancy in the divisions made by a group of observers.

The definition involves three fundamental notions: *language* (or *users of language*), *a situation in which a user of a language is trying to apply a symbol L to an object x,* and *the consistency of application of L to x.* It is impossible to define them in independ-

[33] It needs, therefore, to be clearly distinguished from such features of symbolism as ambiguity. The latter is constituted by inability to decide between a finite number of alternative meanings having the same phonetic form (homonyms). The fact that ambiguity *can be removed* shows it to be an accidental feature of the symbolism. But any attempt to remove vagueness by a translation is defeated by the overspecification of meaning thus produced. Cf. an attempt to replace "The hall was half full" by "The ratio of the number of persons in the hall to the number of seats was exactly half." The presence of *one* person too many would falsify the second, but not the first, of the statements.

[34] In ordinary language, vagueness is shown explicitly by the use of adverbs of degree or number such as *any, many, rather, almost,* etc. These serve as a set of pseudo-quantifiers, generalizations as it were of the "respectable" quantifiers *all* and *any,* forming a sliding scale which can be attached to any adjective. The method of the next section, which reduces to the conversion of propositional functions into propositional functions of an extra variable by the addition of a numerical parameter is thus the generalization of a device already present in ordinary discourse.

[42]

ence of each other, for the first, which is clearly involved in the second and third, is in turn based upon the last. Thus the three notions must be defined in terms of a single process of interpretation, assigning a meaning to any context in which they are used. For the present we shall define a "language" as the vocabuarly and syntax abstracted from the laws expressing the uniformity of linguistic habits of a certain group of persons; and that group of persons we call the users of the language.[35] This definition will be discussed further in the next section, when it will be shown that the whole procedure is not circular. For the present, however, language will be treated as a relatively unproblematic notion, and we proceed to explain the notion of consistency of application. The method is based on the assumption that while the vagueness of a word involves variations in its application by the users of the language in which it occurs, such variations must themselves be systematic and obey statistical laws if one symbol is to be distinguished from another. It will be necessary to refer to situations in which a user of the language makes a decision whether to apply L or $\sim L$ to an object x. (Such a situation arises, for instance, when an engine driver on a foggy night is trying to decide whether the light in the signal box is really a red or a green light.) Let us call such a situation a *discrimination of x with respect to L*, or a *DxL* for short. (Then a DxL will be identical with a $Dx \sim L$, by definition.)

[35] The "set of conventions" determining the vocabulary and syntax of such a language are the simplified expressions, in the imperative mood, of the empirically discoverable rules of usage. While the existence of such a language presupposes, by definition, *some* uniformity in the linguistic habits of its users, the empirical laws expressing the partial uniformity of such habits are complex, in process of variation, and heterogeneous in character. It is necessary to distinguish between rules of logic, grammar, and good taste. The neglect of certain distinctions and discriminations habitually made by users of the language provides a simplified or "model" language bearing some, but not too much, resemblance to their actual habits. Then the first crude analysis can be corrected by a supplement which considers the facts neglected. Thus the definition proceeds by a series of successive approximations.

For some x's, the result of a DxL is almost independent of the observer; most users of the language, and the same user on most occasions, decide either that L applies or that $\sim L$ applies. In either case there is practical unanimity among competent observers as to the correct judgment. For other x's (in the "fringe") there is no such unanimity.

In any number of DxL involving the same x but not necessarily the same observer, let m be the number which issue in a judgment that L applies and n the number which issue in the judgment that $\sim L$ applies. We define *the consistency of application of L to x* as the limit to which the ratio m/n tends when the number of DxL and the number of observers increase indefinitely. (The second number is of course limited to the total number of the users of the language.) Since the consistency of the application, C, is clearly a function of both L and x, it can be written in the form $C(L,x)$.

In a previous section we claimed certain systematic features in the variation of application of a vague but unambiguous symbol. It is now possible to specify these features more exactly. As we pass from left to right along the series S of terms x, the corresponding values of $C(L,x)$ will have large values at

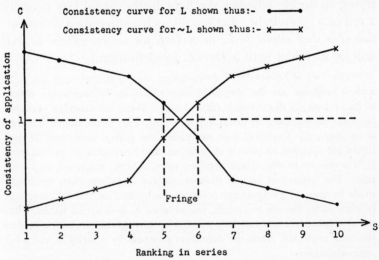

Figure 1. Consistency of application of a typically vague symbol.

[44]

the outset (region of "certain" application of L), decrease until values near to one are reached (fringe), and decrease again until values near to zero are reached (region of "certain" application of $\sim L$). A list of the exact values of $C(x,L)$ corresponding to each member x of S will be an exact description of L's vagueness. In Fig. 1, a typical set of consistencies is shown in graphical form.

The numbers along the horizontal axis denote the position of terms in the series S, while the height of a point above a number vertically beneath it represents the consistency of application of the symbol in question for the corresponding term of the series. The points marking the values of the consistencies associated with each member of the series have been joined to form an open polygonal line. It will be convenient to call the curve thus obtained a *consistency profile* for the application of L to the series S. In practice the number of terms in S will usually be very much greater than 10 (e.g., there are said to be something like 700 distinguishable shades of gray), and the consistency curve will approximate to a smooth curve having a continuous gradient.

The exact shape of the consistency curve will, of course,

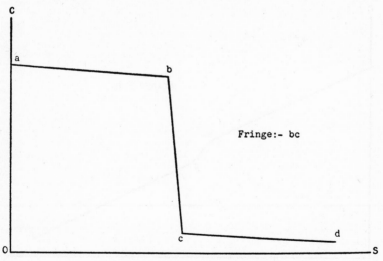

Figure 2. Consistency curve of a very precise symbol.

[45]

vary according to the symbol considered. It has been assumed that the typical symbol, L, is unambiguous, but an ambiguous symbol will be easily detected by the presence of more than one fringe in its consistency curve. In other words the steady decrease of consistency as we move from left to right is taken as a definition of unambiguity. Further, the introduction of consistency profiles allows us to define the relative vagueness of symbols on the basis of a classification of their corresponding consistency profiles. Thus the very precise symbol would have a consistency curve made up of a straight line almost parallel to the horizontal axis, and at a great distance from it, followed by a steep drop to another line almost parallel to the horizontal axis and very close to it, i.e., the curve is marked by the narrowness of the fringe and lack of variation in the symbol's application elsewhere.

The very vague but unambiguous symbol, on the other hand, would have a consistency profile approximating to a straight line of constant negative gradient, i.e., the fringe merges into the whole field and there is continuous variation in the symbol's application (Fig. 3).

Intermediate cases could be classified according to their

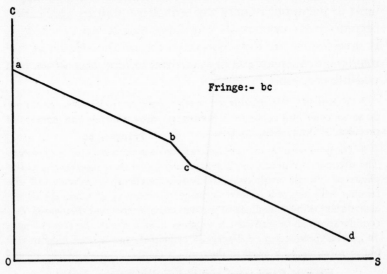

Figure 3. Consistency curve of a very vague symbol.

[46]

deviation from the extreme types illustrated in Figs. 2 and 3.

In order to do this, it might be more convenient to plot, not the consistency as above defined, but the deviation of the consistency from the extreme values. Let m be the number of the *more favored* judgments in a total of n DxL, made as before with respect to the same x. And let z be the limit approached by $2m/n$ as the number of DxL increases. Then z lies always between 0 and 1, is high in the fringe and low in the regions of certain application, whether of L or $\sim L$. A curve connecting z with the rank of x would approximate in shape to the frequency curves studied in statistics, and the determination of a symbol's degree of vagueness would then reduce to well-known statistical problems such as the determination of the area or flatness (kurtosis) of a frequency curve.

It is to be noticed that the existence of a series of relatively less vague symbols does not imply the existence of a symbol of zero vagueness[36] any more than the existence of greater lengths implies the existence of a greatest or least length.[37] The limits to the application of the term *length* are of exactly the same kind as the limits to the application of *red* or *chair* or any other vague word. It is not possible to set any upper limit to the application of the term *length*, but its application becomes less consistent as very large lengths are reached. It is unnecessary in this context to follow the details of the mathematical treatment of vagueness beyond this sketch of a possible procedure.[38]

[36] Cf. Russell, "We are able to conceive precision; indeed if we could not do so we could not conceive of vagueness which is merely the contrary of precision" ("Vagueness," p. 89).

[37] The final term in any case differs from its predecessors in *some* respects. The situation is indeed complicated in physics by the existence of a multiplicity of different methods for measuring length in accordance with the familiar tendency of a science to extend the meaning of a concept by the assimilation of new methods of measurement as they are discovered. But consideration can be restricted to *length measured by a ruler* (the case of length 'in general' produces no difference in principle), and we can imagine this phrase substituted for *length* in the text.

[38] Cf. Appendix 2 (pp. 54-58) for further details.

We have seen that the relations exhibited in the consistency profile can be regarded as generating a numerical function correlating a numerical value of the consistency to each member x in L's field of application.[39] The consistency curves of L and $\sim L$, or the equivalent numerical functions, constitute the complete analysis of the implications of L and $\sim L$ so far as concerns this vagueness. We eliminate the difficulties due to the inadequacy of the dichotomy of Lx and $\sim Lx$ by providing a more adequate symbolism in which explicit account is taken of those quantitative relations in the field of reference of which the difficulties in interpretation of the dichotomy are a sign.

If the analysis of L (i.e., the specific consistency profile) be denoted as L', an alternative mode of formulation would be to regard the consistency distribution as indication of the *degree* to which L', the more explicit symbol, is applicable to the corresponding terms of the series S. We then regard L in its analyzed form as the incomplete expression of a propositional function having *two* arguments, reading $L'(x, C)$ as L' *is present in x with degree C*. In this form of expression attention is drawn to the objective relations between L' and S which determine the consistency distribution.

To remove a possible source of misunderstanding it may be as well to add that the analysis of Lx in the manner suggested does not involve the claim that a person asserting Lx in a DxL should know the analysis, i.e., the corresponding distribution of consistencies of application, either at that or at any subsequent time. Any assumption that ability to use a symbol correctly involves extensive statistical knowledge of the behavior of other users would involve a vicious circle. But

[39] On a frequency theory of probability the assertion of the value of $C(L,x)$ for a given argument x could be interpreted as an assertion concerning the probability of L's application to x. This would involve interpreting all statements of the form Lx as statements of probability lacking a numerical parameter. Such a theory bears a formal resemblance to the theories of, say, Keynes or Reichenbach (*Wahrscheinlickheitslehre* [Leiden, 1935]). But the argument in the text is independent of any particular interpretation of probability.

[48]

we can very well use a symbol correctly, i.e., in statistical conformity with the behavior of a certain group of users, without knowing in detail to what we are committed by the linguistic habits of the group.

7. DEFINITION OF THE USERS OF A LANGUAGE

The sense in which language is used in the previous section is clearly a technical one, which needs further discussion.

We need a sense which is narrower than the ordinary sense in which French, Italian, or German are called languages. For "In a country like France, Italy or Germany . . . every village or, at most, every group of two or three villages, has its own dialect. . . . The difference from place to place is small but, as one travels in any one direction, the differences accumulate, until speakers, say from opposite ends of the country, cannot understand each other, although there is no sharp line of linguistic demarcation between the places in which they live."[40] Thus "correct" German or "correct" Dutch are better regarded as specially important dialects abstracted from languages which shade into each other by a continuous series of intermediate local variations.[41] We need a sense, however, which is slightly narrower even than that of the "official" dialect. For if it is a question of obtaining a consistency profile for the name of a color, we shall want to exclude certain persons who cannot speak the official dialect. The observations of the color-blind or those who claim to perceive distinctions in shade invisible to all other persons are valueless in constructing the profile. Thus, without attempting to achieve the empty ideal of strict uniformity we shall find it necessary to exclude from the group of users of the language persons having unusual powers of discrimination. The element of arbitrary convention in the use of the term language in our technical sense is unavoidable and characteristic of all attempts at definition. If, however, in view of the enormous variation on geographical, social, technical, and

[40] L. Bloomfield, *Language* (New York, 1933), p. 51.
[41] Bloomfield, *op. cit.*, p. 44.

even sexual grounds to be found in linguistic behavior, we reject the assumption of *strict* uniformity as too crude an approximation to be useful, it will be necessary to specify how the amount of *permissible* variation is determined. We shall do this by using the process of deriving the consistency profile of a vague symbol simultaneously as a definition of the privileged users of the symbol.

We can begin by considering such a large group of persons that the problem reduces to that of identifying some selection from the group as *the* set of users of the symbol L. It has been assumed that *no* set of persons thus selected (not even a set consisting of a single person) will show absolute uniformity in applying L. For each set, however, we can apply the procedure of the preceding section,[42] making the number of DxL for each x increase indefinitely, for each x in turn, but keeping the group of observers constant. In this way *some* of the subgroups will provide their own characteristic consistency profiles for the symbol L.

Now the various subgroups can be classified and amalgamated on the basis of the mutual deviations of their respective consistency profiles. In the simplest case in which the subgroups separate into a number of nonoverlapping classes, each having exactly the same consistency profile, we say that there are as many different usages of L as there are distinct forms of consistency profiles produced by this statistical analysis, and define *the* subgroup of users of L in any one of its meanings as the *largest* subgroup having the corresponding consistency profile.

In practice, however, the situation is likely to be complicated by the existence of a great many consistency profiles with gradations between extreme types. In this case the notion of privileged users whose behavior determines the vague-

[42] Actually to do this would seem to involve examination of the limiting behavior of *each* subgroup. The practical difficulties this would involve and the subsequent modifications required in practice in determining the uses of a language in any specific case need not be considered in a discussion of the principles.

ness of L' will itself be a relatively vague notion. The decision whether to extend any provisionally selected subgroup by the inclusion of new members will depend upon the modifications in the shape of the consistency profiles which such admissions entail. When such modifications are slight the group will be extended, but not otherwise. Newcomers whose admission would entail radical modifications in the shape of the profile will be said to use the terms L and $\sim L$ in a different way from that of the group already established. Thus the process of selecting a group of users and of discovering the consistency profile of a symbol are complementary and interact upon each other.

The whole analysis may be compared with the process by which species are defined in biology. There, too, the group of animals constituting a species is defined not by exact correspondence in habits or characters but by a statistical distribution of variation in habits around a mean position.[43] When a grouping of properties round a mean position is discovered, it is regarded on the one hand as the *definition* of the species, and on the other as a *property* of the species once it is defined. So too statistical regularity in deviations of linguistic habits is used both to isolate a privileged group and simultaneously to define those habits by the invention of an appropriate symbolism.

[43] Thus if we adopt a recent definition of species in genetic terms as a "group of individuals fully fertile inter se, but barred from interbreeding with other similar groups by its physiological properties (producing either incompatibility of parents or sterility of the hybrids or both)" (T. Dobzhansky, "Critique of the Species Concept in Biology," *Philosophy of Science* [1935], 353) we are compelled to admit the qualification that "neither the mechanisms producing incompatibility, nor those producing sterility, function on an all-or-none principle. For instance, sexual isolation may be incomplete, and individuals belonging to different groups may sometimes, though seldom, copulate. Similarly, some hybrids are only semi-sterile or sterile in one sex only" (*ibid.*). Nor is the situation fundamentally altered if a genetic definition of this sort is replaced by a taxonomic definition in terms of the possession by the members of the species of certain common characteristics.

[51]

APPENDIX I. AN EXPERIMENT IN VAGUENESS

It was hoped that the following experiment might illustrate the formation of a consistency profile and the manner in which consistency of application can be an index of objective relations in the field of reference. Each subject was asked to make a single division, at what seemed "the most natural place," in the series of rectangles shown in Fig. 4 and, having made a unique choice, to analyze the reasons for his decisions. (The instructions used are reproduced at the end of this Appendix, so that the results obtained can be checked by others.)

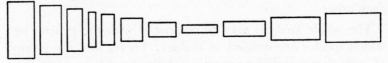

Figure 4. Series of rectangles used in experiment on vagueness.

Careful inspection of the series will show at least three[44] criteria for dividing the series which are covered by the deliberately vague word "natural" used in the instructions for the experiment. The rectangles diminish in height by equal steps from left to right until the eighth from the left is reached, and then increase in height again by the same amounts until the end of the row is reached; exactly the same is true of the *breadths* of the rectangles considered in the opposite direction from right to left. In addition to this the heights and breadths are so correlated that each rectangle is geometrically congruent to another rectangle distant the same number of places from the nearer end of the series, and is obtained from it by a revolution of 180° about an axis perpendicular to the paper. Thus the first and eleventh rectangles, the second and tenth, third and ninth rectangles, etc., have the same shape and size. If the criterion of diminishing heights be called *H* for convenience of reference, the criterion of increasing breadth

---

[44] In fact, of course, there are an indefinite number of criteria which might be applied; those described as merely the most "natural," i.e., those which most people tend to use.

B, and the criterion of symmetry (which is a kind of combination of *H* and *B*) *S*, it will be seen that application of *H* would result in a decision at a point between *7/8* and *8/9* inclusive (see instructions at end of this Appendix for explanation of the notation), application of *B* at a point between *3/4* and *4/5* inclusive, application of *S* at the point 6. Thus conflicting criteria produce overlapping fields of application, as in the case of the color spectrum. When the experiment was performed on eighty-three persons it was found that criterion *B*

Table of Experimental Results

PLACE AT WHICH DIVISION WAS MADE	NO. OF PERSONS MAKING THE DIVISION AT THAT PLACE
1 to 3/4	None
4	1
4/5	2
5	None
5/6	4
6	36
6/7	6
7	4
7/8	16
8	14
8/9 to 11	None
	Total: 83

was seldom employed, the most usual reaction being an application of *H*, *S*, or a compromise between the two.[45] Although no particular care was taken to ensure homogeneity of the group subjects, who were in fact of all ages and types, drawn from the writer's acquaintances and students, the corresponding consistency profile, even with the small number on whom the experiment was tried, has quite a distinctive shape of the kind associated with a simply ambiguous symbol. It is to be expected that the characteristic concentration of the number of divisions at or near *6* and *7/8* would be preserved as the number of subjects increased.

[45] Any tendency to make a division in the middle of a series could have

[53]

[TYPEWRITTEN INSTRUCTIONS ISSUED WITH THE SERIES OF RECTANGLES]

You are supplied with a series of rectangles arranged in a horizontal line. Do not turn the sheet round; keep them in the horizontal position. You are asked to divide the set of rectangles by a *single* vertical line, at what seems the most NATURAL place. The division may be either between two rectangles or through the middle of one of them; e.g., if all rectangles to the left were red and all the rest were black, the "natural" place to make the division would be between the red and the black rectangles. *Do not draw any lines*, but show your decision on a separate sheet of paper in the following way:

A division between the third and fourth rectangles from the LEFT is shown by writing 3/4, and so on.

A division through the middle of the tenth rectangle from the LEFT is shown by writing 10, and so on.

You can take as much time as you like but must make one and only one division.

[The following was issued after the first part of the instructions had been performed:]

If you can, try to explain in writing *why* you made the division in the place you did, and add any comments you think interesting (e.g., whether you hesitated between several places).

[Actual dimensions of rectangles: 4 cm. x 2 cm., 3.5 cm. x 1.5 cm., etc. (unit of increase in linear dimension 0.5 cm). Space between rectangles: 0.5 cm.]

APPENDIX 2. EXTENSION OF THE ANALYSIS TO THE LOGICAL RELATIONS BETWEEN VAGUE SYMBOLS

One of the main problems with which this essay has been concerned is the applicability of logical principles when vague symbols are involved. The notion of an ideal universe in which the laws of logic and mathematics have unconfined validity having been rejected, it remains to show how the undoubted usefulness of the formal sciences in a field of vague symbols can be explained by an extension of the method already sketched in the earlier sections.

---

been avoided by prolonging both ends of the series a considerable distance or by using a series pasted round a cylinder.

From the formalist standpoint, the analysis of vagueness in terms of consistency functions can be regarded simply as the introduction of more complex symbolism, replacing the propositional function Lx of a single variable by a function of two variables, $L(x,c)$ (read: "L applies to x with consistency c"). The relations between symbols in a calculus whose symbols are assumed to be "absolutely precise" will then appear as a limiting case of the relations between symbols having an extra argument, c, and obtained from the general case by allowing c to tend either to zero or to infinity in every formula in which it occurs, i.e., in effect simply by suppressing that argument.[46] Thus the validity and usefulness of the relations applicable to the limiting case (logical relations between "absolutely precise" symbols) will depend upon the degree to which they can be represented as a standard to which the more general case approximates. In particular, the purely logical relations between the incomplete symbols attained by suppressing parts of vague symbols would appear as limiting cases of relations between vague symbols.

The generalization of the usual notions of material implication or negation of propositional functions of a single variable will be relations connecting the corresponding values of the consistency arguments in two propositional functions. It follows from the definition of the consistency function that if $L(x,c)$ and $\sim L(x,c')$ for the same x, the products of the two consistencies, c and c', is unity. Thus the principle of excluded middle is replaced by the operation which permits the transformation of $L(x,c)$ into $\sim L\left(x, \dfrac{I}{c}\right)$.[47]

---

[46] The limiting process and the suppression of the argument are assumed to produce equivalent effects.

[47] If this principle of transformation is itself formalized (corresponding to the use of the law of excluded middle as a premise as well as a logical principle), it will be necessary to introduce a further consistency variable. The generalization of the assertion (x) $(Px \text{ v} \sim Px)$ will then be

$$(x, c) \{P(x, c) \text{ v} \sim P(x, f(c))\}$$

where f is some specified function of c (nearly equal to c when c is near to I, very small when c is large and very large when c is small; the exact form

[55]

The consistency profiles of vague symbols can in fact be regarded as a generalization of the circles in the Euler diagrams traditionally used by logicians to represent the relations of inclusion and exclusion between classes.[48] Just as the operation of negating a propositional function corresponds in the usual spatial analogy to the movement from the interior of a circle to its exterior, so also, in the spatial illustrations of this essay, the corresponding transition is from L's consistency profile to the reciprocal curve for $\sim L$ (cf. Fig. 1).

This in turn suggests a generalization for the relation of implication between propositional functions, or the equivalent relation of inclusion between their extensions. We take as the *type* of the case when L's field of application includes M's field the case in which M's consistency profile lies wholly *underneath* L's consistency profile, i.e., for every x, M's consistency of application is less than L's consistency of application to that x. It is necessary to say that this definition specifies only the type or standard case of the relationship between two functions, because, in accordance with the general standpoint of this essay, deviations from the type must be allowed. If the consistency of M is greater than the consistency of L in *very few* of the x's, we shall still say $Mx \supset Lx$ to *some* extent. We can imagine a number $i(L,M)$ which measures the degree to which the relation between the consistency profiles of L and M deviates from the standard case of inclusion.[49] Then i, which might be called an approximation index for

of $f(c)$ would depend on the exact form of the consistency curves in the special case).

[48] Since such diagrams habitually assume a two-dimensional field of application, the corresponding diagram of consistencies of application should strictly be three-dimensional and consist of a (polyhedral) surface obtained by joining the top of adjacent ordinates erected not upon an axis (OS in Fig. 2) but upon a plane of reference. The argument of the section can, however, be sufficiently illustrated by supposing that the field of application is a one-dimensional series as in Figs. 1-3.

[49] $i(L, M)$ might be, for example, the ratio of the number of x's when M's consistency is greater than L's to the number when M's consistency is less than L's. The exact definition which is chosen is unimportant.

the relation of inclusion is a function of the consistency distributions of L and M.

Thus the statement that $Mx \supset Lx$ will be generalized into some such form as

$$\supset \{i(L,M), c\}$$

i.e., a propositional function of two variables, viz., the approximation index for inclusion and the usual consistency variable. Hence the syllogistic law which permits of transition from the two formulas $\supset (L,M)$ and $\supset (M,N)$ to the formula $\supset (L,N)$ is generalized into some rule connecting the different approximation indices in

$$\supset \{i(L,M), c\}, \supset \{i'(M,N), c\} \text{ and } \supset \{i''(L,N), c\}.$$

Thus if the approximation index were suitably defined it might follow that i'' must be $< i + i'$. The rule for passing from $\supset (L,M)$ and $\supset (M,N)$ to $\supset (L,N)$ would then become: Whenever $\supset \{i(L,M), c\}$ and $\supset \{i'(M,N), c\}$ are asserted for the same value of c and specific (but not necessarily identical) values of i and i', then $\supset \{i''(L,N), c\}$ can be asserted, with the same value of c, the value of i'' certainly being less than the sum of i and i'. In the special case where $i = i' = o$ (strict inclusion) we shall have $i'' = o$, and the ordinary relation will hold.

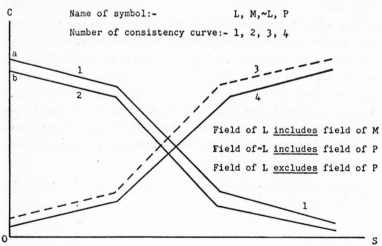

Figure 5. Logical relations between vague symbols spatially illustrated.

[57]

We can characterize the preceding interpretation very roughly in this way: the ordinary rules for the logical transformation of sets of statements (e.g., the syllogistic rules) produce conclusions whose degree of vagueness is of the same order[50] as those of the premises. In proportion as the relations between the consistency curves approximate to the definitions of inclusion and negation given above, the resulting laws of logical transformation approximate to those of the traditional forms.

By means of the notions of inclusion and negation it is easy to define the relation of *exclusion* between consistency functions. We say that L's field *excludes* P's if $\sim L$'s field includes P's. The standard cases of the relationships arising are shown in Fig. 5. It is easily verified that the new definitions of inclusion, exclusion, and negation preserve the usual formal properties of these relationships. Thus both inclusion and exclusion remain transitive: also if L's field includes M's, $\sim M$'s field includes $\sim L$'s, etc. (see Fig. 5).

Thus, if the logical forms are interpreted as standard cases to which the relations between consistency functions may approximate, the formal properties on which the theory of formal logic are based remain valid in the approximatory sense discussed.

For while the vagueness not only in the terms of the premises but in their relations prevents us from asserting the conclusion of an argument in applied logic or applied mathematics without a qualification as to the degree of consistency (whose amount depends on the precision of the terms and logical relations), the *form* of the transformation is independent of the actual consistencies, provided we are satisfied with a final precision which increases indefinitely when the precision of the premises increases.

[50] This means, roughly speaking, that it tends to zero when the degree of vagueness of all the premises tend to zero.

III

The Justification
of Induction

SO MUCH LABOR has been expended upon the attempt to "justify induction" that it is surprising to find little attention paid to the meaning of "justification." It should have been clear, for instance that "justification" is a relational notion, whose exact specification varies with the type of *standard* of justification to which appeal is to be made. Where *no* standard of justification is acceptable, the notion of justification becomes vacuous; where divergent standards are accepted, different, but not necessarily conflicting types of justification will be sought.

In determining whether induction can be "justified," we should first ask what type of standard of justification *we* are prepared to accept. And if we are interested in refuting the sceptical conclusions of Hume and his successors, we must first discover what type of justification *they* are prepared to accept. (We may hope, also, to be able to decide which standard of appeal has proper authority.)

Nearly all writers on the subject have upheld a *deductive* standard of justification. Hume himself made it abundantly clear that his scepticism arose from the impossibility of a "demonstration" or *deductive proof* of assertions concerning matters of fact. And later students of the "problem of induction," with hardly a single exception, have followed Hume in this. They have thought the problem to consist in showing that the premises of inductive inference, with or without supplementary "assumptions," *deductively entail* the conclusion.

Considerable ingenuity is needed to make the program seem plausible. It may be urged that categorical assertions with respect to the future must be replaced by statements of probability; or that the conclusions of scientific inquiry are conditional upon the truth of some grand postulate of the "uniformity of nature" or the equivalent; or even that it is necessary to reinterpret empirical laws and theories as a priori mathematics.

Such attempts, however ingenious, are doomed to be futile. In all this debatable ground, we can be sure at least of this: that *some* of the arguments by which we infer characteristics of the unobserved are *not* deductive. Indeed, it is a distinguishing sign of all the arguments properly described as "inductive" that their premises are compatible with the logical negation of their conclusion. It is true

[61]

by definition that induction is not deduction. All the ingenuity of those who still fight the lost cause of rationalism can succeed only in dressing up the platitude that the one mode of argument is not the other.

But why should this be a cause for alarm? If the fact that induction cannot be reduced to deduction is ground for disquiet about the validity of the former, why should it not, by parity of reasoning, cast equal aspersions upon the validity of deduction? More generally, what reasonable ground can be given for arguing from the mere difference of two things to the lesser cognitive value of either term of the inequation? When stated in such bald terms, the "problem of induction" seems to dissolve into absurdity.

The sceptical arguments against the possibility of justifying induction are not trivial, however. The source of their formidable persuasiveness is to be found in a series of unconscious equivocations, all the more difficult to detect because so natural to commit. A careful examination of the language used by writers on induction shows them to slide from the use of "justification" in a "common" or "everyday" or "practical" sense to that of "justification" in some "strict" or *deductive* sense. (The same is true of the other related logical or epistemological terms—"proof," "possibility," "knowledge," "evidence"—which figure prominently in the discussion.) A philosopher's assertion that "we are not justified in believing that the sun *will* rise tomorrow" might send the prudent man scurrying to take precautions against the impending catastrophe; but his alarm will change to wry amusement on hearing that exactly the same type of "warning" will be regarded as appropriate *no matter how much we know in the "ordinary" sense of know.*

On the basis of such linguistic analysis, some writers have suggested that the sceptic is making "linguistic recommendations." They say that the sceptical critics of induction (i.e., almost all who have written on the subject) wish to *change* the language of everyday life in such a fashion that, speaking roughly, "know" shall mean the same as "know *deductively* or *intuitively*" (in the manner in which the theorems and axioms of mathematics are known). But this analysis is almost as paradoxical as the discussions to which it is supposed to be an answer. For the critics of induction will not be appeased by a mere change of terminology.

Those who take deductive principles as a standard of inquiry are supposing deduction to be somehow *superior* to induction. But in relation to *which* ends? The attraction of deductive method is its supposed "certainty" or "infallibility." If the aim of cognitive inquiry were "the complete intellectual peace" attainable in mathematics, the preference for deduction might be less absurd than it is. But in the empirical sciences we seek comprehensiveness of knowledge no less than systematic organization and reliable method. If deduction is valuable as a mode of organizing empirical data, induction has the great merit of permitting inference to hitherto unobserved phenomena. To make invidious comparison between the two is as absurd as to assert that the walls of a house are more important than its rafters.

Having rejected the claims of deduction to be a superior standard of justification of inductive inference, we can now explain in what sense we believe "justification" of induction to be necessary or possible. Principles of inductive inference (e.g., those of statistical sampling) need not be used dogmatically. If serious question arises as to their reliability, we may either seek to deduce them from more securely grounded general principles (deductive justification); or we may try to show that they *work in practice* (inductive justification). Inductive justification of induction involves no circularity. For we are not aspiring to furnish a *demonstration* of the validity of induction. It will be sufficient if we can show on the basis of experience that inductive methods are to be trusted. And this can indeed be shown, at any rate within restricted fields of experience. That the inductive methods characteristic of science have worked better than other methods *in the past* is a reasonable ground for confidence in their applicability in the future. Lamentation over the impossibility of a "stronger" or "less invalid" defense of induction is not a sign of superior philosophical enlightenment. It is a sign of misguided allegiance to a deductive standard which is, in this instance, irrelevant.

2. THE GENERAL MEANING OF "JUSTIFICATION"

A demand for justification is normally taken to imply a *discrepancy with some acceptable standard.* And a satisfactory justification is one which neutralizes the apparent discrepancy by showing it to be consistent with, or deducible from, the relevant standard.

When a man who tells a lie is called upon to "justify" his action, the standard is constituted by the moral injunction against lying; and a justification satisfactory in form (though

[63]

not necessarily so in substance) might consist of a proof that telling the truth in the instance in question would produce great avoidable suffering. (Here the discrepancy is removed by modifying the form of one relevant standard and invoking a second standard. If both men agree about the facts of the case, agree that the sound ethical principle is that lying is generally, but not universally, wrong, that avoidable suffering ought to be prevented, and that the problematic course of action is consistent with, or even deducible from, these principles, the justification will be considered satisfactory.)

If a mathematician is asked to "justify" the division of equal quantities by a quantity equal to zero, the discrepancy is between his procedure and the general algebraic rule forbidding division by zero. Should he be able to show that he had not in fact divided by zero, the mathematician would remove the discrepancy by showing that the rule is not violated by the case in question; but if he were to argue that, in the special calculus in question, division by zero never produced contradiction or ambiguity, he would achieve consistency by modifying the standard. To modify the standard is to substitute, for reason shown, *another* standard.

Unless I am wrong, such examples as these show the following assertions to be true:

(i) Where no *standard* of justification is acceptable, it makes no sense to speak of justification.

(ii) The kind of justification appropriate will vary with the type of standard acceptable.

(iii) Standards of justification may themselves need justification. This can be done only by showing them to be consistent with, or deducible from, some more inclusive standard of justification accepted as authoritative.

If these conclusions seem all too obvious, so much the better. I shall argue that the failure of philosophical critics to see clearly the character of the principles of justification which would satisfy them has blinded them to the irrelevance of these standards. And I shall try to show that the notorious "hopelessness" of a defense of induction testifies only to the misdirection of the attempt to achieve its justification.

3. THE STANDARD OF JUSTIFICATION EMPLOYED BY CRITICS OF INDUCTION

There is no mystery about the *kind* of justification which, if it could be produced, would satisfy the philosophical critics of induction, from Hume onwards. Roughly speaking, they ask for a proof that induction *must* "work." Ewing, for instance, says: "How can we possibly be justified in deducing the effect from the cause unless we suppose that it is dependent upon or follows necessarily *from* the cause and does not merely follow it? . . . entailment there must be if our inference is to be justified."[1] And another writer, who claims to have *found* a justification for induction, therefore asserts, "The principles of induction and hypothesis are no less *a priori*, no more mental or operational, than the syllogism or the calculus."[2] Both philosophers, and with them the majority of those who have written on the subject, are committed to an a priori or deductive standard of justification. They desire, and would be satisfied by, a *proof* that conclusions of inductive arguments are true, or at least probable. By a proof is to be understood here, as in mathematics or logic, a valid deduction from self-evident first principles. I shall say that such critics demand a deductive justification of induction. And I shall call such a critic a "deductionist."

What, then, is the discrepancy with the deductive standard which occasions the demand for the justification of induction? It is not, as might be supposed, the fact that inductive methods are fallible, i.e., that even the most careful and well-founded types of inductive arguments sometimes yield false conclusions. For inductive arguments having the highest degree of reliability still fail to satisfy the critic. I do not suppose that a spun coin ever comes to rest on its edge, or that pure water

[1] *Aristotelian Society Proceedings*, 33 (1932–33): 116.

[2] Donald Williams, *The Ground of Induction* (Cambridge, Mass., 1947), p. 124. Cf. p. 182: "The principle of induction . . . provable *a priori* . . ."

at room temperature is ever solid, or that sulfuric acid will ever slake thirst. If, in these, and countless other familiar cases, we succeed, on the basis of inductive evidence, in making predictions which *in fact* are always verified, the critic writes them off as cases of *"practical"* or *"moral"* certainty. The practical disquiet with regard to the reliability of a conclusion drawn on *insufficient* inductive evidence is uninteresting to the philosophical critic of induction, except insofar as it indicates a more pervasive "defect" of inductive methods in general. For even in the cases where nobody would doubt that all the "practical" criteria of certainty had been met, it would still be maintained that the conclusion was "problematic."

What renders even the best inductive conclusion illegitimate, on this view, is its failure to satisfy the deductive standard. So long as the negation of the conclusion of an inductive argument is compatible with the premises, i.e., so long as the conclusion is not *entailed* by the premises, the critic will be dissatisfied. Conversely, in order to make an honest woman of induction it is required to show that her offspring may be duly certified as products of deductive relationships.

4. NO DEDUCTIVE JUSTIFICATION OF INDUCTION POSSIBLE

Now if I am right, it can be shown deductively that no deductive justification is possible. Thus the deductionist's quest for a solution of the "problem of induction" is hopeless—even by his own standards.

In order to show this, we need some agreed definition of "inductive argument." Let us take, for the sake of illustration, Peirce's definition: "Induction is where we generalize from a number of cases of which something is true, and infer that the same thing is true of a whole class."[3] Any argument conforming to the definition will clearly not be deductive. For the premises will have the form: (p_1) A_1 is B, (p_2) A_2 is B, . . . , (p_n) A_n is B; while the conclusion will have the form: (c) all A are B. Now I take it to be beyond dispute that the conjunc-

[3] *Collected Papers of Charles Sanders Peirce* (Cambridge, Mass., 1932), 2: 375.

tion of all the premises $(p_1 \cdot p_2 \cdot \ldots \cdot p_n)$ is compatible with the negation of the conclusion $(\sim c)$. For there would be no logical contradiction in asserting that n of the A's were B, while all the other A's were not-B. The conjunction of all the premises and the negation of the conclusion $(p_1 \cdot p_2 \cdot \ldots \cdot p_n \cdot \sim c)$ is a *logically possible* assertion.

Suppose now it is desired to validate the argument in question, by adding a *logically necessary* (or a priori) premise (P). Since we have supposed that the conjunction of the original premises and the negation of the conclusion $(p_1 \cdot p_2 \cdot \ldots \cdot p_n \cdot \sim c)$ *may* be true (i.e., without contradiction), and since P *must* be true in all cases, we see that the conjunction $(P \cdot p_1 \cdot p_2 \cdot \ldots \cdot p_n \cdot \sim c)$ may also be true.[4] Thus adding a logically necessary principle as a premise cannot convert the inductive argument into one which is deductively valid.

Peirce's definition of induction was used above only for the sake of illustration: the line of argument is sufficiently general to apply to most definitions of induction that have been proposed or accepted. (But we shall have to make an exception, as will be seen later, for definitions which require the conclusion of an inductive argument to take the form of a probability assertion.) For whatever differences such definitions may show, they will be found to agree in permitting the negation of the conclusion to be consistent with the joint assertion of all the premises. (Unless this were so, induction would be a species of deduction, and there would be no problem.) And so long as this is so, our argument will apply: no addition of a logically necessary (a priori) premise can prevent the negation of the conclusion from remaining compatible with the joint assertion of the *new* set of premises; the argument remains incorrigibly inductive.

To put the matter briefly: *induction, by definition, is not a species of deduction*. Hence we can see in advance that the search for a deductive justification of induction is hopeless.

Nevertheless a tremendous amount of ingenuity has gone

---

[4] The principle used in this paragraph is that the logical product of a necessary proposition and a possible proposition is a possible proposition.

[67]

into the search for deductive justifications of induction. One reason why such undertakings have not seemed hopeless from the outset is that philosophers have modified their definition of inductive argument in such a way as to allow the conclusion to appear as a probability assertion. In view of the prevalent obscurity of the notion of "probability" it has been possible for those who proceed in this way not to be clear whether they were making the "inductive arguments" deductive or nondeductive. But when the ambiguity in the notion of probability is removed, it will be found (as will now be shown) that no contribution is made to the "problem of induction" by such recourse to a probability interpretation.

5. THE PROBABILITY INTERPRETATION OF INDUCTIVE ARGUMENT
   NO SOLUTION OF THE "PROBLEM OF INDUCTION"

The clearest statement known to me of one form of what I propose to call the "probability interpretation" of inductive argument has been given by Broad: Having argued that induction by simple enumeration involves a formal fallacy, he continues:

The conclusions of inductive argument must therefore be modified, and the most reasonable modification to make is to state them in terms of probability. . . . With the suggested modification of our conclusion the logical difficulty vanishes. Suppose the conclusion becomes that it is highly probable that all *S*'s are *P*. There is then no illicit process. We argue from a certain proposition about *some S*'s to the probability of a proposition about all *S*'s. This is perfectly legitimate.[5]

This view, that *categorical* inductive conclusions are not "legitimate" and ought to be replaced by probability statements, is very popular today. (Indeed it is commonly taken as almost too obvious for discussion that inductive conclusions ought not to be regarded as more than probable.)

What does it mean to say *P is probable*, in a sense in which this statement is contrasted with *P* (or *P is true*)? This ques-

[5] C. D. Broad, *Mind*, 27 (1918): 391. The quoted passage incidentally shows that Broad, like Ewing, is looking for deductive justification.

tion is not to be dismissed offhand, as if the answer were obvious. Certainly we use probability notions successfully, and sometimes with great accuracy (as in actuarial forecasts), but there is no general agreement on the *analysis* (or definition) of probability.

But, at any rate, all analysts agree in accepting the following two statements:

(i) "*P* is probable" does not mean the same as "*P* is true."

(ii) "*P* is probable" is compatible both with "*P* is true" and with "*P* is false."

Indeed, unless statements (i) and (ii) are accepted, there is no point in substituting *P is probable* for *P* as the conclusion of a typical inductive argument. For unless (i) is the case, no change is being made. And if (ii) is not the case, it must be possible to deduce from *P is probable* either *P is true* or else *P is false;* while, if this were so, the original premises would "legitimately" entail a conclusion (*P is true* or *P is false*) not in the probability form—so, again, nothing has been gained.

All of this is sufficiently obvious, perhaps. It may be that no advocates of the probability interpretation would deny that *P is probable* is compatible both with the truth and with the falsity of *P*. But none of them seem to be dismayed by the consequent lack of verifiability of the inductive conclusions in the form they take to be standard. The view I am criticizing asserts that I am not justified in claiming *that I have two legs at this moment* (*P*)—to take that as an illustration—and am at best justified in claiming *that it is highly probable that I have two legs at this moment* (*Q*). Now suppose, in some way or another, I find *Q* to be true;[6] then *P* has not been verified, since *Q* might have been true even if *P* were false. Or, again, suppose *Q* is found to be false; then *P* has not been falsified, for *P* might be true even if *Q* were false.

It seems, then, that if we were to follow the recommendations of the advocates of the probability interpretation, we could not be shown to be right by the verification of *P*, nor

[6] It is hard to see how, on the probability interpretation, this could be done—and that is an extra difficulty.

[69]

wrong by the verification of $\sim P$. We can be sure, then, that on this view, the statement substituted for "P" (viz., "P is probable") is not about what P is about but about something else. But *what* else?

The answer will depend upon the analysis of probability which we find it proper to adopt. I shall consider only the "classical" (or "Laplacean") type of view and the frequency type.

On the classical view (or current modifications of it), the meaning of *P is probable* (in some specified degree) is explained in terms of the logical relation of P to some set of conditions constituting the evidence for P. In the older forms, if we know that P expresses one of a set of n "equally possible" alternatives, P is said to have a probability of $1/n$; while in modern variants the alternatives may be so weighted as to call for a more complex rule of calculation. The critical point, however, is that the (appropriate) evidence conditions *entail* that P is probable (in the corresponding degree). No doubt when Broad, in the passage cited above, regarded the passage from *some S's are P* to *it is probable that all S's are P* as legitimate he had some such neo-Laplacean notion of probability in mind.

So conceived, *P is probable* is undoubtedly entailed by the premises of the inductive argument; we have *deductive* assurance that if the premises are true the conclusion will be true. But is this what we want? The original inductive argument (from *Some S's are P* to *All S's are P*) was of interest because we were hopeful of being permitted to infer the character of *S*'s hitherto unobserved; but the substituted conclusion (*All S's are P* is probable), on the present interpretation, follows deductively from the evidence (*Some S's are P*) and tells us nothing about the unobserved cases. If we supposed that the fact that *All S's are P* is probable provided *any* good reason, on this view, for expecting unobserved *S*'s to be *P*, we should be mistaken.

Consider what reason could be supplied for preferring the "more probable" to the "less probable" conclusion of an inductive argument (probability understood in the Laplacean

JUSTIFICATION OF INDUCTION

sense). All that so far distinguishes the two cases is that the two propositions between which we have to choose have different logical relationships to the available evidence. But why should this difference be of any importance? What verifiable differences will result if we perversely choose the conclusion which, on this view, is the *less* probable? To such questions, the theory has no satisfactory answer.[7]

Let me try to make the difficulty plainer. A lunatic, compelled to choose between two alternative conclusions of an inductive argument, might regularly adopt that proposition in whose verbal formulation the more letters occurred. Why should *verbal prolixity* be regarded as inferior to probability (defined in the neo-Laplacean way) as a guide to the future? For *both* notions are defined in such a fashion that their applicability to a proposition can be established independently of that propositions's truth, and independently of any future outcome of attempts at verification. Where a proposition is probable (in the neo-Laplacean sense) it remains so, in relation to the evidence, *no matter what the outcome*. It seems impossible, then, that any verifiable consequences *with respect to matters of fact* can follow from an inductive argument terminating in such an assertion of probability. In the attempt to certify the conclusions of inductive arguments in relation to a deductive standard of justification, the neo-Laplacean succeeds, but at the expense of removing all empirical content from the conclusion. What he justifies is not an inductive conclusion of any interest, but a sorry substitute for it; we wanted

[7] Cf. J. M. Keynes: "Probability begins and ends with probability. That a scientific investigation pursued on account of its probability will generally lead to truth, rather than falsehood, is at best only probable. The proposition that a course of action guided by the most probable considerations will generally lead to success, is not certainly true and has nothing to recommend it but its probability" (*Treatise on Probability* [London, 1921], p. 322). But if probability is no more than some logical relationship between a proposition and a class of propositions (or, on Keynes's view, an undefinable relation between propositions), the choice of probable conclusions seems to have very little to "recommend" it.

to be sure that milk would nourish us—he insists that water will do no harm.[8]

On the frequency view,[9] probability statements do indeed have verifiable consequences with regard to unobserved instances. Hence the frequency view is exempt from the criticisms elaborated above and needs separate consideration.

Neglecting refinements of detail, we may say that the frequency view interprets probability statements as statistical summaries of frequencies in indefinitely extended series of observations. Suppose all Manx cats hitherto observed to have had no tails; the conclusion *Any (unspecified) Manx cat will probably be tailless* means, on this view: The proportion of Manx cats who have no tails is greater than one half. Thus if we use the conclusion to predict the nonoccurrence of a tail in the case of one Manx cat after another we shall, if the inductive argument was sound, be right more often than not "in the long run."[10]

If we had drawn the categorical conclusion, *Any S is P*, we would have been committed to asserting that each observed *S* would prove to be *P*; by saying, instead, *Any S is probably P*,

[8] I do not say that Laplace, Keynes, or others of this way of thinking are in fact unreasonable in their choice of criteria of rational action with regard to matters of fact: I contend only that they cannot know reliance upon probability, in their sense, to be rational without appeal to induction. It seems obvious to me that the rationality of any criterion must involve some kind of reference to the frequency of *success* of the favored procedure. If this is so, the *kind* of defense which a neo-Laplacean can give for his reliance upon probability must take the form of some principle connecting probability with successful predictability. But such a principle can only be inductively grounded.

[9] For representative versions, see R. von Mises, *Probability, Statistics and Truth* (London, 1939), or E. Nagel, *Principles of the Theory of Probability* (Chicago, 1939).

[10] I am deliberately ignoring, as unnecessary for the purpose in hand, the technical difficulties connected with the definition of a ratio of frequencies in *infinite* classes. It will be noticed that I am here considering a conclusion of the form *Any S is probably P* rather than *All S's are probably P*, as before. This is to make it easier to sketch the frequency view and is immaterial to my main argument.

we weaken the conclusion, since we maintain only that a *majority* of the observed *S*'s will be *P*. Thus the substitution of the modified conclusion (*Any S is probably P*) for the original conclusion (*Any S is P*) does, on the frequency view, weaken the force of the argument's conclusion and thereby strengthen our assurance of the argument's reliability.

It will be obvious, however, that on this view, the new and weaker conclusion is not a deductive consequence of the premises. There is certainly no inconsistency involved in maintaining on the one hand that all the members of a sample drawn from a class have a certain characteristic and, on the other hand, that a majority of the members of the class do not have that characteristic.[11] The deductionist critic will find the same kind of difficulty in making predictions concerning frequencies in series or classes of events as he found in making predictions about single events. For the evidence that allows us to conclude to the frequencies in classes of events of which a sample is before us is again inductive in character. The reason for asserting that series of events yet unobserved will have some describable statistical property is that other *observed* series have been found to have the same, or a similar, statistical property. And this is still an induction, though of different form from those we were examining before. The inference from evidence about the statistical distribution of frequencies in observed classes to the statistical distribution to be expected in classes yet unobserved is just as "risky" or "subject to error" as any other inductive inference. For we may well remind ourselves, once more, that the deductionist is *not* interested in practical questions of the *relative* reliability of alternative conclusions for inductive arguments. There are good, practical reasons for sometimes confining our inductive conclusions to cautious assertions of probability (notably so in cases where the evidence is not homogeneous); and if the de-

[11] Let the class be that of positive integers. And let the sample consist of the integers smaller than six. Then all members of the sample are less than six; but practically none of the integers (i.e., the members of the class from which the sample was taken) have that characteristic.

[73]

ductionist's attempt to modify the conclusions of inductive argument is persuasive it is through confusion with such practical considerations. But we have seen that the deductionist attack on induction is more radical in its character: he objects to induction solely because the negation of the conclusion is compatible with the assertion of the premises, i.e., because the premises do not *entail* the conclusion, i.e., because the argument is inductive and not deductive. Nothing but the impossible would satisfy the critic, viz., that induction should cease to be induction and become deduction instead. Thus no probability modification of inductive conclusions will resolve the difficulty. Either the new substituted conclusion *will* be entailed by the premises (as in the classical view)— and then the conclusion will no longer have reference to the unobserved, so that the purpose of inductive inference will be stultified; or else the inductive argument will not be trivialized in this way, and the modified conclusion will continue to refer to unobserved cases—but then the premises will not entail the conclusion, and the argument will remain inductive, to the critic's everlasting dissatisfaction. (The critic of induction would like to have the advantages of inductive argument without its "risks"—he hopes for implication of the conclusion by the premises to be both *synthetic* and a priori.)

6. IS THERE ANY "PROBLEM OF INDUCTION"?

When we have clearly recognized that the ground of complaint against induction is that induction, by definition, is not deduction, the misgivings of the critic of induction promise to dissolve into absurdity. There is something absurd in criticizing anything for being what it would be logically impossible for it not to be. And there is something oddly unsymmetrical about the criticism, also. For if induction cannot be deduction, neither can deduction be induction. If the sheer difference of the two modes of argument were sufficient ground for criticism we might with equal plausibility or lack of it bewail the inability of deduction to be induction. We are not entitled to argue, in general, from the mere difference of two things to the superior cognitive value of either term of the inequation. At some point it would seem requisite to show that deduction is, in some way, *superior* to induction. Now it is instructive that this crucial step in the attack upon induction is seldom made explicitly. What happens, instead, is (i) that it is simply taken for granted, as too obvious for discussion, that deduction is "better" than induction for cognitive purposes; and (ii) such key terms as "evidence," "proof," "knowledge," and "validity" are used in *partly normative* senses which presuppose the correctness of (i). When a deductionist critic of induction says, "We don't *really know* that the sun will rise tomorrow," he means, by *"really* know," know in the deductive fashion of mathematics or logic; and it is because he believes that "real knowledge" is better than what "commonly passes for" knowledge that his comment has power to disturb the unsophisticated. Remove the evaluative or normative implications of the statement and we are left again with the undisturbing platitude that we don't know that the sun will rise tomorrow as we know the binomial theorem or De Morgan's rules in the algebra of classes. (Why should we?)

7. THE LINGUISTIC ASPECTS OF THE PROBLEM

It does not require much linguistic penetration or acquaintance with "ordinary usage" to appreciate that the use of language made by the critic of induction deviates in a misleading manner from some ordinary usage. There is *a* usage of "know" (and cognate terms such as "really know" or "seem to know") in which it is *correct* to say that I know all manner of matters of fact on inductive evidence. It would be speaking in a very ridiculous fashion to say that the assertion, "I know that I have two ears" (made as I write this), is incorrect. This type of case is unquestionably one of the cases for which the term "know" is intended to be used according to the habits and rules governing correct English usage. When I say that the word is used correctly, I do not mean that no rules of grammar are breached, so that one is speaking "good English."

[75]

By "correct" I mean to imply more than this. To say that a word is correctly used, in accordance with a normal usage, in certain circumstances, is to say that a certain sentence containing the word is, in those circumstances, true. Hence, to say, as I do, that it is correct for me to say now, "I know that I have two ears," is to imply that I *do* know now that I have two ears. This, in turn, implies that I do *have* two ears.

Perhaps the critic will not deny this. He may grant that in an *ordinary* and common usage, I *am* entitled to claim now that I know I have two ears; but he will very likely continue to insist that I do not "strictly" or "really" know it. And if he does this, there is serious risk of ambiguity. If a mathematician tells a carpenter that he will be unable to mark points on his drawings or models in future, the good man may properly be alarmed, suspecting some change in the order of nature which will destroy the basis of his livelihood. When the carpenter learns, however, that the mathematician is talking about the kind of point which it is logically impossible to draw on paper, he may take heart. For he now realizes that the criticism amounts to no more than the observation that the point drawn on paper is not a "mathematical point." Since he is also to be permitted to talk, albeit vaguely and unphilosophically, about "ordinary" or "approximate" points, his practice and his expectations remain unaffected by the criticism. The permission to retain a common-sense distinction between "strict" (or "mathematical") and "ordinary" (or "approximate" or "physical") points leaves the original terminology essentially unchanged.

In such a concocted illustration, the shift in use of words (from "ordinary" point to "strict" point) is too conspicuous to be overlooked. But when the deductionist criticizes inductive argument, and the uses of key terms such as 'know' which go with it, he easily falls into a similar trap. We are told that "strict" knowledge occurs only when a conclusion is deduced from unquestionable premises; that it is logically impossible for predictive assertions concerning matters of fact to be so deduced; and we are persuaded to assume that these remarks are pertinent to the sense of knowledge used in contrasting *knowledge* about the unobserved with *hypothesis* or mere *conjecture*.

In one way, indeed, the procedure of the critic of inductive knowledge is more misleading than that of the geometer who claims that "real points" cannot be drawn upon paper. The geometrical notion of a point having position but no magnitude yields a helpful standard of successive approximation for the draftsman. One may be said to draw *better* points insofar as he succeeds in reducing their magnitude and thereby renders their positions more definite. But to suggest that the goal of procedures by which we seek to acquire knowledge about matters of fact should be that of deducing conclusions from unquestionable premises is to propose a worthless ideal. There are obvious criteria for determining the degree of approximation of a physical point to the ideal geometrical point; but there is no way in which an inductive argument can approach the ideal of deductive argument. Mere increase in evidence does nothing to bridge the "gap" between induction and deduction. If all the particular facts about the past history of the universe were known to us at this moment, the passage to a prediction about the character of the very next instant of our own experience would remain inductive, not deductive.

Similar remarks would apply to the use of the related words "evidence," "proof," "doubt," "certainty," and "justification." For the usages of such epistemic words depend upon one another. If we say, "Such and such is known," we are committed to saying, "*There is no doubt that* such and such is true," and again, "*It is certain that* such and such is true," and, "*We are justified* in saying such and such is true"—at any rate in perfectly normal and familiar senses of the epistemic terms in question.[12]

So in quite familiar senses of the words "doubt," "certain," and "justified," nothing that the critic of induction has to say

---

[12] The different phrases are not exact synonyms, however, and consequently show different patterns of variation of meaning.

has the slightest tendency to throw doubt upon the truth of the proposition that I have two ears or to suggest that it is not certain that I have them, or that I am not justified in claiming that I have them.

It seems, therefore, that what the critic of induction is mainly doing is proposing a change of terminology. While maintaining the distinctions we *now* make between knowledge, probable hypothesis, and conjecture (in common or ordinary senses), he wants to use other labels. Where we say "know with certainty," he prefers to say "practically know" or "have a belief which is practically certain"; where we say "know by deduction from a priori premises," he wants to say "really know." This leads some writers to say that the critic is merely recommending a "change in language."

8. IS THE CRITIC ONLY MAKING LINGUISTIC PROPOSALS?

A number of philosophers have claimed that the critic of induction is offering a "recommendation" to change ordinary language.[13] Impressed by the incorrigibility of statements about logical or mathematical relationships, he is said to favor reserving such terms as "knowledge" and "certainty" for those cases, abolishing for that purpose the common or ordinary senses in which the words are used.[14]

This analysis of the dispute between the defenders of induction and their critics is illuminating, so far as it goes. Our disagreement with the critic *is*, in part, merely verbal. He *does* wish the term "knowledge" and the associated terms "certain," "justified," and so on to be reserved for a priori propositions; and we, on the other hand, want the term "knowledge" and its cognates to continue to be applicable to a much wider class of cases, so that it may continue to be correct to claim knowledge of all manner of matters of fact.

If our dispute consisted in no more than this, it might be

[13] Thus N. Malcolm, in "Certainty and Empirical Statements" (*Mind*, 51 [1942]: 36): "Let us consider another aspect of the recommendation to discontinue the application of 'certain' to empirical statements."

[14] N. Malcolm, *op. cit.*, p. 35.

swiftly settled. The critic, as we have already noted, does not propose to abolish the distinctions now made at the common-sense level: he grants that *practical* certainty may be distinguished from hypothesis or conjecture. We, on the other hand, are not at all unwilling to recognize a difference between knowledge of the truth of a priori statements and knowledge of the truth of empirical statements. Thus the proposal or recommendation we have to consider is that there shall be a change of verbal *labels:* the choice is between two intertranslatable philosophical dialects, and anything that either disputant can say in his language, his opponent can say in his. There remain, it is true, some differences. Every philosophical idiom stresses some analogies at the expense of others, and it may be that one idiom rather than another may be found especially misleading. But this can hardly give ground for extended debate between reasonable men.

Yet the fact is that the critic will by no means be pacified by any such interpretation of what he is asserting. The critic is not so doctrinaire as to insist that ordinary men shall speak philosophically when engaged on their familiar occasions,[15] nor will the critic be satisfied by a proposal merely to *speak* in a way he is supposed to be recommending. This is enough, perhaps, to show that the recommendation, if there is one, must be a very queer recommendation indeed. For (i) the man who might be supposed to know best whether he is making a recommendation strenuously resists the suggestion;[16]

---

[15] Cf. Hume's statement: "Tho' everyone be free to use his terms in what sense he pleases; and accordingly in the precedent part of this discourse, I have followed this method of expression [in terms of probabilities], 'tis however certain that in common discourse we readily affirm, that many arguments from causation exceed probability, and may be regarded as a superior kind of evidence. One would appear ridiculous, who would say, that 'tis only probable the sun will rise tomorrow, or that all men must dye" (*Treatise*, part 3, section 11).

[16] Cf. Moore's retort to a similar suggestion: "I see no reason to accept [the] . . . view that those who say 'We don't know that there are any external objects' are merely making a recommendation as to how 'know' *ought* to be used" (*The Philosophy of G. E. Moore* [Evanston, 1942], p. 674).

(ii) the verbal changes in question may be freely conceded by both sides; (iii) the "changes" in question are matters of emphasis rather than substantial innovations of usage—the deductionist speaks as good English as his opponents. Even the most liberal supporter of the use of terms in Pickwickian senses should hesitate before calling what is here at stake a "recommendation." (We may say, indeed, that the use of "recommendation" here is metaphorical—itself, on this view, a recommendation to use "recommendation" in an unusual fashion.) It might, indeed, be less misleading to say there is *no* dispute between the parties, whether about words or matters of fact. But this would still leave us to explain how the appearance or semblance of a dispute arises.

I am inclined to think that the deductionist believes that one form of expression (restriction of the term "knowledge" to cases of necessary truths) is *better* than the other—because it "conforms more exactly to reality." So that however willing he may be to concede the practical convenience of using "knowledge" in other senses, he wishes to reserve the eulogistic connotations of the favored epistemic terms for cases which are sufficiently deserving. He will *not* be satisfied if we merely pronounce the noise "knowledge" in the cases he designates; he wants us to agree that knowledge of a priori truths is superior in value to the modes of apprehension (whatever we like to call them) by which we are led to accept empirical statements; he is sure that deduction is superior to induction. If we are to defend induction against its ablest attackers we must try to understand and refute this view.

9. IS DEDUCTION "SUPERIOR" TO INDUCTION?

The superiority supposedly attaching to knowledge of necessary truths (e.g., in mathematics) results from the supposed "certainty" or "infallibility" of the means by which such knowledge is acquired. By contrast with the "certainty" with which one may claim to know that the sum of three and four is seven, a belief that there will be at least one storm before the year is out appears fallible, unsure, subject to correction or disproof.

Or, at any rate, this is how the comparison is presented. We are often invited to compare some mathematical proposition (that the sum of three and four is seven), whose truth is established beyond any question, with some empirical proposition (that there will be at least one storm before the year is out) whose truth is, at best, questionable. If an empirical proposition supported by stronger evidence were compared with a less trivial mathematical proposition, it is not so clear that the verdict would not be reversed. If I had to compare the proposition *that I have a body* with that in which the Binomial Theorem is formulated, I should be inclined to say that the former is *more* "certain" than the latter. If I have any reservations, it is because I am so unclear as to what is meant in such contexts by "certainty." When the term is construed as a psychological predicate, its application in a eulogistic sense to true mathematical propositions becomes philosophically trivial. For to say that mathematical theorems are certain in this sense is to say only that men feel certain about them; but the same is true of a vast number of true empirical propositions. And if it is said that such feelings of certainty are a *safer guide* in mathematics than in predicting the outcome of matters of fact, the point may be conceded. But it is possible to make serious blunders in mathematics, and it is not uncommon to make empirical predictions of high precision and accuracy.

Apart from such psychological, or semipsychological, senses of the term "certainty," what other meaning can be given to saying that the mathematical theorems are certain? Regarded in abstraction from what men think, correctly or incorrectly, *about* the theorems, those theorems are neither certain nor doubtful. They either do, or do not, follow from relevant premises: they either are, or are not, in accord with the properties of the mathematical entities to which they refer. The same is true, however, of *empirical* propositions. Regarded

[81]

in abstraction from what men think, correctly or incorrectly, *about* empirical propositions, such propositions are neither certain nor doubtful. They either do, or do not, follow from the relevant premises: they either do, or do not, describe what further observations will show to be the case. The notion that mathematical assertions have "superior certainty" is the outcome of unwarranted attribution of psychological predicates ("certain," "doubtful") to nonpsychological subject matter (that to which the propositions of mathematics refer).

Some rationalists will object at this point that no account has been taken of the superior *intelligibility* of mathematical reasoning. "Suppose the inductive inference from *P* (that moving billiard balls come into contact) to *C* (that the balls rebound) does in fact continually prove to be reliable," we may imagine them to say, "it still remains a brute matter of fact that the predicted result is verified. After the ten thousandth collision I understand no better than after the first *why* the result should have occurred. Contrast this with the situation in mathematics where I can *see* why a closed plane curve must have an inside and an outside."

There is a twofold answer to this objection. On the one hand, there is no reason to admit that physical occurrences (or the propositions formulating truth claims with regard to them) must be "unintelligible." We can very well explain *why* billiard balls rebound after collisions, e.g., in terms of what we know about their elasticities. If *this* kind of explanation (in terms of other empirical uniformities) is rejected *in principle*, the critic is once again surreptitiously introducing a special ideal of intelligibility and explanation. If by "intelligible" he means "intelligible in the way mathematical theorems are intelligible," we may grant that matters of fact are unintelligible. But so long as we refuse to accept the relevance of the implicit standard, the concession is negligible.

We may also counterattack with advantage. Mathematical intuition may be subjectively satisfying, but no more than any other means of cognitive apprehension does it carry its own warrant of assurance. Intuitions may be mistaken, and

[82]

those that masquerade as trustworthy guides are distinguishable by no infallible symptom from the impostors. Intelligibility is never enough to certify the reliability of mathematical thought.

It may be useful to remind ourselves of some general considerations. If induction and deduction are compared with regard to their relative values, it can only be their *instrumental* values that can be in question. For I do not suppose that anybody who seriously maintains induction to be "better" than deduction holds this to be so, *independently of any purpose which induction and deduction are to serve.* In any case, such a judgment would be irrelevant to the present discussion. It may be that some men get aesthetic pleasure from contemplating the proofs and theorems of pure mathematics; and perhaps induction by contrast seems lumbering, untidy, and opportunistic. But the formal beauty of logic and mathematics is no ground for ascribing to them any preferential *cognitive* value: beauty is not truth, in spite of Keats, nor is the more aesthetically satisfying the "more likely" to yield the truth.

I take it for granted, then, that induction and deduction are to be compared with respect to their relative capacity to serve some common end (or, at least, different ends whose values are in turn comparable). That common end can surely be nothing else than that of *knowledge, rationally achieved.*

Once again, as so often before in the course of this discussion, we must beware of so *defining* the common end of both induction and deduction that the superior instrumental value of one follows automatically from the definition. We could *define* the common end of eating and drinking as the quenching of thirst; and then it would be necessarily true that drinking was superior to eating with respect to the achievement of *that* end. But this would be a trivial conclusion, mischievously expressed; for it would amount to saying that drinking is better than eating for the purposes which drinking, but not eating, can serve; and this is a tautology from which nothing of importance follows. We might just as well choose to say that the satisfaction of hunger is the "common end" of both eating

[83]

and drinking; and it would then follow, necessarily, that in this highly misleading sense eating was "superior" to drinking.

On no account, therefore, ought we to say that deduction is "superior" to induction as yielding "certainty." For "certainty" is a synonym for "necessity," which is a defining characteristic of what we mean by "deduction." To use certainty as a criterion for the preferential value judgment in favor of deduction is to nail to the mast the tautology that deduction is a "better" means to the attainment of whatever ends it, but not induction, can attain. And we might just as well (or just as foolishly) retort that, on the contrary, induction is better than deduction, as yielding conclusions *not* entailed by the premises. For this is the tautology that induction is better fitted to achieve the ends which it, but not deduction, can by definition achieve.

Can we try to escape from this judgment of the triviality and irrelevance of using certainty as a criterion of cognitive value by arguing that induction and deduction have *different, though comparable* values? But what could it mean to say that knowledge of a necessary truth was, somehow, "better" than knowledge of a well-grounded inductive truth? What would be the basis of comparison? Would it not be as if to say that a quadratic equation was better than a weather forecast?

Yet I want to maintain that the two processes do have a common end, in relation to which a comparison of relative value would be neither trivial nor absurd. In determining the ends which are intended to be served by human activities we have no better recourse than to observe how we employ those activities in practice. On this basis I suggest that the common end of induction and formal insight is that of *establishing by reliable*[17] *methods conclusions which are comprehensive, systematic, and true.* (This is, of course, an attempt to formulate in outline the dominant aim of science, and to a lesser degree, the cognitive pursuits of everyday affairs.) In saying that both induction and formal insight are intended to serve the end suggested,

[17] The deductionist might say that the use of this term begs the question at issue.

I am making a significant empirical statement, which does not follow tautologically from the definitions of either process or both. And a judgment of relative efficacy in achieving this end would be significant and free from the defects of the versions previously rejected.

But is it *true* to say that formal insight serves better than induction the ideal of comprehensive, systematic, and truthful conclusion from evidence? There is something absurd about this question—as there would be in asking whether the bricks or the beams contribute more to the building of a house. The fact is that formal insight and inductive inference are not competing and mutually exclusive means for the achievement of the general aims of cognitive inquiry; on the contrary, the conduct of scientific investigations constantly illustrates the need to supplement each process with the other. It is a travesty of scientific method to suggest that much progress toward the discovery of comprehensive and systematic truth can be made without appeal to the formal disciplines of mathematics and logic; but it is equally so to deny the indispensability of induction.

We must remember that the high reliability of deduction is counterbalanced by the corresponding poverty of content of its products; induction may often be attended by a high risk of error, but the predictions resulting from its use are often of striking novelty and practical importance. There is no single scale on which to measure the relative merits of induction and deduction: Certainly there can be no sense in saying reliability is better than comprehensiveness when both are essential aspects of the only procedures which seem to serve the aims of rational inquiry. The most that we are entitled to say is that, in respect of reliability, deduction has advantages not shared in the same measure by induction; while in respect of comprehensiveness of reference to matters of fact the latter has advantages absent from the former. But all this gives no grounds for saying that one is "better" than the other; or that eulogistic epistemic terms should be reserved exclusively for the products of either method; or that one, but not the other,

[85]

is inherently defective and a fit subject for pessimistic animadversion.

I conclude that the preferential value judgment which underlies the deductionist's "recommendation" for the use of language has no foundation except confusion. Irrational preference for deduction would be less mischievous than it is but for the futile labors it encourages. So long as deduction is cherished as the paradigm of cognitive method, the illusion will persist that induction is an imperfect approximation to deduction; and that the aim of empirical inquiry is to increase the probability of inductive conclusions until it reaches the limit of deductive certainty. So we are led to search in a fashion which is bound to be self-defeating for principles which will "guarantee" or "justify" induction; or for some "necessary connection" between matters of fact. These efforts lead nowhere. So long as induction is by definition not deduction, no amount of effort by contemporary rationalists will do more than to dress up the same platitude in more or less ingenious disguise.

10. INDUCTIVE JUSTIFICATION OF INDUCTIVE METHODS

Yet, after all, there is a kind of justification of induction which is sometimes both possible and necessary. There is no sense, to be sure, in attempting to justify induction in general—for there is no relevant and authoritative standard of justification to which appeal could be made. Specific principles of inductive procedure (e.g., those which constitute the basis of statistical sampling), however, need not be used dogmatically and may sometimes be properly challenged.

Suppose a statistician to draw inferences concerning "populations" of a certain kind by examining a sample of 10 per cent of those populations. If the mode of inference be criticized, it may be defended by examining a *sample of inferences*. We might examine a large class of cases where an inference was made according to the procedure in question: should it be the case that in a very large proportion, say 95 per cent, of the cases the inference proved to be correct, we might properly argue that the inductive procedure had been justi-fied. (If, however, the systematic examination of the method showed a large proportion of mistaken inferences, the original procedure would have to be modified or abandoned. This shows that the examination of samples of inferences is not merely a prolongation of the original procedure.)

This way of justifying an inductive procedure is, of course, inductive in character. In order to show that the original sampling procedure was reliable, we had ourselves to argue from a set of examined inferences to inferences as yet to be performed. As a proof of the general validity of sampling (arguing from *Some S are P* to *All S are P*) our justification would clearly be circular. But we were not trying to *prove* anything, in the deductive sense; and since we were adducing *new* evidence, our justification could not be regarded as viciously circular.

Such inductive justification cannot be final. If the method used in the course of justification is itself challenged, we could devise a further inductive test of *its* reliability. And the last method used could always itself be put to further test.

It is not to be supposed, in the light of what has been said, that sound inductive method requires the performance of an infinite series of justification, justification of justification, justification of justification of justification, and so on, without end. At the simplest level of inductive argument, in which methods are used uncritically, it is sufficient for the correct-ness of an inductive inference from A to B that a method be used which *in fact* works in such cases (or a large majority of them). By observing the title on the outside cover of a book I may correctly draw the inductive inference that the same title will appear on the title page. The inference is correct be-cause it *in fact* works in such cases; and I may properly be said to know the truth of the conclusion. Yet to know is not the same as to know that I know. And for *some* purposes it may be desired to check the inductive method used in the inference by appeal to *further* inductive evidence based upon an examination of a sample of similar inferences. For other

[87]

purposes, however, it may be satisfactory and proper to draw the correct inference habitually without subjecting the principle of the inference itself to inductive test. It is easy to make the mistake of supposing that the first inductive inference must be strengthened by successful inductive test and, conversely, is weak without it. But this is not the case. If an umbrella in fact keeps the rain off my head, it does all that can be expected of it; to raise a second umbrella above the first does not improve the situation; and to demand an infinite series of umbrellas would be to destroy the utility of that convenient domestic object. We may always reconsider the methods used in inductive procedures, and we may, thereby, serve the desirable end of unifying branches of inductive inquiry previously separated. No matter how refined or searching our methods become (as principles of inductive procedure are made explicit and precise) there will be some places in the entire structure where we use a method *without producing justification*. (A house rests upon a foundation, and that in time may be supported by a deeper foundation, but at the very bottom there is a last foundation which supports without being supported.) But we may always produce further justification if challenged. Every inductive principle can be justified—but not all at the same time.

IV

The Semantic
Definition
of Truth

WAS LED TO WRITE this essay by a suspicion that others, too, had found it hard to understand the significance of the so-called "semantic" definition of truth constructed by Professor Alfred Tarski.[1] Part of the trouble is due to the fact that Tarski defines the term "true in L," where L is one of a number of *artificial* languages of relatively simple structure. His definition is complex. But when its technicalities have been mastered, one is left wondering how far the definition could be adapted to "ordinary" English or any other "natural" language. And one may wonder how far the results illuminate the *"philosophical* problem of truth."[2]

I shall try to describe, as simply as possible, the distinctive features of Tarski's procedure. Then I shall consider what modifications are needed if a similar definition of truth is to be framed for a *natural* language ("ordinary English"), and I will end with some critical remarks about the philosophical significance of the semantic definition.

2. THE NEED FOR SEMANTICAL TYPES

One feature of Tarski's procedure which we must be care-

[1] The basic source is Tarski's famous essay, "Der Wahrheitsbegriff in den formalisierten Sprachen," in *Studia Philosophica* (Lwów, 1935), 1: 261–405. This is a German translation of a Polish work published in 1933. A more popular outline, containing replies to criticism, is the same author's "The Semantic Conception of Truth," *Philosophy and Phenomenological Research*, 4 (1944): 341–375. I shall refer to these works as *WFS* and *SCT*, respectively.

[2] Tarski himself claims *philosophical* significance for his work: "Its central problem—construction of a definition of a true statement (*Aussage*) and establishment of the scientific foundations of the theory of truth—belongs to the domain of theory of knowledge, and is even reckoned as one of the main problems of this branch of philosophy. So I hope that this work will interest epistemologists (*Erkenntnistheoretiker*) and that they will be in a position to analyze critically the results contained therein, and use them for further research in this field . . ." (*WFS*, p. 392, translated).

Cf. also *SCT*, pp. 342–343, where Tarski's definition is represented as a refined version of the "classical Aristotelian conception of truth" and the "correspondence theory."

[91]

ful to imitate is a rigorous observance of the distinction between an "object-" and a "meta-" language. The need for this, or an equivalent, is easily shown by an argument making use of the following figure:

> The statement printed within a rectangle on this page is false.

To save tiresome verbiage, let "*c*" be agreed to be an abbreviation for the words, "The statement printed within a rectangle on this page." If the reader will consider the meaning of "*c*" and then *examine this page*, he should be led to accept:
(1) *c* is identical with the statement "*c* is false."

On the other hand, it seems hardly possible to deny:
(2) "*c* is false" is true if and only if *c* is false.

From (1) and (2) there follows:[3]
(3) *c* is true if and only if *c* is false,

which is a self-contradiction. From an empirical truth (1), and a statement apparently true by definition (2), a contradiction has been deduced.[4]

This paradox arises through ambiguous use of the term "statement" and may be resolved by introducing an appropriate distinction. If statements containing the term "true" or "false" are systematically labeled "secondary" to distinguish them from the "*primary*" statements, from which those terms are absent, no paradox will arise. For the rectangle on this page must now be supposed to contain the words, "The *primary* statement printed within a rectangle on this page is false," which themselves constitute a *secondary* statement, say *s*. Since no primary statement is in fact printed within the rectangle, it is easily seen that *s* is false[5] but not self-contradictory.

Similar puzzles can be constructed by using such "semantic'›

[3] (2) has the form k is true $\equiv l$; (1) has the form $m = k$; substitution of m for k in (2) yields (3).

[4] This version of the Epimenides paradox is attributed to J. Lukasiewicz (cf. *WFS*, p. 270).

[5] Assuming Russell's analysis of the definite description, "*the* so-and-so."

terms as "designates" or "name of." A general distinction between object- and meta-language will prevent any of them
from occurring. A further precaution is an injunction against
the admission of such semantic words as primitive or undefined terms; it is a major task of semantics, in Tarski's program, to provide clear *definitions* of these suspects.

How this is to be done in the case of "truth," I shall soon
illustrate by means of an example (section 4).

3. THE CENTRAL IDEA OF TARSKI'S METHOD

The ideas which guide Tarski's search for a semantic definition of truth are deceptively simple: (i) He decides to interpret "true" as a predicate of object-language *sentences* (so
that a sentence of the form "*s* is true" belongs to the *meta-*
language). (ii) He tries to construct a definition of "true" of
which the following will be consequences:

"Today is Monday" is true $\equiv$ Today is Monday,[6]
"London is a city" is true $\equiv$ London is a city,
"Tom loves Mary" is true $\equiv$ Tom loves Mary,
and so on.

The enumeration of instances is deliberate; for it is impossible to give an adequate formal translation of the words
"and so on." In order to see the point of Tarski's work, it is
essential to understand why this is so.

The natural way to generalize the condition (ii) above
would be to say:

(Θ)   For all x, if x is a sentence, then "x" is true $\equiv x$.

But this formula is easily seen to be nonsensical. According to
the usual conventions for quotation marks, the symbol occurring immediately after the word "then" (in Θ) refers to
a constant, not a variable. In fact, "x" is the twenty-fourth *letter*
of the alphabet, and not even a sentence. Thus to say " 'x' is
true" is as nonsensical as to say "Tom is true."[7]

---

[6] Here " $\equiv$ " is the sign of logical equivalence, synonymous with "if and
only if."

[7] For reasons against interpreting " "x" " as the name of a variable
sentence, see *WFS*, pp. 274–276.

[93]

We might try to replace Θ by some such formula as:

For all x and y, if x is a sentence and y uniquely designates x, then y is true $\equiv x$.

But this does not belong to the *meta*-language, in which we wish the definition of "true" to be formulated: it is a sentence of the *meta-meta*-language.[8] And the undefined semantic term, "uniquely designates," is no less problematic than the term "truth" which is to be defined.

In default of a *simple* definition expressing the intent of condition (ii) above, the best we can do is to write a *schema*:

(S) s is true $\equiv x$.

We may say, informally and inexactly, that an acceptable definition of "true" must be such that every sentence obtained from S by replacing "x" by an object-sentence and "s" by a name or definite description of that object-sentence shall be true. But we must remember that to talk in this way is equivalent to paraphrasing the unacceptable formula Θ. At all events, S is *not* a definition of truth, but at best a criterion to guide us in the search for a definition.[9]

As the simplified language now to be described will illustrate, Tarski's definition of truth has quite a different form from that of the schema, S.

4. AN ILLUSTRATIVE MODEL[10]

We suppose our object-language, L, to contain the following vocabulary:

    "a"   "b"   "r"   "s"   "p"   "n"

The first four of these symbols are to be understood as respectively synonymous with "the Amazon," "the Baltic,"

---

[8] It refers to "primary" and "secondary" terms and must itself, therefore, contain *tertiary* terms.

[9] This point, made emphatically in both *WFS* and *SCT*, has been overlooked by many critics. Wrongly assuming S or some equivalent to be the proposed definition, they remain understandably puzzled by the pointlessness of the further maneuvers.

[10] Another helpful model may be found on p. 154 of M. Kokoszynká's illuminating paper, "Über den absoluten Wahrheitsbegriff und einige andere semantische Begriffe," *Erkenntnis*, 6 (1936): 143–165.

"is a river," and "is a sea"; "*p*" is the sign of a logical product, "*n*" the sign of negation.

As illustrations of *sentences* of **L** we take "ra," "*n*sb," and
"*np*rasb." These mean the same as "the Amazon is a river,"
"the Baltic is not a sea," and "it is not the case that the
Amazon is a river and also the Baltic is a sea."

The meta-language, **M**, in which we talk about signs belonging to **L**, includes (i) all signs belonging to **L**, (ii) the
signs "A," "B," "R," "S," "*P*," "*N*," which are names for
"a," "b," "r," "s," "*p*," "*n*," respectively, (iii) a convention
stipulating that "RA" shall be a name for "ra," "*N*RA" a
name for "*n*ra," and so on,[11] (iv) the usual symbols of the
logical operations, " $\sim$," "V," "(*x*)," " $=$," etc.

The definition of "true in **L**" proceeds in two stages. First
we define "sentence in **L**" or, as we shall say for short, "Sentence" (a term belonging to **M**, of course).

Using English, rather than **M**, as our meta-language, we
can say informally that a sign, u, (belonging to **L**) is a Sentence if and only if one of the following three conditions is
satisfied:

(i) u is "ra" or "rb" or "sa" or "sb,"

(ii) u is a sign composed of a Sentence preceded by "*n*,"

(iii) u is a sign composed of a Sentence preceded by a
Sentence preceded by "*p*."

The formal definition, expressed in **M**, will be:

u ϵ Sentence $=_{\text{Df}}$

$\{$ [(u $=$ RA) V (u $=$ RB) V (u $=$ SA) **V** (u $=$ SB)]

V [($\exists$v)(v ϵ Sentence $\cdot$ u $=$ Nv)]

V [($\exists$v)($\exists$w)(v ϵ Sentence $\cdot$ w ϵ Sentence $\cdot$ u $=$ Pvw)]$\}$.

This is a "recursive" definition: it supplies us with a means
of deciding in a finite number of steps whether any given
formula belonging to **L** is or is not a Sentence.[12]

[11] In a formal presentation, this vague description would have to be replaced by formal rules for the "concatenation" of symbols belonging to **M**.

[12] Thus suppose the formula is *PRAN*RB. Clause (iii), or its formal
equivalent, reduces the question whether this is a Sentence to the question
whether both RA and *N*RB are Sentences. Clause (i) shows RA to be a

[95]

Now we supply a definition of "true in **L**." Informally, using English again as a meta-language, we may say that a sign, u (belonging to **L**), is True provided that u is a Sentence (as previously defined) and, in addition, one of the following three conditions is satisfied:

(i) (u is "ra" and ra is the case) or (u is "rb" and rb is the case) or (u is "sa" and sa is the case) or (u is "sb" and sb is the case),

(ii) u has the form "*nv*" and v is *not* True,

(iii) u has the form "*p*vw" and both v and w are True.

The formal definition, expressed in **M**, is:

u ϵ True $=_{\text{Df}}$

(u ϵ Sentence) &

$\{$ [(u = RA $\cdot$ ra) V (u = RB $\cdot$ rb) V (u = SA $\cdot$ sa) V (u = SB $\cdot$ sb)

V [($\exists$v)(u = Nv $\cdot$ $\sim$(v ϵ True))

V [($\exists$v)($\exists$w)(u = Pvw $\cdot$ v ϵ True $\cdot$ w ϵ True)]$\}$.

Even in this highly simplified model, the definition of "true" has a formidable appearance. Yet its central notion is easy enough to grasp. Our object-language, **L**, has an infinity of sentences belonging to it, all of which, however, are constructed in a particularly simple fashion out of the four simplest sentences, RA, RB, SA, and SB, either by prefixing N to a given sentence, or by prefixing P to the combination of two given sentences. In the case of the simplest sentences, "RA ϵ True" is defined to be equivalent to "ra" ("The Amazon is a river" is true if and only if the Amazon is a river) and similarly for the other three simplest cases; while the more complex cases are reducible to the simpler ones, by means of the recursive definition provided.

An example may help to make this clearer. We wish to determine whether *PRANRB* is true. We already know *PRANRB* to be a sentence (see p. 95, note 12). The third clause of the definition requires us to determine whether *both*

Sentence, while clause (ii) shows NRB to be a Sentence if RB is one, which clause (i) again guarantees. Thus *PRANRB is* a Sentence.

RA and NRB are true. According to the first clause, RA is true if and only if ra; and according to the second and first clauses, NRB is true if and only if $\sim$rb. Now our *geographical knowledge* entitles us to affirm both "ra" and "*n*rb" (the Amazon *is* a river and the Baltic is *not* a river). Thus we may affirm that $PRAN$RB is true.

In all cases the procedure will be similar. A given complex sentence of **L** will either have the form "*n* (. . .)" or the form "*p* (. . .) (– – –)." If the first, we shall need to inquire whether "(. . .)" is *not* true; if the second, whether *both* "(. . .)" and "(– – –)" are true. In either case the problem has been reduced to that of the truth of simpler sentences.

It will be noticed that "$PRAN$RB" is the name of the sentence, "*pra*nrb"; and that the criterion of the truth of $PRAN$RB is explicitly expressed by "*pra*nrb." A similar situation will arise in general, *though we are not allowed to say so*. We can "see" that the test of the assertion "NRB is true" is expressed by "*n*rb"; the test of "$PSASB$ is true" is expressed by "*p*sasb"; and so on.[13] But every attempt to *say* this leads back to the illegitimate formula, Θ, rejected in section 3 above.

It is not hard to see the relation between our definition of "true in **L**," and the schema (**S**) of p. 94 above. The *technical* interest of the definition arises from its success in, as it were, generalizing the particular instances of this schema. And we can now see how this was done. In place of the futile attempt to treat " "*x*" " in

$$\text{"}x\text{" is true} \equiv x$$

as a variable, we achieved the desired end by *enumerating* the criteria in the simplest cases, to which all the more complex cases were made reducible.

[13] In our special case, we might even formulate a maximum of procedure: To test a statement of the form " . . . is true" where " . . . " is wholly composed of capital letters, test the statement " – – – ", derived from " . . . " by substituting the corresponding small letters. This maxim, however, is subject to the criticisms explained in section 3. If we formulate the maxim explicitly, we get a statement similar to Θ or **S**.

5. TECHNICAL APPLICATIONS OF TARSKI'S DEFINITION

The model I have used differs from the simplest case discussed by Tarski in the following respects. His simplest object-language contains an infinite number of variables (where **L** contains none), no individual constants (where **L** contains "a" and "b"), no predicates with a single argument (while **L** contains "r" and "s"), a single two-termed relation of inclusion (none in **L**), and a universal quantifier (none in **L**). Whereas **L** consists only of trivial combinations of four trivial statements, Tarski's first object-language is already sufficiently "rich" to express a general theory of class relationships.[14]

To those interested in the formal aspect of such studies, the most interesting of Tarski's results concern the conditions in which a definition of truth of the type he desires (i.e., conforming to schema **S** above) is possible. It appears that the meta-language used must be "essentially richer" than the object language (i.e., roughly speaking, must contain variables of higher logical types). And if this condition cannot be fulfilled (as in the common cases where the object language contains an infinity of logical types), an *explicit* definition of truth in the meta-language becomes impossible.[15]

An important by-product of Tarski's work is a method for demonstrating the undecidability of certain propositions in "sufficiently rich" deductive systems.[16]

[14] This higher complexity of the object-language calls for the use of ingenious special devices in order to formulate a recursive definition of truth. Thus Tarski first defines the notion of "satisfaction" of a sentential *function*, reaching the definition of truth of a sentence only indirectly. For the definition, see *WFS*, pp. 303–316; for an explanation of the need of the detour, see *SCT*, p. 363.

[15] The best we can then do is to introduce "true" as an undefined term by means of axioms.

[16] This provides a method of investigating the "completeness" of deductive systems, alternative to the well-known methods used in proving Gödel's Theorem. Cf. A. Tarski, "On Undecidable Statements in Enlarged Systems of Logic and the Concepts of Truth," *Journal of Symbolic Logic*, 4 (1939): 105–112.

The technical interest of Tarski's work, however, is independent of its philosophical significance. Indeed it seems to me that if he had replaced "true," throughout his formal studies, by "T," "X," or another arbitrarily chosen symbol, his important results regarding the consistency and completeness of deductive systems would have followed just as well. The question of the adequacy of his work as "philosophical reconstruction" of the preanalytical notion of truth is quite distinct from that of the value of his contributions to the exact study of formal deductive systems.

6. CAN TARSKI'S PROCEDURE BE APPLIED TO "ORDINARY LANGUAGE"?

Tarski's definitions of truth are formulated in connection with "artificial languages," i.e., generalized deductive systems of varying degrees of formal complexity. The philosophical relevance of his work will depend upon the extent to which something similar can be done for colloquial English (E say).

Bearing in mind the presence in E of the semantic paradoxes discussed in section 2 above, we must expect certain modifications to be made in E. The most important of these will be the rigorous enforcement of the object-language/meta-language distinction and the introduction of suitable typographic devices to distinguish terms belonging to the object-language (L_E, say) from those belonging to the meta-language (M_E, say). Equally obvious, in the light of our earlier discussion, will be the demand that the formation and transformation rules of L_E (rules of syntax and logical deduction) be completely formalized; and that all semantic terms such as "true," "false," "expressing," "name," and their cognates be deleted from M_E (though they may be reintroduced *by definitions*). More important for our purpose are the following requirements:

(i) All the terms defined in E must be supposed replaced by their definitions, and *a complete inventory of the undefined terms of L_E must be available*.

[99]

(ii) Every undefined term in L_E must have a distinctive name in M_E,[17] and *a complete inventory of such names must be available.*

With the exception of those I have called (i) and (ii), the above conditions express obvious modifications required in *any* exact treatment of an admittedly inexact vernacular. If *all* of them could be satisfied (which there is no reason to doubt except in the case of [i] and [ii], there would be no difficulty in principle[18] in applying Tarski's procedure, appropriately modified. As in the case of our simplified model (section 4) we should first need to *enumerate* defining conditions for *every* sentence of the form "(. . .) is true," where "(. . .)" is replaced by the name of a *primitive sentence* in L_E (i.e., one containing no logical signs). And then we would have to formulate a recursive definition of "true in L_E" of a kind reducing the test of "(– – –) is true," where "(– – –)" is replaced by the name of a *complex* sentence of L_E, to the test of simpler cases.

The technical difficulties in completing this program are of no importance here. It is the first steps—the exhaustive enumeration and designation of the primitive signs of L_E (conditions [i] and [ii] above) that need careful scrutiny. For the consequences are highly paradoxical. If a single proper name, say "Calvin Coolidge," were omitted from our inventory, the notion of truth would not have been defined for sentences in which that name occurred. Of the sentence "Calvin Coolidge was a president of the United States" we

[17] This could be done in various ways: We might arrange for each undefined term in L_E to have a number correlated with it; or "catcat" might be the name of "cat," "manman" of "man," and so on; or the familiar device of quotation marks might be used. But although the names might be regularly formed in some such fashion, M_E could not contain a rule to determine that they *be* so formed. It must, for instance, be a kind of logical accident that the name of a word in L_E is obtained by inserting it between commas. No official notice could be taken of the structural relations between a word of L_E and its name in M_E.

[18] Except insofar as L_E proved too "rich" for a definition of "true in L_E" to be possible. Cf. section 5 above.

[100]

could say neither that it was true, nor that it was untrue. The proper comment would be that since no reference to the name "Calvin Coolidge" occurred in our definition, the term "true in L_E" had no application to the case in point. (Or we might say that "Calvin Coolidge" did not belong to L_E, as L_E was defined by us.)

It might be said that the omission of a proper name already in use by speakers of the English language would merely be a symptom of carelessness in the framing of our definition. And no doubt it would. But no matter what care were taken to obtain a "complete" inventory of primitive terms in the English language, *the resulting list would become obsolete every time a new name came into use.* Every time an infant was christened, or a manuscript received a title, the inventory and, consequently, the definition of truth depending upon that inventory, would become inaccurate. The "open" character of a natural language, as shown in the fluctuating composition of its vocabulary, defeats the attempt to apply a definition of truth based upon enumeration of simple instances. The attempt is as hopeless as would be that of setting out to define the notion of "name" by listing all the names that have ever been used.[19]

7. FURTHER CRITICISM OF THE SEMANTIC DEFINITION

Let us waive for the present the objections stated in the last section. The relativity to which I have drawn attention might, after all, prove unavoidable, so that "truth" would be a predicate whose definition would vary with the varying fortunes of the English language. And let it be supposed that a

[19] The reader may find it a useful exercise to show in detail why the use of general linguistic predicates in M_E, such as "name," merely leads back to the formulas Θ and S of section 3 above. It seems, indeed, that the extensional or enumerative character of the proposed definition is essential to it. And if this is so, we must either resign ourselves to the transitory and fluctuating nature of the "concept" of truth offered or look for some other way to define it. Since the paradoxical consequences result from the attempt to interpret "truth" as a property of linguistic objects (sentences), it might be worth while, after all, to try to formulate a "realist" alternative.

[101]

semantic definition of the proposed type had been offered of say "true in the English language as of January 1, 1940."

To what extent could a competent reader of such a definition *understand* the term "truth" thereby defined? If he could follow the technicalities of the recursive definition supplied, he would certainly be in a position to eliminate the term "true" from any context in which it occurred. To this extent, then, he would be able to *use* the term correctly as intended, making the correct inferences from all asserted sentences in which it could occur. But he would surely be strongly inclined to say also something like "I understand the *principle* of the definition." And we ourselves, to come closer home, seem to *understand* Tarski's procedure (in the fashion in which one may grasp the "point" of a mathematical proof without attending to all its details). We seem to see quite clearly that what Tarski is doing is so to define truth that *to assert that a sentence is true is logically equivalent to asserting that sentence*. And in so doing, we feel that we *understand* the definition, besides being able to apply it. But if we try to *say* what we think we understand, we sin at once against the canons of syntactical propriety. The phrase "to assert that a sentence is true is logically equivalent to asserting that sentence," which is intuitively so clear, is in fact, a crude formulation in colloquial English of the inacceptable formula Θ of section 3.

Anybody who is offered a definition of "true in the English language as of January 1, 1940" must, therefore, resolutely abstain from supposing that he "understands" the principle of the definition, in the sense of being able to give an explicit definition[20] of the concept defined. If he tries to give such a formulation, he will succeed only in talking nonsense (uttering a sentence which breaks the syntactic rules of the language to which it belongs).

[20] It is possible to give an *explicit* definition of semantic terms as of other terms introduced by recursive definition. But this involves the use of variables of higher types than those occurring in the original recursive definition and does not resolve our difficulty. On this point see *WFS*, p. 292, n. 24.

It might be said, in answer to this, that too much is being demanded, by implication, of a recursive definition. After all, the operation of multiplication (of integers) is defined *recursively* in arithmetic, yet nobody could reasonably complain, *on this account*, that "the concept of multiplication" is not "understood." If we can use the multiplication sign correctly in all the contexts in which it occurs, so that we make no mistakes in calculation, we "understand" multiplication as well as it can be understood. The rest is psychology. Whether a mathematician has a subjective feeling of "grasp" or "insight" or "understanding" has nothing to do with the question of the logical adequacy of the mathematical definition.

This is all very well for the case of multiplication (and similar terms recursively defined in mathematics). Here "multiplication" is defined, uniquely, *once and for all*,[21] and it is sufficient that we shall be able to *use* the sign of multiplication correctly in all its possible occurrences. But the case is different for "truth."

If we were to insist rigorously upon the absurdity of any attempt to generalize the definition of "true in English as of January 1, 1940," we should have to insist also that the recursive definition had exclusive *application to the "language"* *in question*. To the request to find *another* definition of "true in French" or even "true in English as of January 1, 1950," the response would have to be that we had not the least notion of how to begin.

It is as if I were to "define" the term "telephone number in New York" for a child by enumerating the telephone numbers of all those persons in New York who have telephone numbers. A moderately intelligent child would soon "spot" what I was doing. He might say, "I understand: you always give the number which has been assigned by the telephone company." But if I am to retort, "No, that has *nothing* to do with the case—attend to the definition!" he would be helpless to extend the definition to other cases. If my admonition

[21] When the operation of multiplication is generalized to apply to an indefinite variety of number systems the case is altered.

were intended seriously, no principle would have been given to determine the extension of the original definition: a "telephone number *in London*" might be a man's height, or his waist measurement, or *any* number associated with him.

Similarly, if we are to take the semantic definitions at their face value, we must suppose "truth" to have been defined *only* for the cases actually discussed, with no indication at all for extension to other languages. But to pretend that this is the case is self-deception. No account of the semantic approach to the definition of truth can be regarded as satisfactory which prevents us from saying what we undoubtedly understand from the exposition of the theory.[22]

It is worth noting that the formulation of a general criterion of truth is indispensable for a direct[23] solution of the "philosophical problem of truth." For the philosopher who is puzzled by the nature of truth wants a satisfactory *general* description of usage. To be told that such and such are *instances* of truth will not serve to assuage his thirst for generality. A philosopher who is investigating "the nature" or "the essential nature" of man, will find little assistance in the information that all American citizens are men.

8. THE SEMANTIC DEFINITION AND THE "PHILOSOPHICAL PROBLEM OF TRUTH"

The clinching argument for this conclusion is that adherents of the correspondence, the coherence, or the pragmatist "theories" of truth will all indifferently accept the schema **S** of section 3 above. They would all be prepared to agree[24] that

[22] A general criterion of truth might perhaps be formulated in a meta-meta-language (cf. *WFS*, p. 306, n. 38), but it remains to be shown that this can be done without reinstating the semantic paradoxes. There is a constant temptation in the formal study of semantics to relegate important questions to a "language" whose structure has not been studied.

[23] I mean an answer *to* the question asked by the philosopher—rather than an attempt to show that the question is illegitimate and should not be asked.

[24] Subject to certain possible qualifications, however. On certain "realist"

[104]

"It is snowing today" is true $\equiv$ It is snowing,
"London is a city" is true $\equiv$ London is a city,
and so on.

And insofar as the semantic definition of truth has such consequences as these *and no others*, the philosophical dispute stays unsettled.[25] The philosophical disputants are concerned about what *in general* entitles us to say "It is snowing" or "London is a city" *and so on*. In other words, they are searching for a general property of the designata of true object-sentences. To this inquiry, the semantic definition of truth makes no contribution.

Nevertheless, the semantic definition does suggest another *philosophical* theory of truth (though one which few philosophers would find attractive). The central idea of this adaptation consists in introducing the term "true" into *the object language*, by means of recursive definitions paralleling those of Tarski.[26]

We might indeed stipulate:

(1) (s)(that s is true $=_{Df}$ s),[27]

(2) (s)[that $\sim$s is true $=_{Df}$ $\sim$(that s is true)],

(3) (s) (t) [that (s & t) is true] $=_{Df}$ [(that s is true) & (that t is true)].

Further clauses of the recursive type might be added, as needed.

On this view, the locution "that . . . is true" would be regarded as a linguistic device for converting an unasserted

---

theories of truth, it might be held that the truth of a proposition does not presuppose the existence of a sentence expressing that proposition. On this view, the sign of logical equivalence should be replaced by that of one-way entailment.

[25] I cannot accept Tarski's claim that his definition favors the "classical Aristotelian conception of truth." I regard his view as neutral to this and all other *philosophical* theories of truth.

[26] Cf. Carnap's discussion of his "absolute" notion of truth (*Introduction to Semantics* [Cambridge, Mass., 1942], p. 90).

[27] Notice that the word "true" is here attached to a sentence, not to the name of a sentence. Thus truth must now be a property of what is designated by a sentence (perhaps a proposition?), not a property of a sentence.

[105]

into an asserted sentence.[28] Truth would then tend to lose some of its present dignity. One might be inclined to call the word "true" redundant, and to baptize the theory, in the customary misleading fashion, as a "No Truth" theory. Such consequences ought not to abash us, however. For *any* defined term can be viewed as redundant, if we are prepared to suffer the practical inconvenience of dispensing with its use.[29]

We need not be afraid, either, that the proposed notion of truth would allow the reappearance of the semantical paradoxes. For we can continue to "stratify" (separate into semantic types) all terms having linguistic reference in our language. And this is enough to remove the known paradoxes.[30]

More serious is the objection that this proposal would make no provision for such expressions as "*The truth* is hard to discover," or others in which reference to truth or falsity is made by means of *substantives*. But in this respect the proposed theory is in no worse case than that of Tarski; and it may claim to be at least as close to common usage.

Yet I am not seriously backing a "No Truth" theory against its more orthodox competitors. My own view is that any search for a *direct* answer to the "philosophical problem of truth" can at best produce a formula that is platitudinous and tautological or arbitrary and paradoxical: and that a more hopeful method for investigating the "problem" is to dispel the confusions of thought which generate it.

9. SUMMARY

I have illustrated the semantic method for defining "truth," using for this purpose a simplified, "model," language. The occurrence in "ordinary language" of semantical paradoxes was seen to make imperative a distinction between "object-

[28] So that "true" would be an "incomplete symbol" forming a part of the "signpost," "⊦ ", of Frege or Whitehead and Russell?

[29] Cf. Tarski's answer to a similar objection, *SCT*, pp. 358–359.

[30] An unsupported assertion of this sort is not worth much. But I believe it would not be hard to show the consistency of the proposed rules for the use of "true."

[106]

language" and "meta-language." This, in turn, suggested a leading notion of Tarski's method, viz., that of treating "true" as a predicate of object-*sentences*, definable in an appropriate *meta*-language. Examination of the steps needed to adapt the procedure to "ordinary English" brought paradoxical consequences to light. For the definition would become obsolete whenever new names were introduced into the language; and the "point" or principle of the definition could be "seen" but apparently not *stated* without inconsistency. The semantic definition can therefore not be regarded as a satisfactory "philosophical reconstruction" of preanalytic usage. Indeed, the neutrality of Tarski's definition with respect to the competing philosophical theories of truth is sufficient to demonstrate its lack of *philosophical* relevance. His exposition does, however, suggest a "No Truth" theory, which was outlined; but neither this, nor any formal definition of truth, goes to the heart of the difficulties which are at the root of the so-called philosophical problem of truth.

[107]

V

Russell's
Philosophy of
Language

The influence of language on philosophy has, I believe, been profound and almost unrecognized.—Russell

I. INTRODUCTION

RUSSELL'S INFLUENCE. For the purpose of preliminary definition we might adapt a remark of William James and identify philosophy of language as "what a philosopher gets if he thinks long enough and hard enough about language." This characterization may serve as a reminder of the persistence and intensity of Russell's preoccupation with language, displayed in much of his philosophical writing during the past twenty-five years.[1] The flourishing condition of present-day "semiotic" is a sufficient testimony to the fertility of Russell's ideas; today, some twenty years after the epigraph of this essay was composed, it would be more accurate to say: "the influence of language on philosophy is profound and almost universally recognized."[2] If it is true that "language has, so to speak,

[1] The quotation at the head of this essay is taken from the article "Logical Atomism," in *Contemporary British Philosophy* (1924), vol. 1, which is, for all its brevity, the best statement of Russell's early program for philosophical inquiries into language. It is a matter for regret that the earlier lectures, published under the title of "The Philosophy of Logical Atomism" in *The Monist* (28 [1918]: 495–527; 29 [1919]: 32–63, 190–222, 345–380), have never been reprinted. Language is a topic of central importance also in "On Propositions: What They Are and How They Mean" (*Aristotelian Society Proceedings*, Suppl. vol. 2 [1919]: 1–43), in *The Analysis of Mind* (London, 1921), especially ch. 10: "Words and Meaning", and in *Philosophy* (New York, 1927), ch. 4: "Language". *An Inquiry into Meaning and Truth* (New York, 1940) is, of course, almost entirely devoted to the same topic.

[2] Contemporary concern with philosophy of language is most apparent in the members and sympathizers of the philosophical movement known as "Logical Positivism" or "Scientific Empiricism." In this instance the transmission of ideas can be traced with rare accuracy. It is known that the Vienna Circle was much influenced, in the postwar years, both by Russell's own work and that of his pupil Wittgenstein. Although the *Tractatus* owes much to Russell, there can be no question that the influence here was reciprocal, as Russell has frequently and generously acknowledged. The *Monist* articles are introduced with the words: "The following articles are ... very largely concerned with explaining certain ideas which I learnt from my friend and former pupil, Ludwig Wittgenstein" (*The Monist*, 28

[111]

become the *Brennpunkt* of present-day philosophical discussion,"[3] hardly another philosopher bears a greater share of the responsibility.

Philosophical study of language, conceived by Russell as the construction of "philosophical grammar,"[4] may have been regarded by him, at an early period, as a mere "preliminary" to metaphysics; it soon became much more than this. Philosophical linguistics may be expected to provide nothing less than a pathway to the nature of that reality which is the metaphysician's goal. To this very day the hope persists that "with sufficient caution, *the properties of language may help us to understand the structure of the world.*"[5]

So ambitiously conceived, as a study potentially revealing ontological structure, philosophy of language cannot be restricted to the examination of uninterpreted formal systems, still less, as with earlier philosophers, to the rhetorical art of avoiding unintentional ambiguity. Its successful pursuit requires the use of data drawn from logic, psychology, and empirical linguistics and the formulation of reasoned decisions concerning the scope of metaphysics and the proper methods of philosophical research. Such questions as these arise constantly in Russell's discussions, even on occasions when he is most earnestly avowing the "neutrality" of his devotion to scientific method.

Since the full-bodied suggestiveness of Russell's work on language is a function of his refusal to adopt the self-imposed limitations of the mathematical logician, it would be ungrateful to regret the complex interweaving of themes which results.

[1918]: 495). A more detailed discussion of sources would call for some reference to the work of G. E. Moore. Cf. *The Philosophy of G. E. Moore* (Evanston, 1942), pp. 14 ff.

[3] W. M. Urban, *Language and Reality* (London, 1939), p. 35.

[4] "I have dwelt hitherto upon what may be called *philosophical grammar*. . . . I think the importance of philosophical grammar is very much greater than it is generally thought to be . . . philosophical grammar with which we have been concerned in these lectures" (*The Monist*, 29 [1919]: 364).

[5] *An Inquiry into Meaning and Truth*, p. 429 (italics supplied).

But any selection of topics, considered in abstraction from the context of Russell's general philosophical doctrines, is bound to be somewhat misleading. It must be hoped that the aspects of Russell's earlier procedures here chosen for brief critical examination so typically manifest his style of philosophic thought at this period that an understanding of their merits and defects will serve as a guide to the evaluation of the more extensive doctrines of which they are a part.

The Scope of This Essay. The main topics discussed in the remainder of this essay are:

(i) *The consequences of applying the theory of types to "ordinary language."* A new paradox will be presented whose resolution requires extensive reformulation of Russell's theory, and a critical judgment will be made of the value of the renovated theory.

(ii) *The search for "ultimate constituents" of the world.* The procedure here, so far as it is relevant to the criticism of language, will be shown to be, in part, susceptible of a neutral interpretation, and, for the rest, to be based upon an unproved epistemological principle (reducibility to acquaintance), which will, after examination, be rejected.

(iii) *The notion of the "ideal language."* This branch of the investigation concerns the goal of the entire method. The construction of an "ideal language" will be condemned, for due reason presented, as the undesirable pursuit of an ideal incapable of realization.

These headings cover most of Russell's *positive* contributions to philosophy of language.[6] There will be no space for discussion of the genesis of the whole inquiry in the destructive criticism of "ordinary language."[7] The bare reminder must suffice that the English language, as now used by philosophers, offends by provoking erroneous metaphysical beliefs. Syntax

[6] The only serious omission is reference to Russell's behavioristic analysis of meaning (cf. especially the last four works cited in footnote 1 above). The arguments of Essay IX ("Questions about Emotive Meaning") apply with little modification to Russell's position on this matter.

[7] *Contemporary British Philosophy,* 1 (1924): 368.

[113]

induces misleading opinions concerning the *structure* of the world (notably in the attribution of ontological significance to the subject-predicate form), while vocabulary, by promoting the hypostatization of pseudo entities, encourages false beliefs concerning the *contents* of the world. In either case we are "giving metaphysical importance to the accidents of our own speech."[8] It is in trying to remedy these defects of ordinary language by searching for what is *essential* in language that we arrive finally at the "ideal language" and its valid metaphysical implications.

2. CONSEQUENCES OF APPLYING THE THEORY OF TYPES TO ORDINARY LANGUAGE

The Genesis and Character of the Theory of Types. Russell's arguments against philosophers who insist upon reducing all statements to the subject-predicate form amounts to showing that their procedure leads to contradiction.[9] But the "new logic" of relations, whose function it was to take account of complexities of form neglected by syllogistic logic, proved to be infected by the new and more puzzling contradictions of the "mathematical and logical paradoxes." The basis of Russell's cure for this malady is the observation that each paradox involves a characteristic reflexive application of terms (as exemplified typically in the notion of a class being a member of itself). The cure provided in *Principia Mathematica*, as the "theory of types," is, accordingly, a restriction

---

[8] *The Analysis of Mind*, p. 192.

[9] Cf. *Our Knowledge of the External World* (London, 1914), p. 58. It may be noted that the argument, as there presented, is defective in requiring the alleged defender of the universality of the subject-predicate form to propose an analysis which is not of that form. The argument could, however, be patched up. It would then establish that the attempt to express all relational propositions as logical products of functions of *one* variable (i.e., to assert that $xRy \equiv Px.Qy$ for all x and y) would lead to inconsistency with the theorems of the relational calculus. Russell interprets this result as a proof of the inadequacy of exclusive adherence to the subject-predicate form; but an opponent (such as Bradley, against whom the argument was directed) might regard it as one further manifestation of the "unreality of relations."

upon the kind of symbols which may be inserted into a given context.[10] Entities designated by symbols all of which may be inserted into some one context are said *to belong to the same type*. There results a segregation of entities into a logical hierarchy of types, whose members are individuals, functions of individuals, functions of functions of individuals, etc. (or an equivalent extensional hierarchy of classes and relations). Specification of the types of the entities involved is sufficient to reveal as invalid the arguments used in deriving *some* of the paradoxes.

This refutes only the paradoxes expressed in terms belonging wholly to mathematics or logic; but this is all that is required within logic itself, as subsequent logicians have emphasized. They follow Ramsey in rejecting the further subdivisions inside the types (the "branching theory of types"), which were the basis of Russell's contribution to the solution of the remaining paradoxes. They agree with Ramsey that the latter are caused by "faulty ideas concerning thought and language,"[11] and, by claiming that "the fault must lie in the linguistic elements,"[12] they achieve a radical simplification of the original form of Russell's theory. This is no doubt satisfactory for those engaged in constructing a formal logic of maximum manipulative simplicity,[13] but it still leaves to be unraveled an imputed

[10] Cf. the article by Alonzo Church on "Paradoxes, Logical" (in *The Dictionary of Philosophy* [New York, 1942], pp. 224–225) for a convenient statement of the problem and a bibliography.

[11] F. P. Ramsey, *The Foundations of Mathematics* (London, 1931), p. 21. In the group of ogical paradoxes Ramsey puts those arguments, such as that involved in the contradiction of the greatest cardinal number, ". . . which, were no provision made against them, would occur in a logical or mathematical system itself. They involve only logical or mathematical terms. . . ." The remainder ". . . are not purely logical, and cannot be stated in logical terms alone; for they all contain some reference to thought, language or symbolism, which are not formal but empirical terms" (*ibid.*).

[12] F. P. Ramsey, *loc. cit.* (He proceeds to urge the need for further examination of the "linguistic elements.")

[13] The contradictions against which this part of type theory was directed are no business of logic anyway. . . . The whole ramification, with the

[115]

and endemic "ambiguity" of "ordinary language." Russell's discussion of this important residual problem deserves more critical attention than it has hitherto received.

The Definition of the Logical Types of Entities Designated by Words of the Ordinary Language. As contrasted with the definition of logical types in the artificial language of mathematical logic, the main point of difference which arises when the attempt is made to establish distinctions of type within "ordinary language" depends upon the fact that in the latter case modification is introduced into a system of vocabulary and syntax *already in use.* There can be no question, therefore, of attaching unambiguous indications of type to symbols *introduced by definitions* (as in *Principia Mathematica*); the need is rather for a principle which will serve to reveal ambiguities of type within the system of grammatical rules already current.

The leading principle of the theory of types, so far as it applies to ordinary language, consists in the assertion that *grammatically* impeccable sentences often prove to be crypto-nonsense generated by a propensity for substituting in the same context words which agree in grammatical while differing in logical form. "In its technical form, this doctrine states merely that a word or symbol may form part of a significant proposition, and in this sense have meaning, without being always able to be substituted for another word or symbol in the same or some other proposition without producing nonsense."[14]

The benefit to be anticipated from an application of the theory of types to ordinary language will, therefore, consist in a set of criteria specifying *which* substitutions of words are legitimate. Since words which may so replace one another in all contexts are said to belong to the same type (by an extension of the usage of the similar expression in *Principia Mathematica*), the notion of logical types, as *here* used, will be of crucial importance.

---

axiom of reducibility, calls simply for amputation" (W. V. Quine in *The Philosophy of Alfred North Whitehead* [Evanston, 1941], p. 151).

[14] *Contemporary British Philosophy,* 1: 371.

The definition of a logical type [Russell says] is as follows: A and B are of the same logical type if, and only if, given any fact of which A is a constituent, there is a corresponding fact which has B as a constituent, which either results by substituting B for A or is the negation of what so results. To take an illustration, Socrates and Aristotle are of the same type, because "Socrates was a philosopher" and "Aristotle was a philosopher" are both facts; Socrates and Caligula are of the same type, because "Socrates was a philosopher" and "Caligula was not a philosopher" are both facts. To love and to kill are of the same type, because "Plato loved Socrates" and "Plato did not kill Socrates" are both facts.[15]

In the form presented, this definition can be made to generate a new and instructive paradox, whose existence will demonstrate the need for further clarification of Russell's procedure.

The Paradox of Dissolution of Types. Let it be supposed that K and L are of the same type, as defined above, and K and M are of *different* types. Then the following statements are true:

(1) "L is of the same type as K" is a fact,

(2) "M is not of the same type as K" is a fact.[16]

Now the second fact is the negation of what results from substituting M for L in the first fact. And the situation is formally analogous to that used for illustrative purposes by Russell, with L, M, and *being of the same type as* K corresponding respectively to Socrates, Caligula, and *being a philosopher*. Since L and M can replace each other in the manner specified in the definition, it follows that L *and* M *are of the same type*. But this clearly contradicts the initial assumption that M belongs to a type other than that to which both K and L belong. Expressed otherwise, the argument would seem to establish that, if there are at least three entities in the world, it is impossible that they should not all belong to the same type.[17]

[15] *Op. cit.*, pp. 369–370.

[16] The statements have been expressed in ways parallel to those used in Russell's examples.

[17] This contradiction does not seem to have been previously discovered.

Such a consequence would, of course, be quite intolerable. For, since it may be granted that there are at least three entities, it would be permissible to substitute any symbol for another in all contexts, and the application of the theory to ordinary language would achieve precisely nothing.

Two suggestions for the removal of this difficulty, each having a certain initial plausibility, will now be discussed.

The Consequences of Relying upon Ambiguity in the Term "Fact" to Resolve the Paradox. It would be in the spirit of Russell's own exposition to retort that the word "fact" occurs, in the sentences (1) and (2) above, in a sense other than was intended in the definition of logical type. For, according to his account, "the following words . . . by their very nature sin against it [the doctrine of types]: attribute, relation, complex, *fact.* . . ."[18] No doubt it is required that a fact to the effect that K and L are of the same type shall be of an order of complexity other than that of an empirical fact in which K or L are constituents. But if this is maintained, Russell's definition of type becomes itself ambiguous and of indefinite application.[19]

So long as the word "fact" is taken in the colloquial sense in which to say " 'X' is a fact" is merely to say "it is true that X," the definition is plainly intelligible (though itself then sinning against the theory of types). In this sense *every* true sentence must be admitted to express a "fact," and the paradox is unassailable. But if the word "fact," as it occurs in the definition, is to be so restricted in meaning that only *some* true sentences shall be permitted to express facts in this unusual sense, it now becomes imperative to indicate how *such* facts are to be identified. In the absence of such supplementary information the definition will be useless.

Should such specification of the technical meaning of the

[18] *Contemporary British Philosophy*, 1: foot of p. 371.

[19] An alternative proposal that might deserve examination would be to render the relation *being of the same type as* systematically ambiguous according to the type of the entities it relates. But this proposal would itself violate the theory of types.

crucial term "fact," however, be possible there would remain the further difficulty that the definition, now amended to be consistent with the theory of types, would have application only to a restricted class of sentences, viz., those expressing "facts" in the narrow technical sense. There would be no guarantee that the restricted theory of types resulting would not allow paradoxes to proliferate in the area over which it exercised no jurisdiction.

The theory is, then, indefinite and possibly self-contradictory; at best it can hope only to be incomplete. It would seem that Russell's own formulation leads to formidable if not insuperable difficulties.

The Paradox Resolved by Reinterpretation of Russell's Theory. The root of the difficulties above displayed is to be found in Russell's interpretation of the relationship of *belonging to the same type* as holding between "entities." A direct escape is provided by substituting a parallel relation holding between *words.*

Let the locution, "K and L are of the same type," be abandoned in favor of the expression "the *words* 'K' and 'L' are *syntactically similar*" (and let it be agreed that in such cases 'K' and 'L' shall be said to belong to the same *syntactical type*). With this understanding, the sentences (1) and (2) above must be rewritten in some such form as

(3) "λ is of the same syntactical type as κ" is a fact,

(4) "μ is not of the same syntactical type as κ" is a fact,

where λ, μ and κ are now *words*. And from this it will follow only that the *names* of all three words will be syntactically similar. Since the name of a word is not identical with the word itself, no contradiction will now result. Thus this suggestion, which is in line with Russell's own remark that "the theory of types is really a theory of symbols, not of things,"[20] would seem to provide a satisfactory resolution of the paradox.

But only at the cost of considerable increase in complexity. It may be left as an exercise to the reader to show that it will be necessary at the very least to provide an infinite hierarchy

[20] *The Monist*, 29 (1919): 362.

of senses of the expression "syntactically similar" corresponding to the different syntactical levels of the words it relates. There will need to be one relation of syntactical similarity between words, another between names of words, still another between names of names, and so forth. But this hierarchy has the advantage of being generated *by definition;* since the expression "syntactically similar" is specifically introduced into the language by definition, there can be no objection to the supplementary differentiation of several senses; the character of the hierarchy involved makes the identification of the level involved in any particular instance immediate and unmistakable.

The Need for a Negative Interpretation of Russell's Theory. If a linguistic translation of Russell's theory on the lines suggested above should prove feasible, there will still be required further modifications, if contradiction is to be avoided.

There are certain syntactically polygamous contexts able to receive words of the most diverse syntactical types without degenerating into nonsense. It is proper to say both "I am thinking about Russell" and "I am thinking about continuity"; thus nothing that has so far been said would prevent the disintegrating and absurd inference that "Russell" and "continuity" are syntactically similar. Unless further inhibitory measures are instituted, a wholesale merging and dissolution (this time of syntactical types) will once again be in prospect.

There seems no solution for this kind of difficulty, which arises in connection with all sentences expressing propositional attitudes (whether of knowing, supposing, or believing), except to interpret the theory of types negatively as essentially an instrument for establishing *differences* of type. It will be necessary, however, to add a supplementary provision for the transmission of type distinctions to the associates of the ambiguous word in every context. The new procedure consists in asserting that two typographically distinct words are syntactically *dissimilar* if there is *at least one* context in which one cannot be substituted for the other without generating non-

[120]

sense. To this is added the further condition that corresponding elements of contexts capable of receiving syntactically
dissimilar words are themselves to be regarded (independently
of typographical similarity) as syntactically dissimilar. (The
first part of this test shows "Russell" and "continuity" to be
syntactically dissimilar; the second then requires the two
occurrences of "thinking" in "I am thinking about Russell"
and "I am thinking about continuity" to be construed as
instances of *two* words belonging to different syntactical
types.)

Thus the application of the theory of types to ordinary
language is a more complex undertaking than Russell's own
account would suggest. A single attempt at substitution may
establish that "*A*" is not of the same (syntactical) type as
"*B*." Suppose two sentences are typographically identical
except in containing "*A*" in place of "*B*"; then the corresponding symbols, in spite of typographical identity, must be
considered as belonging to different types. Implicit recognition of this consequence may have been responsible for
Russell's criticism of the use of such words as "attribute,"
"relation," etc., and for his subsequent comment that, after
discriminating the type ambiguities, "we usually arrive, not
at one meaning, but at an infinite series of different
meanings."[21]

The Value of Russell's Application of the Theory of Types. The
consequences of Russell's procedure should by now be sufficiently clear. Any interpretation that will be faithful to his
intentions requires the impossibility of substituting two words
for one another in even a single context to be regarded as
sufficient cause for their segregation into mutually exclusive
types. The consistent elaboration of this leading idea involves
the making of ever finer distinctions of "meaning" between
words not customarily regarded as ambiguous. So stringent
does the requirement prove that it becomes difficult, if not

[21] *Contemporary British Philosophy*, 1: 372. It is to be noted that the quoted
statement, by referring collectively to "meanings," itself sins against the
theory of types.

impossible, to state the theory itself without contradiction, such difficulty being only a single instance, though a striking one, of a general tendency to produce a paralysis of the general statements of which philosophical discussion so largely consists.

The case for submitting to such unwelcome consequences is something less than conclusive. It is well to recall that the theory was originally designed to purge discourse of those paradoxes which are not accounted for by the nonbranching theory of types. But it may be supposed that the paradoxes in question might prove capable of a solution having less drastic consequences; indeed, it is plausible to expect that prohibition of a characteristic reflexive type of *definition* might be enough to achieve this end.[22] Whether this suggestion should prove fruitful or not, it may be suspected that Russell's theory does less than justice to the success with which communication is actually achieved in *ordinary* language. The demonstration of distinctions of type, defined in terms of possibility of mutual substitution of words, is on occasion a valuable technique for exhibiting operative ambiguity whose removal is relevant to the solution of philosophical disputes. But the consequences of an attempt to apply such techniques universally may be regarded as a *reductio ad absurdum* of a point of view which seeks to apply to ordinary language segregatory criteria appropriate to an artificially constructed calculus. And this in turn can be traced back to the inclination to regard the relation between language and the world exclusively in the light of identity of structure.

3. THE SEARCH FOR ULTIMATE CONSTITUENTS OF THE WORLD

The Genesis of the Theory of Descriptions. For all their drastic character, the segregatory techniques of the theory of types prove insufficient to cure *all* the philosophical confusions

---

[22] Thus the paradox of the least finite integer definable in a specific number of words depends upon the lack of definition (or the simultaneous use of contradictory definitions) of the term "definable."

[122]

which can be attributed to excessive confidence in grammatical structure as a guide to logical form. A notable instance of such confusion arises in connection with the syntactical properties of phrases of the form "the so-and-so."

If the phrase, "The present king of France," be compared, in respect of identity or diversity of type, with a personal name, say that of Stalin, it will be found that the noun clause may be substituted for the name without producing nonsense.[23] More generally, it is a fact that some descriptive phrases and some nouns can replace each other in some or all contexts without producing nonsense. If the theory of types were to be relied upon to provide a sufficient criticism of ordinary language, it would be necessary to conclude that "Stalin" and "The present king of France" are syntactically similar.[24] This conclusion is maintained in a more colloquial form by anybody who claims that "The present king of France" names or denotes a person.

Upon such a foundation of identification of the syntactical properties of the descriptive phrase and the name, curious arguments have sometimes been erected. Since "The present king of France" refers to a person who does not exist, it must be conceded that there are *nonexistent persons* who can appear as subjects of true propositions. Though nonexistent, they must accordingly be capable of sustaining predicates. Thus it is certain, by the law of excluded middle, that one of the two propositions, "The present king of France is a parent" and "The present king of France is childless," is true. And there must be countless other properties by which the nonexistent present king of France is characterized (among them the property of

---

[23] This statement would need some qualifications for complete accuracy. It is not easy to provide an account of the theory of descriptions that will succeed in being tolerably brief. The best short version known to me is that of Professor L. S. Stebbing in her *A Modern Introduction to Logic*, 2d ed., pp. 144–158 ("The Analysis of Descriptions") and pp. 502–505 ("Logical Constructions"). Cf. also G. E. Moore's article (in *The Philosophy of Bertrand Russell* (Evanston, 1944)) on "Russell's 'Theory of Descriptions.'"

[24] Or that Stalin and the present King of France belong to the same type.

being under discussion in this essay). It can scarcely be doubted that whatever is characterized by properties is not a mere nonentity, that in order to be a subject of which characters are genuinely predicable it is required to have some kind of objective "being," not to be confused with the vacuity of sheer nothingness on the one hand or the full actuality of "existence" on the other.

The argument culminates, then, in the assertion that the present king of France has some shadowy mode of participation in the world—some tenuous sort of "reality" compatible with nonexistence. And, if so much prove acceptable, the stage is set for similar argument in defense of the right to a recognized objective status of fictions, self-contradictory entities, and even nonentity itself. Hamlet and the Snark, the philosopher's stone and the round square, being all characterized by predicates, must all, in some versions of this position, have their being in a multiplicity of distinct limbos, realms of *Sosein*, *Aussersein*, and *Quasisein* in which to enjoy their ambiguous status of partial or quasi existence.[25] The exploration and portrayal in "a terminology devised expressly for the purpose" of such *Lebensräume* of Being, will, of course, provide philosophers of this persuasion with endless material for mystification and dialectical ingenuity.

That arguments so remarkable should have appealed to some philosophers is a matter of historical record; and many another argument in good standing today might be shown to involve patterns of thought essentially similar. The suppression of such invalid trains of inference, against which, the theory of types provides no protection, is the main object of Russell's theory of descriptions.

This part of Russell's program may still be plausibly interpreted as a contribution to the reform of common syntax; improvement of the vocabulary of ordinary language (which will be remembered as the second plank of the platform) is

[25] The classical source of this argument is A. R. v. Meinong's *Untersuchungen zur Gegenstandstheorie* (Leipzig, 1904). For a sympathetic exposition cf. J. N. Findlay's *Meinong's Theory of Objects* (London, 1933), especially ch. 2.

provided rather by the doctrine of logical constructions. Although this is intimately connected both in origin and content with the theory of descriptions, it requires the use of certain epistemological considerations which need not be invoked in the case of the latter.

The Theory of Descriptions as a Metaphysically Neutral Technique of Translation. That the theory of descriptions can be construed as a method of logical translation, capable of justification independently of adherence to any disputable epistemology, is a point that is commonly overlooked by critics. The reader may be reminded that Russell's contribution to the interpretation of descriptive phrases consists in the circumstantial demonstration that every sentence containing a descriptive phrase can be translated into another sentence having the same meaning but a different, and normally more complex, grammatical form. Thus, to take the familiar illustration once again,

(5) The present king of France is married

becomes

(6) Exactly one thing at present reigns over France, and nothing that reigns over France is not married.[26]

The features upon which the usefulness of this procedure depends is the absence in the expanded form (6) of any ostensible reference to an alleged constituent (a "nonexistent person") designated by the original phrase "The present king of France." Not only has the descriptive phrase disappeared in the course of translation, but no part of the expansion of (5) can be identified as capable of abbreviation by the original descriptive phrase. Thus the procedure is not one of definition, in the dictionary sense, of the phrase "The present king of France," but rather a method for recasting every sentence in which the original phrase occurs.[27]

Mastery of the character of the translations appropriate to

[26] Here again some accuracy has been deliberately sacrificed. Cf. Stebbing, *op. cit.*, foot of p. 157, for a better statement.

[27] There is no reason, however, why the notion of definition should not be extended so as to cover the kind of reduction involved in the example cited.

[125]

the different kinds of contexts in which descriptive phrases may occur having once been achieved, a permanent protection is provided against the blandishments of grammatical analogy which lend the doctrine of Realms of Being its spurious plausibility. Reference to the expanded form (6) above shows that the original sentence (5) differs quite radically in form from such a sentence as "Stalin is married." It becomes obvious that adherence to the principle of excluded middle is consistent with the assertion that *every* ascription of a predicate to the present king of France results in a false statement; more generally, a valuable instrument is thereby provided for the expulsion of illegitimate inferences and the clarification of ideas, as the successful application of methods essentially similar to a variety of other philosophical problems amply demonstrates.[28]

It is important to recognize that the enjoyment of such welcome benefits exacts no prior commitment to any epistemological theses. The gist of the method is the proof of the equivalence in meaning of given sentences. Only if appeal to some philosophical principle is involved in verifying the truth of any such proposed translation will it be necessary to deny that the method is epistemologically neutral.

Now the manner in which the equivalence of two *English* sentences is established does not differ in principle from that involved in proving the correctness of a translation from one European language into another. In both cases there is more or less explicit and direct appeal to congruence of behavior and linguistic utterance in cognate situations. The criteria are of a sociological order and may, for that very reason, provide a basis for agreement between philosophers elsewhere advocating very diverse epistemological or metaphysical doctrines. Since an idealist and a materialist can agree upon the correct translation of a passage from Homer, there seems to be no reason why they should have much more difficulty in coming to an understanding about the soundness of a proposed trans-

[28] A good example is G. E. Moore's article, "Is Existence a Predicate?" (*Aristotelian Society Proceedings*, Suppl. vol. 15 [1936]: 175–188).

lation within their native tongue; they might both therefore make equal and equally good use of the methods provided by the theory of descriptions. It is not extravagantly optimistic to hope that, once the theory has been separated from the more specifically metaphysical components with which it is associated in Russell's presentation, it may ultimately achieve a measure of common agreement (without prejudice to eventual differences of opinion concerning the interpretation and value of the method) such as may be found in the elementary propositional calculus or the other well-established branches of symbolic logic.

The Doctrine of Logical Constructions and Its Reliance upon the Principle of Reducibility to Acquaintance. It is to be noted that the foregoing noncontroversial portion of Russell's theory is concerned with the logical expansion of *logical symbols.* When sentence (5) was equated with sentence (6), such words as "present," "king," "France," etc., occurred *vacuously* (to use a convenient term of Quine's[29]); they were present merely as illustrative variables indicating how "The X of Y is Z" might, *in general*, be translated. Thus the translations offered by the theory of descriptions provide further insight into the manner in which the logical words "the," "and," "of" are used in ordinary language; but no information is yielded concerning the syntactical relationships of nonlogical material words.

The shift from the consideration of logical to that of non-logical or material words corresponds exactly to the line drawn in this brief exposition between the theory of descriptions and the doctrine of logical constructions; it will now be shown that when this boundary is crossed the validity of an epistemological principle concerning the reducibility of knowledge to acquaintance becomes relevant to the criticism of Russell's method.

Anybody who maintains, with Russell, that tables are logical constructions, or that the self is a logical construction, is claiming *at least* that sentences containing the material words "table" or "I" submit to the same type of reductive

[29] W. V. Quine, *Mathematical Logic* (New York, 1940), p. 2.

[127]

translation as was demonstrated in connection with descriptive phrases.[30] If tables are logical constructions it is necessary that every sentence containing the word "table" shall be capable of transformation into another sentence from which that word is absent and no part of which could be abbreviated by the word. It is quite certain that *some* material words, such as "average," satisfy such a condition; and it would seem initially plausible that some elements of vocabulary do and others do not admit of such reduction. If this were the case the claim in respect of any specific X that it was a logical construction would seem to require a specific demonstration. On Russell's principles, however, it can be known in advance of specific investigation that the entities referred to by the vast majority, if not indeed the totality, of the words of ordinary language *must be* logical constructions.

For very much more than mere translation of the kind specified is implied by Russell's contention that tables are logical constructions: the procedure must, on his view, have a *direction*, determined by progressive approach toward a *final translation*. A sentence is a final translation only if it consists entirely of "logically proper names" (demonstrative symbols) for "ultimate constituents"; it may then conveniently be referred to as a *pictorial sentence*.[31] To say that X is a logical construction is to claim that sentences containing "X" may be *finally* translated, in this drastic sense, into pictorial sentences.

What are these "ultimate constituents"?[32] They are, on Russell's view, precisely those entities "with which we can

---

[30] Russell, of course, did not use so linguistic a version. Cf. the statement in the text with the following typical utterance: "The real man, too, I believe, however the police may swear to his identity, is really a series of momentary men, each different one from the other, and bound together, not by a numerical identity, but by continuity and certain intrinsic causal laws" (*Mysticism and Logic* [New York, 1918], p. 129).

[31] The term is due to Stebbing.

[32] "Neither the word [a proper name] nor what it names is one of *the ultimate indivisible constituents of the world*" (*Analysis of Mind*, p. 193; italics supplied).

[128]

be acquainted"; more specifically, sense-data (particulars) now presented to us and universals characterizing sense-data with which we are or have been acquainted. The assurance that every sentence can be finally translated into a pictorial sentence is provided by the principle that "every proposition which we can understand must be composed wholly of constituents with which we are acquainted."[33]

The reasons should now be obvious for distinguishing between the theory of descriptions and the theory of logical constructions. The latter predicts that sentences containing "table" will prove to admit of translation into pictorial sentences in which each element refers to an object with which we are acquainted. But ordinary language contains no logically proper names and can therefore provide no pictorial sentences.[34] The verification of the thesis here requires the invention of a new vocabulary departing drastically in character from that which it is to replace.

The case for the validity of the doctrine of logical constructions accordingly is quite different from that which supports the theory of descriptions. The latter is established by empirical grounds manifested in achieved success in translation; the former is, in the absence of the successful provision of the new vocabulary desiderated, rather the expression of a stubborn aspiration, whose plausibility rests entirely upon the supposed truth of the principle of reducibility to acquaintance.

No mention has hitherto been made of the metaphysical consequences of the doctrine of logical constructions. The reader will hardly need to be reminded that Russell has drawn such consequences freely, characteristically maintaining that matter, the self, and other minds (to cite some striking instances of alleged logical constructions) are "symbolic fic-

[33] *The Problems of Philosophy* (London, 1912), p. 91.

[34] "We cannot so use sentences [i.e., pictorially] both because our language is not adapted to picturing and because we usually do not know what precisely are the constituents of the facts to which we refer" (Stebbing, *op. cit.*, p. 157). "No word that we can understand would occur in a grammatically correct account of the universe" (Russell, *Philosophy*, p. 257).

tions" or even "myths."[35] But for these supposed consequences
it is unlikely that Russell's theory of constructions would have
received the critical attention which has been lavished upon
it. If, as the next section will try to show, the principle of
reduction to acquaintance has no evidential support, discussion of these alleged consequences becomes redundant.[36]

Criticism of the Principle of Reducibility to Acquaintance. Since
the various formulations of the principle which Russell has
given[37] hardly vary except in unimportant details of phrase-
ology, the version of 1905 might be taken as standard: "in
every proposition that we can apprehend (i.e., not only in

[35] The following are typical statements: "The persistent particles of
mathematical physics I regard as logical constructions, symbolic fictions . . ."
(*Mysticism and Logic*, p. 128; ". . . matter, which is a logical fiction. . . ."
(*Analysis of Mind*, p. 306); ". . . [desire] merely a convenient fiction, like
force in mechanics . . ." (*op. cit.*, p. 205).

[36] The standard argument against Russell's attribution of a fictitious
status to logical constructions (viz., the proof that "X is a logical construction" does not entail "X does not exist"), though accurate, does less than
justice to Russell's point, however misleadingly expressed. The critics of
Russell's language of "fictions" would not allow that the average man is a
"fiction" or "unreal"; but they would be prepared to admit that the average *unicorn* is "unreal" (though no doubt stigmatizing the choice of terms
as perverse). Now there is a sense in which the plain man would want to
claim that both the average man *and* the average unicorn are fictions, because the phrases referring to them can be dispensed with in a complete
account of the world. And more generally, if "X" is a dispensable symbol it
is natural to say something like: " 'X' is a mere symbolic expedient, corresponding to nothing ultimate and irreducible in the world." It is this kind
of statement that Russell wishes to make. Now, if all nonpictorial sentences
were finally translatable, it would be natural to say that the world consists
only of particular sense-data and the universals by which they are characterized, and to attribute the apparent presence of *other* entities to unwarranted inferences drawn from the nature of the symbols used in abbreviating
pictorial sentences. It would, in short, be natural to say that facts about
tables are *nothing but* facts about objects of acquaintance. This is the gist
of Russell's position.

[37] "On Denoting," *Mind*, 14 (1905): 492; *Mysticism and Logic*, pp. 219,
221; *The Problems of Philosophy*, p. 91. Cf. J. W. Reeves, "The Origin and
Consequences of the Theory of Descriptions," *Aristotelian Society Proceedings*,
34 (1934): 211–230.

those whose truth or falsehood we can judge of, but in all that we can think about) all the constituents are really entities with which we have immediate acquaintance."[38]

The confidence with which this principle is presented for acceptance contrasts strikingly with the baldness of the grounds offered in its defense. "The chief reason," says Russell, "for supposing the principle true is that it seems scarcely possible to believe that we can make a judgment or entertain a supposition without knowing what it is that we are judging or supposing about."[39] And in another place, after this statement is repeated almost verbatim, there is added merely the comment: "We must attach *some* meaning to the words we use, if we are to speak significantly and not utter mere noise, *and the meaning we attach to our words must be something with which we are acquainted.*"[40]

Whatever persuasiveness attaches to this defense of the principle can be shown to arise from equivocation upon the crucial words "know," "mean," and "acquaintance." It may be just permissible so to use the term "acquaintance" that the sentence, "I know the meaning of '*X*'," is synonymous with "I am acquainted with *X*," where the word "meaning" is used in the sense it has in *ordinary language*. This is hardly a sense of "acquaintance" which can be relied upon not to engender confusion, but a philosopher may nevertheless find its introduction expedient. In this sense of the word, however, the assertion that "the meaning we attach to our words must be something with which we are acquainted" is merely the tautology that "the meaning of our words must be the meaning of our words." This can hardly be Russell's intention in the passages cited. Since we understand the word "Attila" we may be said either to "know the meaning of the word" or, alternatively and synonymously, to "be acquainted with Attila." Now Attila is neither a sense-datum nor a

[38] *Mind*, 14: 492.

[39] *Mysticism and Logic*, p. 219.

[40] *The Problems of Philosophy*, p. 91 (italics supplied). I am not aware of any other defense of the principle by Russell.

universal capable of characterizing sense-data; it is impossible, then, for anybody to be acquainted with Attila in the narrow technical sense of acquaintance which makes Russell's principle, whether true or false, something more than a mere tautology. If his assertion is to have any content, he must be interpreted as meaning "It seems scarcely possible to believe that we can make a judgment without knowing *by acquaintance* what it is that we are judging about" and "It is impossible that our words should have meaning unless they refer to entities *with which we are acquainted*."

The alleged defense of the favored principle ("the chief reason for supposing the principle true") is now seen to be a mere repetition of that which was to be demonstrated. One of two things must be the case. Either Russell is using the term "meaning" in one of its customary senses; in that case the argument adduced in favor of the principle is refuted quite simply by pointing out that "Attila" *means* a certain person with whom we are *not* acquainted in Russell's sense. Or, alternatively, a new sense of meaning is implicitly *introduced* in which only objects with which we are acquainted can be meant by words: in that case the argument is a *petitio principii*. In either case the principle remains unproved.

Grounds for Rejecting the Principle of Reducibility to Acquaintance. It is likely that the reasons why the principle, in default of persuasive argument in its defense, should have seemed to so many philosophers self-evident are connected with the supposed necessity of "directness" in relations of meaning and knowing. Underlying Russell's position throughout is the conviction that in all genuine knowledge or meaning there must be some such ultimate fusion of intimacy between the knower and what is known as is provided by the notion of "acquaintance."

Let the validity of such an approach be tested in some less controversial area. Suppose it were argued that "every proposition about the *possession* of material objects must be reducible to a proposition about *contact* with objects" on the ground that "it seems hardly possible to believe that we can hold an object

[132]

without really being in contact with it." Would it not be clear in such a case that there was being introduced a restricted and misleading sense of "holding" or "possession," in virtue of which it becomes logically impossible to hold anything except the surface with which one is in contact? And would it not be quite as clear that the mere introduction of a stipulation concerning the meaning of a term could succeed in demonstrating precisely nothing?

It may be objected that the analogy is unsound; and it is true that there might be *independent* grounds for supposing the relationship of *meaning*, unlike that of physical possession, to be necessarily direct. But although this may be allowed as an abstract possibility, neither Russell nor anybody else has yet provided good grounds for believing it to be anything more. And there are good opposing reasons for rejecting the principle.

Whenever sentences containing a symbol (such as "the present king of France" or "the average man") can be translated in such a manner that the symbol neither appears explicitly nor can be identified with any portion of the translation, it will be convenient to speak of the symbol as being *dispensable*. Now there is good reason to believe that "table" and "I" are not dispensable symbols, i.e., that there are truths concerning tables and the self which are not capable of being expressed without the use of these or synonymous symbols. It can be demonstrated, in connection with quite elementary examples of deductive theories, that "auxiliary" or "secondary" symbols can be introduced in such a way that they are not capable of *explicit* definition in terms of the basic experiential terms of the theory.[41] This does not render them undefined, in a wide sense of that term, since the mode of introduction of the auxiliary symbols into the system provides both for their syntactical relations with associated symbols and for inferential relations between the sentences in which they occur and the "primary" observational sentences

[41] Cf. Ramsey's discussion of the place of explicit definitions in a theory (*Foundations of Mathematics*, p. 229).

[133]

of the system. This seems to be precisely the situation in respect of such scientific terms as "energy," "entropy," and "field," none of which are "dispensable."[42] There appears to be no a priori reason why this should not be the case also in respect of the names of material objects and other terms of ordinary language.

Indeed a careful scrutiny of the attempts made (especially by phenomenalists) to prove that words denoting material objects are dispensable will render this last suggestion something more than plausible. For these attempts invariably terminate in sceptical conclusions. When Russell, in a later book, undertakes to provide a phenomenalistic analysis of "You are hot,"[43] he arrives at a proposition which in order to be known to be true requires the speaker to know *inter alia* that the hearer is aware of a multitude of events in the same sense of "aware" in which he himself is aware of events and, further, that whole classes of events which *could* be perceived exist in the absence of such perception. Now neither of these truths could be known by acquaintance; the conclusion drawn is that the original proposition analyzed is not *strictly* known to be true. At best we can "assume" its truth, "in the absence of evidence to the contrary."[44] But to assume or postulate the truth of a proposition is only to *hope* that it may be true. There are circumstances in which the truth of the assertion "You are hot" is *certain;* nothing could be more absurd than to doubt that this remark, when addressed to a philosopher in the warmest chamber of a Turkish bath, may sometimes be both true and known to be true. Now if the truth of the principle of acquaintance requires the rejection of even a single certain truth, there would seem to be sufficient reason to abandon it.

4. THE NOTION OF THE "IDEAL LANGUAGE"

The Character of the "Ideal Language." An examination of

[42] Further detail would be needed to prove this statement.

[43] *An Inquiry into Meaning and Truth*, pp. 280–282, 284–291.

[44] *Ibid.*, p. 292.

the character of that "ideal language" which Russell recommends as the goal of the philosophy of language provides a very precise test of the value of his early doctrines. For the "ideal language" is, by definition, the symbolism which would be entirely free from the philosophical defects which Russell claims to find in ordinary language. If language "had been invented by scientifically trained observers for purposes of philosophy and logic,"[45] just this symbolism would have resulted. And it would be "logically perfect"[46] in the sense of conforming to "what logic requires of a language which is to avoid contradiction."[47] The character of the ideal language is calculated, then, to reveal in a vivid fashion the benefits to be expected from a successful outcome of Russell's program of reform.

The discussion of the preceding sections should have made clear the features which would be manifested by such a paradigm of philosophical symbolism. Every symbol will be a "logically proper name" denoting objects of acquaintance: "There will be one word and no more for every simple object and everything that is not simple will be expressed by a combination of words."[48] How closely will these logically proper names for ultimate constituents resemble the words at present in use? By definition, they must be unintelligible in the absence of the entities they denote. Thus no proper names, in the familiar *grammatical* sense, can qualify for inclusion in the ideal language, just because, in virtue of referring to complex series of causally related appearances, they function as logical descriptions. The descriptive character of such a name as "Napoleon" is recognized by the circumstance that the name is intelligible to persons who never met the Corsican.[49]

Similar considerations would seem to disqualify all other types of words in the ordinary language. The names of universals characterizing sense-data (e.g., the name of a specific shade of color) might seem to be exceptions; but it would

[45] *The Analysis of Mind*, p. 193.   [48] *The Monist*, 28: 520.
[46] *The Monist*, 28 (1918): 520.   [49] *The Analysis of Mind*, pp. 192–193.
[47] *Contemporary British Philosophy*, 1: 377.

be hard to deny that even these have meaning in the absence of instances of the universals they denote. Now if universals are among the ultimate constituents, as Russell claims, they must be represented in the ideal language by arbitrary noises of such a character that it is logically impossible that they should be uttered in the absence of instances of the universals concerned.

The attempt might be made to construct illustrative instances of sentences of the ideal language composed entirely of demonstratives, by inventing such words as "thet" and "thot" to supplement the present meager stock of "this" and "that."[50] But even "This thet thot"[51] would still convey to a hearer some such meaning as "Something with which the speaker is acquainted has some relation, with which the speaker is acquainted, to some other thing with which he is acquainted."[52] The proposition understood by the hearer would not then be the proposition intended by the speaker; the "perfect sentence," having meaning only to the speaker and to him only at the time of utterance, would be perfectly unintelligible. If this criticism is based upon a misinterpretation of Russell's intention, and if it were permissible for the names of such ultimate constituents as are universals to be intelligible at a variety of times and to more than a single person, it would still be necessary that the names of particulars should be private; and communication would be possible only by the grace of some kind of pre-established speaker-hearer ambiguity in virtue of which what was a logically proper name for the one functioned as a description for the other.

What becomes under such conditions of the intention that the ideal language shall be "completely analytic and . . . show at a glance the logical structure of the facts asserted or

[50] As suggested by John Wisdom (*Mind*, 40 [1931]: 204).

[51] Somewhat more drastic than Wisdom's "This son that, and that brother thet, and thet mother thot, and thot boy, and this kissed Sylvia" (*ibid.*).

[52] Cf. Wisdom's discussion of this point, *op. cit.*, p. 203.

[136]

denied"?[53] Such a system, containing "no words that we can [at present] understand"[54] would be so remote from our present means of expression and so unsuited to perform the functions of unambiguous and logically accurate communication which may be desired of an efficient language, that to urge its capacity to provide "a grammatically correct account of the universe"[55] is to be extravagantly implausible. The "ideal language" in practice would resemble a series of involuntary squeaks and grunts more closely than anything it is at present customary to recognize as a language.

It is by no means certain that Russell ever seriously supposed that the ideal language could be realized; and some of his remarks suggest that he regarded it on occasion as a mere device of exposition.[56] If, as has been argued above, the ideal language is not capable of realization, it becomes impossible seriously to defend indefinite progression toward such an "ideal" as a desirable procedure for the philosophical criticism of language.

It is not difficult to see, in retrospect, why Russell should have been led into this untenable position of defending as the aim of the philosophy of language the construction of a language which could never work. For the "ideal language" would satisfy perfectly the intention to make the relation of "picturing" the sole essential basis of symbolism. Whatever else Russell is prepared to regard as "accidental" in language, he is unwilling to abandon the notion that language must "correspond" to the "facts," through one-one correlation of elements and identity of logical structure. But there is no good reason why we should expect language to correspond to, or "resemble," the "world" any more closely than a telescope does the planet which it brings to the astonomer's attention.

Consequences of Abandoning the Pursuit of an "Ideal Language." To abandon the image of language as a "picture" of the world, which has, on the whole, wrought so much mischief

---

[53] *The Monist*, 28 (1918): 520.
[54] *Philosophy*, p. 257.
[55] *Ibid.*
[56] Cf. *The Monist*, 28 (1918): 520.

in the philosophy of language, is to be in a position to make the most intelligent use of the products of Russell's analytical ingenuity.

For it would be both unfair and ungrateful to end without acknowledging the pragmatic value of the techniques invented by Russell. Rejection of the possibility or desirability of an "ideal language" is compatible with a judicious recourse to the methods of translation and analysis which have been criticized in this paper. It is a matter of common experience that philosophical confusion and mistaken doctrine are sometimes connected with failure to make type distinctions or to reveal, by the technique of translation, the correct deductive relations between sentences of similar grammatical, though differing logical, forms. And where such confusion is manifested it is helpful to follow Russell's new way of "philosophical grammar." It will be well, however, to be unashamedly opportunistic, making the remedy fit the disease and seeking only to remove such hindrances to philosophical enlightenment as are demonstrably occasioned by excessive attachment to the accidents of grammar and vocabulary. In this way there is some hope of avoiding the temptation to impose, by way of cure, a predetermined linguistic structure—of seeking to eliminate the philosophical ills of the language at present in use by proposing an "ideal language" which never could be used. Nor need such a program be aimless. For the object will be to remove just those linguistic confusions which are actually found to be relevant to doctrines of philosophical importance.

VI

Wittgenstein's
Tractatus

THE WIDESPREAD RECOGNITION of the importance in philosophy of an investigation of language is largely due to the influence exerted by Wittgenstein's *Tractatus Logico-Philosophicus.* The central thesis of that book is summarized in the statement that "all philosophy is 'critique of language'."[1] Critical examination of the language we use is no longer to be regarded as a precautionary measure against ambiguity, vagueness, and rhetoric, a mere preliminary to the serious business of philosophy. In the new interpretation, philosophy or, to be more exact, the subject which replaces the "inextricable tangle of problems which is known as philosophy"[2] is identical with the investigation of language. This program has been elaborated in great detail by the movement sometimes known as "Logical Positivism," of which Carnap is a leading representative. In the book from which the last quotation was taken Carnap urges that "once philosophy is purified of all unscientific elements, only the logic of science remains."[3] The "logic of science" would not commonly be thought to mean the same as "the critique of language." But Carnap explains that by the "*logic* of science" he means "the syntax of the *language* of science."[4] By the "language of science" again he means not the technical vocabulary of scientists but the "universal" language in terms of which *every* fact, whether of common knowledge or of scientific knowledge in a narrower sense, can be expressed. The differences in method and purpose between Carnap's "logical syntax of the language of science" and Wittgenstein's[5] "critique of language"

[1] *Tractatus Logico-Philosophicus* (London, 1922), 4.0031.

[2] R. Carnap, *The Logical Syntax of Language* (London, 1937), p. 279.

[3] *Ibid.*

[4] *Loc. cit.*, p. 281.

[5] Throughout this essay, references to "Wittgenstein" mean references to the opinions expressed in his *Tractatus.* It is hardly necessary to add that its author's views may have changed in the interval of twenty-seven years since his book was published.

[141]

are less important than the agreement that "language" is the whole subject matter of philosophy. A similar view is implicit in Ayer's remark "that philosophy provides definitions"[6] or Wisdom's remark that "all philosophic statements *mention* words."[7] But of those who have been influenced by the *Tractatus*, Schlick has expressed the importance in philosophy of an examination of language with most emphasis. "The whole history of philosophy," he says, "might have taken a very different course if the minds of the great thinkers had been more deeply impressed by the remarkable fact that there is such a thing as language."[8]

If attention to the existence of language may change the course of the history of philosophy, and philosophy is to be confined to the investigation of language, it would seem desirable to have a plain statement of the character of such an inquiry and the respects in which it differs from empirical investigations of the same subject matter. And since views of this sort are derivative from the doctrine of the *Tractatus*, it would be a matter of more than historical interest to have an unmetaphorical statement of what the doctrines of that book are taken to be. Such a statement is not available;[9] the voluminous commentary on Wittgenstein's doctrines (occupying by now a bulk many times greater than that of the original) is remarkably sparing in exegesis. The larger part of this paper is accordingly occupied by exposition and criticism of Wittgenstein's views. The first section explains the more elementary portions of his analysis of language. In the second section objections on the ground of internal inconsistency are answered. The third section discusses the

[6] *Language, Truth and Logic* (London, 1936), p. 55 and *passim*.

[7] *Psyche*, 13 (1933): 155.

[8] *Gesammelte Aufsätze, 1926–1936* (Vienna, 1938), p. 153. (The quotation is from a lecture delivered in the University of London in 1932.)

[9] But cf. the following: (*a*) Russell's Introduction to the *Tractatus;* (*b*) Ramsey's critical notice (*Mind*, 32: 1923; reprinted in *The Foundations of Mathematics* [London, 1931]; (*c*) J. Weinberg, *An Examination of Logical Positivism* (London, 1936), chs. 1, 2.

[142]

extent to which the analysis is applicable to any languages currently in use, and the essay ends with some brief remarks on the general character of philosophical investigations of language.

2. THE ANALYSIS OF LANGUAGE

Wittgenstein's analysis of language, according to Russell, "is concerned with the conditions which would have to be fulfilled by a logically perfect language."[10] On this interpretation "ordinary" language is inaccurate in two respects. It allows nonsensical combination of symbols and, moreover, contains symbols which are vague and ambiguous.[11] The function of the philosopher is to construct a new language in which these defects have been repaired by the provision of precise symbols and explicit rules for their combination.

While this view of the character of Wittgenstein's investigation (which may have been suggested by Russell's own attempts to construct a logically perfect language) is supported by a few of the remarks made in the *Tractatus*, the main trend of the book is against it. Passages such as the following: "All propositions of our colloquial language, are actually, just as they are, logically completely in order,"[12] and, again, "Every possible proposition is legitimately constructed,"[13] can be brought to refute Russell's interpretation and in support of the view that Wittgenstein was interested in "colloquial" language, "just as it is." If the philosophical investigation of language is concerned with language in its present condition the interest of its conclusions is, as Ramsey pointed out,[14] greatly increased. But Wittgenstein is not clear on this point. He is willing to say, "We must employ a symbolism [i.e., a *new* symbolism] which excludes them [i.e., confusions between symbols arising from the physical resem-

[10] *Tractatus Logico-Philosophicus*, Introd., p. 7.

[11] Russell, *op. cit.*, p. 8.

[12] *Tractatus Logico-Philosophicus*, 5.553.

[13] *Ibid.*, 5.5733.

[14] *Foundations of Mathematics*, p. 271.

blance of their perceptible signs] by not applying the same sign in different symbols and by not applying signs in the same way which signify in different ways. A symbolism, that is to say, which obeys the rules of logical grammar—of logical syntax."[15] Such a symbolism, however, *would* be an "ideal" language (or a step toward an ideal language) in Russell's sense.

Such contradictions in Wittgenstein's own formulations of the character of his method, are symptomatic of an attempt to satisfy incompatible demands and will be the basis of the criticisms elaborated in section 4 of this paper. But they are suppressed and superficially resolved in the *Tractatus* by the use of the pair of technical terms, "sign" and "symbol."

The distinction between these two terms is connected, but not identical, with the distinction between "token" and "type" introduced by Peirce.[16] It may be remembered that the object of introducing the latter distinction was to avoid the appearance of contradiction in such a sentence as "The book was fifty thousand words long, but he used only five thousand words in writing it."[17] This is done by saying that the word "word" is used in two different senses: (i) in such a way that the two shapes "and" and "and" in this line are *two* words, (ii) in such a way that there is the *one* word "and" in the English language. The next step is to call the shapes (or corresponding sounds) *token*-words[18] "of" a (single) *type*-word. Each type-word in a language, say W, has then a correlated set of sounds and shapes, say C_W, consisting of all the tokens "of" that type.

By analyzing the different senses in which the word "word" is used in English, Stebbing arrives at a partial analysis of the meaning of "tokens of the same type." "Tokens of the same word" she says "*must* have some degree of similarity

---

[15] *Tractatus*, 3.325.

[16] Cf. L. S. Stebbing, "Sounds, Shapes and Words," *Aristotelian Society Proceedings*, Suppl. vol. 14 (1935): 4.

[17] Cf. Stebbing (*ibid.*) for Peirce's example.

[18] A "token-word" is, of course, not a special *kind* of word.

with other tokens of the same word."[19] This is unhelpful, for all sounds have "some degree of similarity," and two tokens of different words may have a greater degree of similarity than two tokens of the same word. Stebbing wishes to exclude the suggestion that tokens of the same type belong to *that* type in virtue of having the same meaning attached to them.[20] The relations which determine that certain sounds and shapes belong to the same set C_W associated with one type-word W are, on Stebbing's view, sensible relations, e.g., that of differing from certain sounds or shapes, the "norms," by not more than specified degrees of intensity, pitch, or spatial quality, etc. The tokens "fair" and "fair" used to mean blond and impartial respectively are counted as tokens of the same type-word.[21]

Wittgenstein, on the contrary, uses the word "symbol" in order to designate tokens arranged in sets *in accordance with the meaning which is attached to them*. The word "sign" he uses with type-token ambiguity: sometimes to mean a token, as when he speaks of the "sensibly perceptible sign (sound or written sign),"[22] or says that "the sign is the part of the symbol perceptible by the senses"[23] sometimes to mean a type, as when he says " 'A' is the same sign as 'A'."[24] The phrase "belonging to the same symbol," on the other hand, is used only for tokens (but only for *some*) which are used in the same way. Tokens belonging to different types may accordingly belong to the same symbol and vice versa. "In the language of everyday life it very often happens that the same word signifies in two different ways—and therefore

[19] *Op. cit.*, p. 12.

[20] For this view see A. M. MacIver, "Token, Type and Meaning," *Analysis*, 4 (1936–1937): 58–64.

[21] Stebbing, *op. cit.*, p. 12. For the purpose of the present discussion it is of no great importance whether Stebbing's analysis is accurate. Probably considerations of identity of meaning play *some* part in determining common uses of the phrase "the *same* word." But it is convenient to *define* the token-type distinction without reference to meaning.

[22] *Tractatus*, 3.11.   [23] *Ibid.*, 3.32.   [24] *Ibid.*, 3.203.

belongs to different symbols—or that two words, which signify in different ways are apparently applied in the same way in the proposition."[25] But "signs which serve *one* purpose are logically equivalent [i.e., belong to the same symbol], signs which serve *no* purpose are logically meaningless [belong to no symbol]."[26]

We can now reconcile the apparent contradiction involved in maintaining that colloquial language is "logically completely in order" while recommending an *improved* notation. In colloquial language we have two systems of classification of tokens: (i) according to types, (ii) according to symbols. The former is largely, though not entirely, conventional (or as Wittgenstein elsewhere calls it, "accidental"); the latter is the expression of "logical structure." It is because we confuse grammatical distinctions with those of logic that changes in the signs used may be advisable. But any such change is a practical device to prevent confusion, like changing the names of London streets—a "mechanical expedient" for facilitating the recognition of logical relations between symbols. "Whenever we make up 'ideal languages' it is not in order to replace ordinary languages by them; but just to remove some trouble, caused in somebody's mind by thinking that he has got hold of the exact use of a common word."[27] How logical, as distinct from grammatical, structure can be made more explicit is discussed later in this essay.

The distinctions between token and type, on the one hand, and again between sign and symbol, will be found relevant to the detailed description of Wittgenstein's analysis of language, which now follows.

[25] *Ibid.*, 3.323.

[26] *Loc. cit.*, 5.47321. It is to be noticed however that synonyms are not necessarily regarded as cases of the same symbol. In 3.341 there is reference to "all symbols which can fulfil the same purpose." Nor do all the names of a single object belong to a single symbol. It seems that criteria of sensible resemblance between the associated tokens plays *some* part in determining the use of the word "symbol."

[27] From notes of lectures delivered by Wittgenstein at Cambridge, 1933–1934.

[146]

Wittgenstein expresses the result of his examination of language by using a number of technical terms, of which "name," "proposition," "structure," "saying," and "showing" are those with which this paper is primarily concerned. It will be found that none of these can be defined or adequately described in isolation. Like the primitive notions of an uninterpreted formal geometry, their meanings are determined by exhibiting their mutual relations in a set of what is sometimes called "implicit definitions."

A "proposition" (type-sense) is any symbol which has meaning independently of other symbols. It is composed of "names,"[28] but names, unlike propositions, must occur in combination with other names (and logical connectives) in order to convey a complete meaning. "Only the proposition has sense; only in the context of a proposition has a name meaning."[29] Those propositions whose truth-value is independent of the truth-value of any other propositions are called "elementary."[30] "Elementary propositions" constitute as it were the atoms out of which all other propositions are constructed by means of logical operations. The unit of language, like that of matter, has, as the physicists would say, a "fine structure." Every proposition is composite; "it has something in common with *other* symbols";[31] and its elements, the "names," "are combined with one another in a definite way."[32] The way in which the elements are connected in the elementary proposition is called its "structure."[33] The "names" are the smallest units of meaning; they are the "simple signs"[34] which cannot be analyzed further by definitions.[35]

We come now to the correlation between language and that to which language refers. In this three aspects can be distinguished: the reference of names, the reference of propositions, and the correspondence between structure in the proposition and structure in that to which propositions refer.

---

[28] *Tractatus*, 4.21, 4.22.   [31] *Ibid.*, 5.5251.   [34] *Ibid.*, 3.202.

[29] *Ibid.*, 3.3.   [32] *Ibid.*, 2.14.   [35] *Ibid.*, 3.26.

[30] *Ibid.*, 4.21, *et seq.*   [33] *Ibid.*, 2.15.

(i) Names stand for "objects," and the meaning of a name is the "object" to which it refers.[36] (ii) Propositions represent "possible states of affair," and in order to verify a proposition "we must compare it with reality."[37] (iii) The structure of the proposition repeats the structure of the state of affairs which it represents: the names in the proposition are combined in the same way as objects in the corresponding possible state of affairs.[38] In particular the "multiplicity" of both must be the same: "In the proposition there must be as many things distinguishable as there are in the state of affairs which it represents."[39]

In explaining the meanings of the technical terms he introduces, Wittgenstein constantly suggests that he is using "language" in such a way that to say there is a language implies that there are *users* of the language. Thus "the meanings of the simple signs (the words) must be explained to us [i.e., by those who use them] if we are to understand them."[40] Moreover, the criterion of the kind of symbol to which a token belongs is the way in which the token (and the corresponding type) *are used*. "In order to recognize the symbol in the sign we must consider the significant *use*."[41] And again "What does not get expressed in the sign is shown by its application. What the signs conceal, their application declares."[42]

In this brief outline I have tried to keep closely to Wittgenstein's own words, and I have deliberately omitted the more complex parts of the theory (e.g., the discussion of non-elementary propositions, of mathematical equations, of symbols other than names and propositions).

In criticizing Wittgenstein's analysis it is important to remember its purpose. It is primarily directed toward establishing a single negative thesis ("*Mein Grundgedanke*" as Wittgenstein calls it) "that the *logic* of the facts cannot be

---

[36] *Ibid.*, 3.203.   [39] *Ibid.*, 4.04.   [41] *Ibid.*, 3.326.

[37] *Ibid.*, 2.202.   [40] *Ibid.*, 4.026.   [42] *Ibid.*, 3.262.

[38] *Ibid.*, 3.21, 4.0311.

represented."[43] By the phrase "logic of the facts" in this context is meant a system of relations between that "structure" in "states of affairs" which is repeated in the structure of propositions. Wittgenstein makes a sharp distinction between "saying" (or "asserting") and "showing." Propositions *assert* the existence of a state of affairs,[44] but they "*show* the logical form of reality. They exhibit it."[45] Now much of the *Tractatus* is concerned with remarks about the logical structure of symbols; so its method must, on its own principles, consist of "showing." But this seems to involve the unintelligibility of the *Tractatus* itself, since "what *can* be shown *cannot* be said."[46]

The charge of internal contradiction, based upon this distinction between "saying" and "showing," has been so commonly leveled against the *Tractatus* that it will be convenient to answer it at once before proceeding to consider the applicability of Wittgenstein's categories of "name," "proposition," and "structure."

3. IS THE TRACTATUS SELF-CONTRADICTORY?

It has been widely assumed that in maintaining that it is logically impossible to "say" anything about logical structure Wittgenstein is implying the incommunicability of facts about structure and hence the meaninglessness of his own remarks in the *Tractatus*. Russell, for instance, in objecting that "after all, Mr. Wittgenstein manages to say a good deal about what cannot be said"[47] is clearly taking *what can be said* to be identical with *what can be conveyed by means of language* or *what has meaning*. Wittgenstein provides support for this interpretation in the much-quoted passage with which his book ends: "My propositions are elucidatory in this way: he who understands them finally recognizes them as senseless. . . . Whereof one cannot speak thereof one must be silent."[48] It is this passage more than any other which leads Carnap to regard the *Tractatus* as a series of "more or

---

[43] *Ibid.*, 4.0312.   [45] *Ibid.*, 4.121.   [47] *Tractatus*, Introd., p. 22.

[44] *Ibid.*, 4.22.   [46] *Ibid.*, 4.1212.   [48] *Tractatus*, 5.64, 7.

less vague explanations which the reader must subsequently recognize as pseudo-sentences and abandon."[49] Ramsey adopts the same view in his expression of worry at the suggestion that philosophy is nonsense—"We must then take seriously that it is nonsense, and not pretend, as Wittgenstein does, that it is important nonsense."[50]

These critics have taken a single provocative remark too literally. The statement on which the charges of self-contradiction is based itself contains a contradiction. A "senseless" proposition is not a proposition at all, and it is logically impossible that whatever we "understand" should, whether "finally" or at any other time, be revealed as senseless. Either there *was* nothing to understand and we were uttering nonsensical collocations of sounds, or we *did* understand and something *was* communicated.

Closer attention to the remainder of Wittgenstein's argument would show that he is using the crucial words "saying" and "showing" in a technical sense which deviates from the sense which would commonly be attributed to them. It is characteristic of Wittgenstein's sense that the phrase "*p can be said*" is restricted to the cases where *p* is an empirical proposition. This is demonstrated by the following three statements about mathematics and logic: (i) "The propositions of mathematics are equations and therefore pseudo-propositions,"[51] (ii) "The logic of the world which the propositions of logic *show* in tautologies mathematics *shows* in equations,"[52] (iii) "The propositions of logic therefore say nothing (they are the analytical propositions)."[53] It appears, then, that to say that *p* "says" something is to say that *p* is empirical; to say that *p* "shows" but does not say anything is to say that *p* is not empirical. In the respect of "saying nothing" propositions about logical structure, the propositions of philosophy, are in no worse case than the "propo-

---

[49] *Logical Syntax of Language*, p. 283.   [52] *Ibid.*, 6.22.

[50] *Foundations of Mathematics*, p. 263.   [53] *Ibid.*, 6.11.

[51] *Tractatus*, 5.2.

sitions" of mathematics or logic. Now Wittgenstein could not intend to deny that mathematical equations may convey "information" of a certain sort to those who meet them for the first time, but he is concerned to stress the difference between this kind of information and that conveyed by empirical propositions. He is not saying that logical structure is ineffable, but he is drawing attention to a difference in usage between two kinds of propositional symbols. Reserving the word "sense" for empirical propositions is a provocative (and as it seems, misleading) way of emphasizing this difference.[54]

Not only does Wittgenstein not imply the self-defeating doctrine that his own propositions are nonsensical; he supplies us with sufficient clues on which to base a more positive notion of the methods used in exhibiting relations of logical structure. One such method can be illustrated by explaining the analysis of a proposition asserting that some combination of signs is nonsensical, e. g., the proposition, "*The Good is less identical than the Beautiful is nonsense.*"[55]

The grammatical form of this sentence is that of "A is B," where A is some complex object and B is a property of that object. But "The Good is less identical than the Beautiful" does not express a proposition. By adjoining the eight signs we have failed to assert anything. The word nonsense does not indicate a property of a proposition (for there *is* no proposition); it is more like a signal that we have not succeeded in framing a proposition. The failure of the attempt

---

[54] The use of a common word in a new and rather shocking context is an important factor in the *succès de scandale* of Wittgenstein's book. Contrast the rhetorical force of "my propositions are senseless" with "my propositions are not empirical." An important case where the use of a common word in an unusual sense produces confusion is that of "tautology." This word is applied to certain described kinds of truth function, but it has no *explanatory* force. Cf. H. Hahn, *Logique, Mathématiques et Connaissance de la Réalité* (Paris, 1935), p. 31, for a "tautological" theory of the nature of mathematics, wrongly based on the *Tractatus*.

[55] An example used in the *Tractatus*, 4.003. The account which now follows is not to be found in the *Tractatus*.

[151]

makes more vivid, "shows" us, the way in which the signs "Good," "is," "less," etc., are used in the language in which they occur.[56]

"Propositions" such as that used as an example differ from *empirical* propositions in which any or all of the same words may occur. They belong to the category of rules for the manipulation of signs in the language (or deductions from such rules): they may convey information of a certain kind about rules, but it is not the kind of information that is conveyed by empirical propositions. In the latter we *use* signs to make extralinguistic reference: in the statements of logical syntax we use signs in another way in order to reveal and emphasize the kind of ways in which it is permissible in language to use them.[57]

On some such lines as these it would be possible to give more elaborate analyses of the various types of statements which belong to logical syntax.

4. THE APPLICABILITY OF WITTGENSTEIN'S ANALYSIS

Wittgenstein's account of "name," "proposition," and "structure" has been compared in this paper to a formal geometry whose primitive notions are defined by their mutual relations as expressed in a system of "implicit definitions" or axioms. When a formal geometry comes to receive a specific interpretation, i.e., to be applied to a definite subject matter, it is necessary to supplement the axioms by "applicative definitions" or *Zuordnungsdefinitionen* of each of the notions involved. If our analogy holds and Wittgenstein's account of language is to be more than an exercise in formal mathe-

---

[56] Or rather it tells us how they are *not* used.

[57] Cf. the difference between the record of a "move" in chess (say 1.P-K4) and the statement of an impossibility (say that there cannot be ten queens of the same color simultaneously on the board). The latter is about the way in which the pieces may or may not be moved; the former tells us how they *were* moved. The latter is settled before the game begins (belongs to the definition of the game); the former conveys information about the particular game recorded.

matics, it will be necessary to supply criteria for the application of words like "name," "sign," "symbol," etc., to any particular language in which we may be interested. In trying to discover how the "names" and "logical structure" of a language like English are to be recognized we shall see the limitations of Wittgenstein's theory.

First as to names. To those who are familiar with general linguistic theory the hierarchical pattern of Wittgenstein's analysis will not be a novelty. The categories of "name," "proposition," and "structure of proposition" parallel the linguistic categories of "word," "sentence," and "sentence-structure." The student of linguistic theory finds it hard to define these words or to explain unambiguously how they are to be applied in any given language.[58] He is guided by physical characteristics of the tokens used in the language (e.g., by intonation, the isolation of syllables by pauses, etc.). But Wittgenstein has to use criteria which take account of physical characteristics (viz., those which assign tokens to types) without coinciding with the criteria used by the linguistic theorist. For whereas the linguist is searching for something like a minimum unit of *speech* (the "word"), the philosopher needs a minimum unit of *meaning*. Thus the symbol *uncle*, which is a unit for linguistics, will be decomposed in Wittgenstein's scheme by the analysis of the propositions in which it may occur. Only when such retranslation has proceeded so far that each propositional sign appears overtly as a complex of elementary propositions none of which can be further decomposed, shall we be in the position to point out those simple signs which are the "names" in Wittgenstein's sense.

If we try to apply this program seriously to any given "language" (e.g., the brand of English spoken by members of the Aristotelian Society) we shall be faced in our search for names by a difficulty unknown to the linguist. In searching

[58] Cf. L. Bloomfield, *Language* (New York, 1933), pp. 178–179, for a discussion of the meaning of "word."

[153]

for units of speech the latter confines himielf exclusively to the phonemes[59] and compounds of phonemes actually current in the language he is investigating: his task is that of selection and classification. But in the analysis of propositions into complexes of elementary propositions we shall need to invent signs as our analysis proceeds. It is not possible to produce a single "name" in Wittgenstein's sense from our current vocabulary. Nor have we definite criteria for deciding whether any examples which might be produced in fact satisfy the requirements.[60]

It must not be forgotten, of course, that most languages use nonvisual significant features in symbolism, e.g., stress and intonation. The poverty of the printed or written word leaves a loophole for anybody who wishes to argue that language consists of units of meaning—let us continue to call them "names"—while defining these units of meaning only in terms of tokens already used in the language under examination. He might draw, for defining characteristics of his units, upon those significant features of speech which are not explicitly represented in writing. In "inventing" signs, he might proceed to argue: what we are doing is adding a class of shapes to an already existing class of tokens having other physical characteristics and already constituting a type in the language.

A defense on these lines becomes less plausible when regard is paid to the part played by *context* as an element of significance in language. This is most clearly seen by considering the use of demonstratives. In using a sentence like "This is my fountain pen," where I accompany the utterance of the word "this" by showing you my fountain pen, the words used are insufficient to express a proposition unless accompanied by the appropriate demonstration. To my hearers, then, the propositional sign is constituted by

[59] The smallest recognizable significant features of speech.

[60] We can prove that some examples will not satisfy the requirements (by producing analyses of the propositions in which they occur): we cannot prove that a given symbol *does* satisfy the requirements.

seeing my pen as well as by hearing the noises I utter. Only by accepting this would it be possible to maintain that part of Wittgenstein's analysis which demands that complexity in the state of affairs referred to should be reflected in the propositional sign which refers. For I may use the same set of words "This is my fountain pen" on two separate occasions to refer to two different objects. I am then making two *different* assertions, viz., in the one case that my fountain pen is my fountain pen, in the other that some other object, say my hat, is. Since I use the same words on both occasions, the perceptible tokens which allow my hearer to recognize the difference in the two sentences must be diverse on the two occasions. The visual appearance of my fountain pen and my hat respectively must therefore be counted as part of tokens of the propositional sign. A similar analysis could be made of the use of all sentences whose meaning is supplemented by the circumstances in which they are uttered.

The fact that we systematically make use in this way of features of the context, to supplement the meaning of sounds or shapes which would otherwise fail to express complete propositions, will supply the believer in simple signs with further materials for his case. He might argue with some plausibility that, in certain circumstances, when we use the noise "this" to refer to a colored expanse in the visual field, it is the appearance of the visual expanse to the hearer in a certain relation to the sound which is heard at the same instant which constitutes the "name" of the expanse itself.

Such a view involves an awkward extension of the sense of the word "token" to include in addition to the regular use of shapes and sounds, the contextual use of appearances of an object to refer to the appearance itself or the object of which it is an appearance. The extension of the narrower sense of the term "token" is made in the interests of preserving in the propositional token a *perceptible* complexity corresponding to the complexity of the corresponding referent. The appearance of the fountain pen (together with the

[155]

accompanying sound) is to count as a "name" for the pen because we want each object to have its own different but perceptible name.

This desperate expedient will not always serve. Consider the sentence "Today is Monday," which expresses different propositions according to the day on which it is uttered. What is it in the context that determines the hearer to understand that when I now say "Today is Monday" I assert that December 12 and not some other day is Monday? Surely only the fact that I utter the form of words on December 12 and not on some other day. But the fact that I utter the words today is not a perceptible feature of the linguistic situation. To urge in this case that there are *perceptible* differences in the two linguistic situations constituted by the utterance on different occasions of the same form of words "Today is December 12" is utterly implausible. The natural method of describing the situation is to say that we use sentence-tokens belonging to the *same* sentence-type on the two occasions to express two different propositions. That this can be done is no more mysterious than is the fact that we can use the same key to open the front door each day. To suppose that the sentence tokens *must* be unlike would be like arguing that we must use a different key every time we unlock the door.

To sum up this part of our discussion. Suppose we define a language as a logical construction out of the significant *perceptible* tokens used by a certain group of speakers in accordance with certain rules. Among these tokens will be some which we can distinguish as word tokens and propositional tokens. Propositional tokens expressing elementary propositions will be a subclass of all the propositional tokens in the language: Let us call them elementary propositional tokens. Let us call word tokens which occur as parts of elementary propositional tokens by the title of name tokens. Each "name" in Wittgenstein's sense is a logical construction out of a class of name tokens. Whenever x is a name let "C_x" denote the set of the name tokens in terms of which

[156]

x is the logical construction. Then we maintain that there will be *some* values of x, say a and b (with $a \neq b$) such that C_a and C_b contain some common members, i.e., difference in the "name" does not imply mutual exclusion of the correlated sets of name tokens. Moreover, we have no criteria for determining whether any suggested class C of tokens is the correlated class C_x of name tokens of some name x.

The Notion of "Structure" in Wittgenstein's Analysis. I have already pointed out that recognition of the structure of a proposition depends upon ability to identify the elements (names) which are the proposition's constituents. Thus the difficulties in finding applicative definitions for the term "name" automatically involve difficulties in finding applicative definitions for the term "structure." The latter, however, is even less well defined than the former and needs separate attention.

I propose to refer first to the use made by Russell and subsequent writers of the notion of "logical form" and then to point out the modifications from it contained in Wittgenstein's notion of "logical structure."

It is convenient to quote Russell's own account of the notion of "logical form." "In every proposition . . . there is, besides the particular subject-matter concerned, a certain *form*, a way in which the constituents of the proposition . . . are put together. If I say *Socrates is mortal, Jones is angry, the sun is hot*, there is something in common in these three cases, something indicated by the word *is*. What is in common is the *form* of the proposition, not an actual constituent."[61] To this Stebbing adds the comment that "the form of a proposition is what remains unchanged although all the constituents of the proposition are altered."[62]

It is noteworthy that neither Russell nor Stebbing provides a *definition* of logical form. Both assume that there is such a thing. Russell asserts not only that each proposition has a

[61] *Our Knowledge of the External World* (London, 1914), p.62.
[62] *A Modern Introduction to Logic* (London, 1930), p. 125.

logical form but that a number of propositions have the same form in common. Similarly, Stebbing asserts, without proof, that if each constituent of a proposition were replaced by some other term *something* would remain constant. The absence of a definition would not matter if some criteria were given for determining the logical form of a given proposition. Criteria for the *identity of logical form* in two or more propositions are easier to find than criteria for determination of the logical form of a single proposition. Let us examine for identity of logical form the three propositions used as examples in the passage quoted from Russell.

Identity of logical form in two propositions demands, as a partial condition, equality of the number of constituents in each. But none of the three propositions in question are incapable of further analysis, and it is not at all probable that the fully analyzed propositions would be found to have the same number of constituents. To say that the three propositions have the same form is like saying that the mathematical equations $(3x + 7)^2 + 9 = 0$ and $(5x^3 + 4x + 5)^2 + 11 = 0$ have the same mathematical form. Certainly each of these equations contains the square of an algebraic polynomical plus a constant and in this respect are similar, but the fact that the expressions squared are different in the two cases prevents us from asserting identity of form. In the mathematical case, moreover, the equation skeleton "$(\ldots)^2 + --- = 0$" can be preserved, whatever expressions are substituted at the places indicated by "$\ldots$" and "$---$." But the propositional skeleton "$(\ldots)$ is $(---)$" will not be preserved when the proposition is analyzed. In general, therefore, recognition of identity of form in two or more propositions involves knowledge of the full analysis of the propositions. In exceptionally favorable cases, however, close similarity in two propositions may permit us to assert identity of logical form in ignorance of the analyses of the propositions. We can say that "John loves Mary" and "Tom hates Margery" are

[158]

identical in logical form because the corresponding terms are of exactly the same kinds.

In comparing the logical form of two completely analyzed propositions, the only features of the propositions which are relevant are (i) one-one correspondence of the terms in both, (ii) identity of arrangement of the terms, as shown by the disposition of the logical constants, (iii) identity of category of corresponding terms. By saying that two terms are of identical categories we mean that they are either both particulars or both propositional functions with the same number and types of arguments.

To these conditions Wittgenstein adds that corresponding terms must be of the same *kind* in the sense of making sense or nonsense in the same contexts. It is in this respect that his notion of "logical structure" differs from Russell's notion of "logical form." Thus the criteria for identity of logical structure are even more difficult to apply than those of logical form.

The conceptions of logical structure and logical form are probably derivative from the psychologically more primitive notion of *visual* form, and there is consequently a tendency to confuse the former with the latter. Consider, for example, the representation of the simplest integers in the following notation:

I   II   III   IIII   IIIII   IIIIII   IIIIIII. . . .

Here the tokens display certain obvious relations of visual form. But in the sense in which Wittgenstein wishes to speak of structure exactly the same (logical) structure is embodied in the notation

1   2   3   4   5   6   7 . . .

(or rather in the propositions in which they occur). And exactly the same logical structure would be displayed by *any* system of signs used in the same way.[63] For the purpose of determining logical structure it is, for instance, a matter of

[63] How to decide *when* two systems of signs are used "in the same way" is precisely the difficulty.

complete indifference whether we represent certain features of states of affairs by spatial *arrangement* rather than by sounds or shapes. Hence the unimportance in theory of attempts to "improve" symbolism: tokens of *any* properties whatsoever can be used as the material for a complete language. The function of resemblances between propositional signs (e.g., between "*aRb*" and "*bRc*") is the *practical* one of reminding users of the language of the relations between the logical structures of the corresponding propositions. Accordingly, there need be nothing in common between the physical structure of the system of tokens used in the language and the "states of affairs" to which the language refers.

On this view of the matter, the difficulties of discovering relations of logical structure in a given language are of the same nature as those involved in finding "names." "Names" are so defined that no physical characteristics of tokens are a clue to their identification. And the same is true of "logical structure." "What signifies in the symbol is what is common to all those symbols by which it can be replaced."[64] So long as we define identity of symbols in terms of identity of their associated sets of tokens, we shall be bound to say that synonymous symbols (whether names or propositions) need have no common features. If it is objected that propositions may nevertheless have a structure which is not exhibited in the physical relationships of their associated sets of tokens, we must ask for a *definition* of this alleged structure. It is not sufficient to say that the structure *is* the common feature of all symbols which can fulfill the same purpose; it must first be demonstrated that there *is* such a common feature.[65]

Concluding Remarks concerning the Applicability of Wittgenstein's Analysis. It is impossible to obtain from the *Tractatus* exact

[64] *Tractatus*, 3.344.

[65] Cf. the argument that all objects which can open a door must have common features. This is plausible so long as we think of keys. But what is there in common between a key, a door handle, and a battering ram? Only that they can fulfil the same purpose.

[160]

criteria for the application of the fundamental terms "name" and "structure." I suggest that this is due to the attempt to stretch a spatial analogy (which is legitimate in certain restricted methods of symbolism) in such a way as to apply to *every* language. It *is* possible to construct a symbolism in which practically every term of Wittgenstein's analysis can be exactly applied. Consider, for example, a "world" composed of points and bars, as shown in Fig. 6. Each dot is an "object," each continuous linkage a "state of affairs."

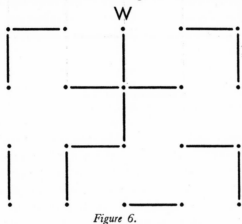

Figure 6.

Consider next a "language" as shown in Fig. 7, where

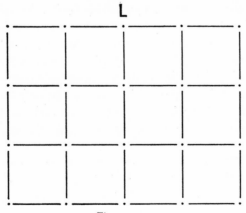

Figure 7.

[161]

each dot represents the corresponding dot in Fig. 6, each bar the corresponding bar in Fig. 6.

Fig. 8 shows an *asserted* (false) proposition in this language.

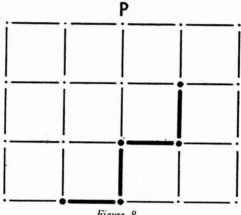

Figure 8.

In this symbolism there *is* something in common between a proposition and its referent; for the state of affairs and the correlated propositional token are geometrically congruent. I am suggesting that the attempt to use this type of symbolism as a pattern for symbolism in general is responsilbe both for the lack of definition of the fundamental terms in Wittgenstein's analysis and for the resulting mysticism. Immediately we allow, in our special symbolism, the system L to be *any* system of signs which can "adequately" represent W, we are led first to allow topological distortion of the symbolizing diagram (by stretching the elastic medium on which we suppose it inscribed), then to replace the dots and bars by words or other shapes until we arrive at a system of signs having no *geometrical* resemblance to W. If we persist in saying that every such system of symbols must have the same structure we are using the word "structure" in a new but undefined sense. To say that all systems which represent W *must* have the same structure is to say no more than that all systems which represent W must represent W.

It is characteristic of "philosophical" investigations of

[162]

language to insist that the propositions expressing the product of the investigation are necessary. We have seen Wittgenstein insisting that equivalent symbols *"must"* have the same multiplicity. I believe the alleged "necessity" of such declarations is connected with a determination to stretch a term like "multiplicity" until it becomes a universal category. I will conclude this essay by saying a little more about the nature of attempts to discover the "essential" characteristics of language.

5. THE CHARACTER OF "PHILOSOPHICAL" INVESTIGATIONS OF LANGUAGE

In a passage quoted at the beginning of this essay, Schlick invited philosophers to pay more attention to the "remarkable fact that there is such a thing as language." In the same lecture Schlick explains that the philosopher is "interested only in those characteristics which all the different methods of communication have in common and which are the *essential characteristics* of Language." He wants "to understand the nature of language in general." The upshot of Schlick's investigation is that "the essential characteristic of language . . . is its capability of *expressing* facts,"[66] providing we understand by "expression" the "showing forth" of "logical structure" and not the communication of "content."[67] Now it will be found that many other writers have also tried to describe the "essential" character of language. I will quote two such attempts:

"The *essence* of language consists in the assigning of conventional, voluntarily articulated sounds, or their equivalent, to the diverse elements of experience."[68]

"The *essence* of language lies in the intentional conveyance of ideas from one living being to another through the instrumentality of arbitrary tokens or symbols agreed upon and

[66] *Gesammelte Aufsätze*, p. 155.

[67] Schlick was strongly influenced by Wittgenstein's views. But he gives us no more definite an account of "logical structure" than is found in the *Tractatus*.

[68] E. Sapir.

understood by both as being associated with the particular ideas in question."[69]

A further remark of Butler's where he says that he is trying to formulate "the essentials, the presence of which constitutes language while their absence negatives it altogether"[70] provides a clue to the character of inquiries which terminate in dicta such as these about the essence of language. For the essential characteristics, "the presence of which constitute language," are simply the *defining* characteristics of language. Wittgenstein, Schlick, Sapir, and Butler are engaged in providing definitions, or explicit rules for the use, of the *word* "language."

The last remark may easily be misleading and needs to be corrected by the following considerations.

(i) Philosophers are not puzzled about the meaning of the word "language" in the way that a foreigner who did not know English might be. Philosophers know how to use the word "language"; they wish nevertheless to make the rules for its use more explicit or to reduce the variety of different ways in which it is used to a single pattern.

(ii) The "philosophical" definition of "language" is not arbitrary: there are correct and incorrect definitions (or more correct and less correct definitions). The test of correctness is agreement with the usage of the language in which the word occurs. But the rule for using the word "language" is not a statement *about* the way in which the word is used in the language in question. The latter is, of course, an empirical statement.[71] We must distinguish between rules *of* usage and statements *about* the usage. A rule in chess is not a statement about the behavior of chess players. If it were we could never formulate the rules of a game which had not yet been played. Nor is a "rule," whether in a game or in language, a command or prescription, as some philosophers who have been impressed by the differences between rules and statements

[69] Samuel Butler, *Essays on Art, Life and Science* (London, 1904).

[70] *Ibid.*, p. 184.

[71] Cf. C. D. Broad, *Aristotelian Society Proceedings*, Suppl. vol. 15 (1936): 107.

[164]

have supposed. (For *who* commands, and what are the penalties for disobedience?) It would be nearer the mark to regard a rule in chess as a description of ways in which the pieces might be moved. Similarly, we can regard a definition such as " 'owl' = 'kind of large-headed small-faced hook-beaked large-eyed soft-plumaged nocturnal bird of prey' " (*Oxford Dictionary*) as a rule for the mutual substitution of the two expressions united by the sign of equality. Like other descriptions, a "rule" is a sentence fragment to which we can add other sentence fragments in order to produce sentences expressing propositions.

Thus from the rule "A" = "B" . . . (r) we can form the sentence "Most educated speakers of the Class C in situation S (e.g., Englishmen who speak English correctly) substitute "A" for "B" and vice versa" . . . (s). Now the sentence s expresses an empirical proposition. And s is formed from r in a regular way which could be followed in manufacturing a corresponding s for *each* rule of substitution r. The test of a proposed rule r is the truth of the corresponding empirical proposition expressed by the corresponding sentence s.

If this account is accurate, the philosopher of language, though the products of his analysis are not empirical propositions but recommended rules for the use of the word "language," may nevertheless need to employ empirical methods in searching for the rules. (Just as somebody who did not know the rules of chess might find it necessary to observe the behavior of chess players in order to arrive at the rules of chess). The empirical methods will not coincide with those at present used by students of linguistic theory because they will be concerned with relations of meaning and not of linguistic structure in a narrower sense. It is certain that language is a great deal more complex than the accounts supplied by any of the authors mentioned in this essay would suggest. The defect in their answers is not in the character of their method but in the fact that their fragmentary and approximatory conclusions are presented as if they were complete analyses.

[165]

VII

The Semiotic of
Charles Morris

HILOSOPHERS of language are sometimes in the predicament, exasperating to themselves though entertaining to their critics, of being unable to comply with their own prescriptions for clarity of discourse. The author of the maxim, "What can be said at all can be said clearly," wrote a treatise of disconcerting obscurity; and his successors have been found, too often, talking nonsense about nonsense. Progress in this difficult subject awaits the creation of a language of criticism that can be used with assurance of common understanding.

Those who expect much from "semiotic," or the theory of sign-using behavior, will therefore open Professor Morris' new book[1] with lively anticipation of profit. Professor Morris' earlier monograph[2] had the merit of establishing a threefold division of the field of semiotic which many have found useful; and if some readers felt there was too much reliance upon the unanalyzed notion of *taking account of by means of*, the new book will answer the criticism. For Morris has there undertaken to provide "a set of terms to talk about signs (taking account of current distinctions but attempting to reduce for scientific purposes their vagueness and ambiguity)."[3] This should revive the flagging spirits of philosophers, literary critics, and other professional manipulators of difficult language who, in the familiar and querulous complaint "despair of making themselves understood." "Accounts of meaning," says Morris, "usually throw a handful of putty at the target of sign phenomena, while technical semiotic must provide us with *words which are sharpened arrows*" (p. 19; italics inserted). But "must" here implies "can," and more than

[1] Charles Morris, *Signs, Language, and Behavior* (New York: Prentice-Hall, Inc., 1946).

[2] *Foundations of the Theory of Signs* (Encyclopedia of Unified Science, I, 2) (Chicago: University of Chicago Press, 1938).

[3] *Signs, Language, and Behavior*, p. 4. The page references that follow are to that book.

[169]

one frustrated putty thrower will be eager to see if semiotic *can* do what it *must* do.

As it is obvious that the virtues of a technical terminology can be properly judged only in relation to the ends it is designed to serve, it is wise to say explicitly, as Morris often does, that the end here in view is the construction of a *"behavioral"* science of signs. Morris' practice provides sufficient indication of the meaning of the laudatory adjective, "behavioral," or its synonym, "biological," though no explicit definition is given. His analysis is intended to include only such undefined terms as might occur in description of the *overt* behavior of a lower organism; but the complex terms thereafter defined by reference to such elementary acts are intended to be applicable to *all* sign-using behavior and more especially to that of human speakers. A central issue in an examination of Morris' semiotic must be that of the extent to which "behavioral" definitions, so narrowly circumscribed, can provide a vocabulary fit to describe the full range and complexity of the human uses of language.

Has Morris been able to show that a simple vocabulary of "stimulus," "response," and cognate "behavioristic" terms is all we need for the description, analysis, and evalaution of all discourse? Or does his careful and detailed discussion reveal, rather, the inadequacy of the tools with which he has chosen to work? I shall try to show that the second alternative is the right one.

More specifically, I propose to show that Morris' terms are ill-defined and excessively narrow for fruitful application to human language; that the attempt to apply them to concrete instances of complex sign-using behavior leads him to use them in extended senses, neither well defined nor "behavioral"; that such endemic ambiguity is compensated by mythical psychological assumptions; and that the whole procedure rests upon a disturbingly circular appeal to the uncriticized structure of the common English vernacular.[4]

[4] The sections of central importance to Morris' analysis are those in which the general notion of a sign is defined (ch. 1) and different kinds of signifi-

2. THE "BEHAVIORAL" DEFINITION OF "SIGN"

In setting out to define the term "sign," "on a biological basis and specifically within the framework of the science of behavior" (p. 2) Morris proves to be committed to some version of "stimulus-response" psychology. And this in turn leads him, like many others, to formulate a *causal* theory of meaning.[5]

Let us say (in order to avoid using words to which Morris ascribes more definite meanings) that a sign stands for, or represents, its *referent:* all causal theories agree in defining a sign as some kind of causal substitute or surrogate for its referent. Anybody who is familiar with theories of this type knows that they usually come to early grief in the attempt to meet the following conditions:

(i) A sign ought not to be represented as having *exactly* the same causal efficacy for an organism as the referent whose substitute it is; for otherwise the sign-referent relation would be symmetrical, in contradiction to the preanalytic meaning of the term "sign" or its synonyms. A conditioned animal that tried to *eat* the dinner bell would not be interpreting the sign but rather succumbing to that "word-magic," or confusion of sign and referent, which popular semanticists view with such understandable alarm. Let this be called the *condition of asymmetry.*

(ii) A sign ought not to be defined in such a way that its interpretation *must* be accompanied by simultaneous *overt* response. Every plowboy, as Macaulay might have said, knows that satisfied cows do not necessarily respond to the sight of corn by anything more than indifference. And if humans manifested understanding by some unmistakable

---

cation are distinguished (ch. 6). The present discussion will have to be confined to these topics and their relevance to human discourse; there will be no room to consider Morris' interesting discussion of "formators," or logical and mathematical signs (ch. 6), the characteristics distinguishing "language" from other sign systems (ch. 2), or his able criticism of other work in the field.

[5] Though Morris does not so characterize his theory.

gleam of eye or twitching of nostril, teaching would be an easier profession than it is. Let the condition that interpreted signs need evoke no simultaneous overt response be called that of *latency of response*.[6]

To see how Morris (unlike some of his predecessors) succeeds in meeting the above conditions, we shall have to analyze his definition of "sign" in some detail.

The condition of asymmetry is met by distinguishing between what may be called *direct* and *preparatory* stimuli.[7] This distinction depends upon the associated notions of *goal-object*, *response-sequence*, and *behavior-family*. A direct response to a stimulus emanating from an object is a response *to that* object as a *goal-object*. A series of direct responses motivated by a *need* of the organism, and ending in a response to the associated goal object in such a way as to remove the need, is called a *response-sequence*:[8] "Thus the series of responses of a hungry dog which sees a rabbit, runs after it, kills it, and so obtains food is a response sequence" (p. 9). And the rabbit is the dog's goal-object.[9]

A preparatory stimulus, on the other hand, *qua* preparatory, evokes no response to the object which causes it but, roughly speaking, modifies the organism's subsequent *direct* responses. In Morris' own words, a preparatory stimulus is "any stimulus which *influences* a response [i.e., a nonpreparatory response] to some other stimulus" (p. 8).

Thus if the sound of a bell causes a dog, when hungry, to go hunting for a rabbit, the bell's sound is a *preparatory* stimulus; for the dog then responds to *other* stimuli (e.g., the visual signals received from its environment) in a way in which it would not otherwise have done.

[6] These conditions and their names are not formulated by Morris.

[7] Morris speaks only of "preparatory" stimuli and has no distinguishing adjective for nonpreparatory stimuli.

[8] I am italicizing technical terms.

[9] Since the rabbit is escaping from the dog, the latter may be supposed to be also some sort of avoidance goal-object for the rabbit. But Morris does not mention such negative "goal-objects."

Before we are ready to define a "sign," we need also the notion of a *behavior-family*, defined as a class of response sequences initiated by similar needs in the organism: "all the response-sequences which start from rabbits and eventuate in securing rabbits as food would constitute the rabbit-food behavior-family (p. 10).

Given this somewhat elaborate apparatus, Morris is at last in a position to define a sign, formally, as follows:

"If anything, A, is a preparatory-stimulus which in the absence of stimulus-objects initiating response-sequences of a certain behavior-family causes a disposition in some organism to respond under certain conditions by response-sequences of this behavior-family, then A is a sign" (p. 10).

And, again, "anything which would permit the completion of the response-sequence to which the interpreter is disposed because of a sign will be called a denotatum of the sign" (p. 17).

Thus the *denotatum* of a sign, if it exists, is the goal-object which, as we may say, in fact "satisfies" the disposition aroused by the sign.

It is now easily seen that this definition fulfills the condition of asymmetry, for in Morris' system the denotatum *must*, and the sign, *qua* sign, *cannot* be, a goal-object. Moreover, if the organism can be "disposed" to behavior without actually performing that or any other behavior (as Morris intends) the condition of latency of response is also met; thus Morris meets both conditions and successfully crosses the first hurdles of a behavioristic semiotic.

In so doing, however, does he make exclusive use of terms which (a) are sufficiently well understood to be taken as primitive, without further definition, (b) refer only to the overt behavior of organisms, (c) apply, without metaphorical extension of meaning, to human use of language? Serious misgivings arise on all three counts.

Are Morris' primitive terms sufficiently well understood to be serviceable for analytic clarification of sign-using behavior? If reference is made to the crucial terms of Morris' own meta-

[173]

language (italicized in previous paragraphs) they will be seen to fall into two classes: (i) those drawn from the language of the descriptive psychology of rats and other lower organisms, including *goal-object, stimulus, response,* and *need;* (ii) more general terms, notably *disposition, influence, cause, set* (or *class*), *similar,* which presumably occur in the meta-language of any empirical science.

A critic in no position to make expert criticism of the claims of animal psychology may accept on authority the assurance that the terms in the first group have definite and well-established uses in that field; but he may properly question this usefulness when organisms more complex and less docile than *Mus norvegicus albinus* are in question; it is very much to be doubted that human "needs," "goal-objects," and the rest can be catalogued in any but the most schematic fashion. Psychologists are generally willing to recognize only a few highly abstract types of human needs or organic drives. Identification of such general human "needs" as food, sex, play, rest, and the associated abstract goal-objects will not serve at all for the specific interpretation of human signs, with which so much of Morris' book is properly concerned.

To take a single instance at random: Morris treats the English word "black" as a sign (p. 78), and any definition of the term "sign" which did otherwise would be useless for the purposes for which semiotic is intended. Consider what Morris is required to assert of this instance: First, there must, according to him, be some identifiable set of human goal-objects such that, having certain identifiable needs, human interpreters would perform response-sequences terminating in just those goal-objects; secondly, in the absence of those goal objects, the sound of the uttered word "black" must dispose the hearer to perform a set of response sequences leading to precisely *such* a goal-object. Now where are these goal-objects which anybody hearing the single word "black" is specifically disposed to seek? Are they to be considered as constituting the set of all things which are black? And are we to suppose that some *specific* human "need" is satisfied or removed by coming into possession of a black object, irrespective of any other characteristic it possesses?

Morris gives an undaunted affirmative answer to this and to all similar inquiries concerning the alleged response-sequences associated with human signs. " 'Black,' 'deer,' 'taller'," he says, "appearing in sign-behavior, dispose the interpreters to response-sequences which would be terminated by something black, by a deer, by something taller than something else. . ." (p. 77). It would be pleasant to see a Thurber cartoon of a man hearing the word "taller" and thereby disposed to "expect something taller than something else" and *nothing more*.

By parity of reasoning, every distinct human sign has, according to Morris, its own distinctive family of response-sequences and its corresponding family of eligible goal-objects. Is this surprising consequence to be understood as an empirical assertion? Have psychologists somehow overlooked these tens of thousands of distinguishable needs? I think not. The "response-sequences" and "needs" are fictions, invoked in order to allow Morris to talk about men as he found it satisfactory to talk about rats. This is mythological psychology in which the explanation needs more explanation than the explicandum ever did. If, however, "goal-object" is given a relatively definite and unmetaphorical meaning, Morris' definition becomes too narrow; for a sign may denote much that is not a goal-object.[10]

[10] There is one point in his argument where Morris shows some awareness of the difficulties which have been discussed above. He says that his definition of "sign" is to be regarded as determining merely *sufficient* conditions for application of the definiendum: "It does not say that something is a sign if and only if the conditions laid down are met, but merely that if these conditions are met, then whatever meets them is a sign" (p. 12). This procedure would be tantamount to the definition of a restricted class of signs (viz., those used by primitive organisms), leaving other signs to be determined by different criteria. In practice, however, Morris *does* use his defining criteria as both necessary *and* sufficient: "the behavioral formulation is the primary one with which the other sets of condition are to be correlated" (p. 14). And in all specific instances the behavioral criteria

[175]

Let the point of the adequacy of Morris' definition of sign in its application to human signs be waived for the present. Regarded even as an attempt to identify the relevant features of the use of signs by lower organisms, his definition is still seriously defective. For if it is too narrow in its specification of the type of object which can serve as a denotatum (as argued above), it is also demonstrably too wide on the side of the sign.

A stimulus is preparatory, Morris said, if it *"influences* a response to some other stimulus," and, roughly speaking, such a preparatory stimulus is a sign denoting a goal-object, if it "influences" the initial response to *that* goal-object.

A critic expecting to find well-defined terms in technical semiotic may well rub his eyes when he finds so vague a word as "influence" used without further explanation. Does it mean the same as "have some causal effect upon"? Then consider the following possibility: Just before the dog of the semiotic fable is free to chase his goal-object-rabbit, he is given an injection of morphine. Does this bring into play "some physical energy which acts upon the receptor" (p. 8) of the dog, i.e., a stimulus? Undoubtedly. Does there result any modification in the dog's subsequent response to the sight of a rabbit? The most casual glance will show it. But it would be absurd to say that the stimulus due to the morphine injection *denotes* a rabbit which is yet to be presented to the dog or *signifies* the presence of food.

Nor is there the least difficulty in generalizing the point: *Any* stimulus which has some causal influence upon subsequent behavior will, if we insist upon the letter of Morris' definition, have to count as a sign. We urgently need some further specification of the character of the imputed sign-referent relation if such absurdities are to be avoided. Morris apparently is not prepared to follow behaviorists of a liberal

take preference: "Semiotic as a science gains nothing by the introduction of mentalistic terms in its primitive terms, for *insofar as these terms are not synonymous with behavioral terms they prove to be scientifically irrelevant"* (p. 29, italics inserted).

persuasion, like Tolman, who have tried to make specific "expectancies" (produced by signs) causally effective in the organism's behavior.[11] But he fails to provide any alternative view of his own.

3. CRITERIA OF THE EXISTENCE OF A "DISPOSITION"

Equally serious difficulties of a different kind arise in connection with Morris' overworked notion of "disposition" by means of which, as seen above, he satisfies the condition of latency of response.

A sign, it will be recalled, is not required actually to cause responses to be performed; rather does it "cause a *disposition* . . . to respond under certain conditions by response-sequences" (p. 10). And this disposition is called the *interpretant* of the sign in question. An organism may have an interpretant, in the absence of observable behavior: the definition of "sign," to quote Morris again, "did not stipulate that the organism for which it is a sign *actually performs* response-sequences of a given behavior-family, but merely that it be disposed to perform them, that is, *would* perform them under certain conditions" (p. 13). Supposing, then, we had some way of determining that an organism had acquired an interpretant, by a procedure which did not call for recognizing any observable responses made by the organism at the time of the sign's presentation: if this were so, the condition of latency of response would undoubtedly be satisfied.

Unfortunately, Morris is as vague in his indications of the meaning of "disposition" as he was seen to be about the meaning of "influence." It is, however, possible to supply a relatively definite meaning along the following lines, which will square with Morris' vague description of the term's meaning but will hardly do for the uses he proposes.

Let us take as a preliminary illustration the case of a hen that is conditioned to "expect" corn on hearing a bell (and

[11] I do not wish to be understood as committed to any view on the still controversial question whether such "expectancies" are in fact causally effective.

so to go seeking it in some place *if hungry*). The hen's corn-seeking behavior prior to conditioning is already "dispositional," that is to say is not unconditionally elicited by the sight of the corn.[12] We may say, then, that the hen's behavior *before* conditioning is a very complex function of its needs, N, and the stimuli it receives, S. This may be represented schematically, in the form $R = f_1 (S, N)$.[13] To say that the hen has *a* disposition to respond to the sight of corn by pecking it is to say there exists *some* functional connection, f_1, (not otherwise specified) between its needs, stimuli, and correlated responses. *After* conditioning, the general pattern of the hen's responses to stimuli will have changed (for it may, when hungry, turn to the feeding tray in the absence of visible nourishment); and the altered situation may be represented schematically in the form $R = f_2 (S, N)$.

To generalize: The suggestion is that in speaking of the creation of an "interpretant" or "disposition to respond," Morris *may* intend to assert that some previously established general relationship between needs, stimuli, and correlated responses has become modified, so that the form of the connection has changed from $R = f_1(S, N)$ to $R = f_2(S, N)$. Along these lines, it may be possible to give some account of "disposition" which will render that term relatively well defined.

The proposed line of analysis would accord well with what Peirce and others have meant when they called a sign a *habit* of response; and on this view the learning of a sign will no more require a unique overt response than the acquisition of a habit does. This may be what Morris had in mind. All that can be said, in the absence of any clear

[12] Morris seems to overlook this.

[13] The formula may be interpreted in this way: "f_1" is to be supposed to be an abbreviation for the name of some complex descriptive function, such that if the name of any definite stimulus is substituted for "S" and the name of any definite need for "N," the description so resulting designates the correlated response R.

[178]

indication of Morris' intention, is that much more definition would be required before the term "disposition" would do the work required of it. It would be necessary, for instance, to explain the meaning of *"kinds"* of disposition, a notion indispensable to Morris' classification of signs in terms of their modes of signification.

In the light of the above strictures on the vagueness and general inadequacy of the primitive terms of Morris' system, it may seem surprising that he is able to emerge with definite decisions on the interpretation of linguistic signs whose significance is controversial. Further examination will show that in the specific applications of semiotic criticism, Morris largely abandons his apparatus of "behavioral" definition in favor of other but unacknowledged criteria. Such unconscious deviation from narrowly behavioral principles is strikingly manifested in his discussion of the "significata" of signs.

4. THE NOTION OF "SIGNIFICATUM"

Though he does not say so, Morris is here trying to reproduce, in "behavioral" terms, a distinction between "connotation" and "denotation" (Mill), or "intension" and "extension," or "Sinn" and "Bedeutung" (Frege), or "depth" and "breadth" (Peirce) which in some form or another has been recognized by all philosophers of symbolism. For very few signs, if any, are "logically proper names"; and Morris, like his predecessors, wishes to give an intelligible account of how signs function in the absence of the particular objects (the denotata) which, in his terminology, *would* terminate the relevant response-sequence by satisfying the organism's motivating need.

Such nondenotative "meaning" or "significance" Morris locates in the properties common to the denotata. He says: "Those conditions which are such that whatever fulfills them is a denotatum will be called a *significatum* of the sign" (p. 17), and again: Terms referring to significata "refer only to the properties something must have to be denoted by a sign, that is, to permit the actualization of the response-sequence to which the interpreter of the sign is disposed" (p. 67).

Whatever else a significatum is, it must, according to the account given, be a set of "conditions" or "properties" or "characteristics" (p. 77); and it might be expected that some further elucidation will follow. It does not. Apparently the term "condition" or its synonyms are so unproblematic in a behavioral semiotic that the fact that "significatum" refers "only to properties" (p. 67) is regarded as a sufficient answer to a hypothetical questioner "who fears that we are in this way peopling the world with questionable 'entities' " (p. 67). This is admirably nonchalant, but will hardly satisfy the doubter. Perhaps even the most positivistically inclined of logicians should not boggle at talking about "properties"; but when such nonquestionable non-"entities" are confidently classified as *locata, discriminata, valuata, obligata, formata* (not to speak of a dozen other kinds), one begins to wonder how "behavioral" the procedure really is.

Such doubts can be dispelled only by attempting some explicit account of the crucial term's usage. And, as before, it can be done, though not in a fashion admissible within a behavioral semiotic.

Roughly speaking, it would seem that a predicate "Ax" may be said to be a necessary and sufficient condition for "Bx" if and only if the two predicates are L-equivalent, i.e., if the proposition "(x) $(Ax$ if and only if $Bx)$" is a "necessary truth." Here the reference to L-truth rather than F-truth is essential: It will not do, for Morris's purposes, to substitute material equivalence for L-equivalence in this explanation; for what is relevant to the significatum of a sign is not the properties which happen *as a matter of fact* to be common to all the actual referents of the sign but rather the properties which *would* be manifested by all *possible* denotata of the sign.

But this is not all. In order to use the term "condition" in the way desired by Morris, it will be necessary to refer to the existence of variable predicates: for A to be a sign it will be necessary that there shall be *some* "condition" which all the corresponding denotata meet; we shall need to refer to and quantify variable predicates. It seems to me, then, that a formal definition of "conditions" will call for the use of a meta-language sufficiently comprehensive in vocabulary to permit of reference to the L-truth of statements and the designation and quantification of variable predicates. Now for all I know, it might be possible to provide ostensive definitions (*Zuordnungsdefinitionen*) of the basic terms of so rich a meta-language in such a fashion that the entire language could still be approvingly characterized as "behavioral": this may be all the more readily conceded in the absence of clear specification of the meaning of the terms "behavioral" or "biological." But, at any rate, if "condition" is to be defined in some such fashion as that suggested above, it is certainly far from being epistemologically primitive; nor can it be used, without definition, in a rigorous semiotic system, as if its meaning were so obvious as to arouse no disquiet.

This line of approach, however, seems to involve a disturbing relativity. In the light of what has just been said, the test to determine whether a given set of goal-objects have any common properties will involve reference *both* to those objects *and to the language used in describing them.* Suppose we have some reason to believe that all the members of a certain class, C, are "similar goal-objects" for "similar needs" of some organism. Whether or not the members of C constitute the extension of some predicate not involving reference to the behavior of the organism in question will depend upon the stock of available predicates and upon what is accordingly to be called a "predicate" or a "condition." Suppose bees have been trained to respond selectively to uniformly tinted-color expanses, as indicative of the presence of sirup (von Frisch's experiments): Are we entitled to say a priori that there *must be* a common color shown in all the cards to which the bees will respond positively at any given period of this training? The answer seems to depend upon what shall be called a "color." If we determine in advance of the experiment the number and specifications of the different color classes, the question whether the bees' responses will correspond to any single one of such predetermined classes is a definite one; but it is then not "necessary" that the bees shall respond to a *single* color. If, on the other hand, we do not determine, before the experiment, what shall count as a single color, the assertion that the bees *must* respond to a unique color becomes empty; for, no matter how the bees respond, we shall say—now uttering an a priori statement— that they *must* be responding to a common color characteristic.

Similar considerations will, I think, apply to Morris' use of "interpretant" and "significatum." He can, of course, *choose* to say: "No sign without interpretant: no interpretant without significatum: no significatum without common conditions present in all possible denotata"; and then it will be *necessary* and a priori that every sign have a significatum. But since, in the suggested analysis of "condition," the test of there being a "condition" is that all the possible denotata shall be describable *by means of an available predicate* (presumably drawn from the current English vocabulary comprising the meta-language), Morris' procedure will then amount to the use of the syntax of some preferred language as a criterion of meaningfulness. If the denotata associated with a set of given preparatory stimuli are all describable by means of a predicate available in the English language (or whatever language the semiotician prefers), the stimuli will be "signs," and otherwise, not. Since there is no way to identify the "disposition to respond" or the "behavior-family" except by finding a set of associated denotata, verification of the alleged presentation of a sign reduces to this: A is a sign if and only if the circumstances which would remove the needs motivating certain associated response-sequences (or, roughly speaking, the circumstances to which the sign is applicable) *can be described in the English language*. But this leaves us helpless to discriminate sense fron nonsense, or the empirically meaningful from the nonsensically unverifiable, in the case of signs belonging *to the English language itself*. Just at the point where semiotic might be expected to become useful, in ways other than that of speculative interpretation of the signification of animal responses to conditioned stimuli, the circularity of the entire procedure brings us to a halt.

Similar considerations will apply to Morris' stipulation that a sign have a unique "significatum." Given any set of objects (the class of possible denotata of some "sign," in Morris' sense), there will normally be an indefinite number of predicates whose extension coincides with that class. Whether the sign is regarded as ambiguous or not will then, for all that is here shown, be a matter for arbitrary decision. Morris says that "a sign-vehicle is *unambiguous* when it has only one significatum . . . otherwise ambiguous" (p. 21). But how do we find out that there is "only *one* significatum"—except by description of the denotata in English terms *assumed to be unambiguous?* Of course, it is easy to define "sign" in such a way that a sign *shall be* unambiguous (top of p. 22)—but this gets us nowhere.

It by no means follows from what has been said that the use of some preferred language as a standard of significance is formally indefensible. But where such a criterion is used implicitly, without explicit acknowledgment, the resulting interpretative judgments of meaning may be expected to be dogmatic. And this is indeed the case at point after point of Morris' discussion. If Morris is found, for instance, referring to the "property of *alternativity*" (p. 157) as the significatum of the "either . . . or" sign, no criterion is discoverable except his own intuition that there *is* such a "property." And so also for the *formata, locata, discriminata, valuata, obligata,* and other "properties" of his ontology.

Nowhere is such implicit and, one may be sure, unintended dogmatism as much in evidence as in Morris' account of "prescriptors" or valuative symbols, which may serve as a last illustration of the defects of his method.

5. THE MEANING OF "APPRAISOR"

We are told, simply, that an appraisor is "a sign which signifies to its interpreter a preferential status of something

[183]

or other" (p. 79). A preferential status is, then, a "property," not only a significatum but indeed a special kind of one. But how are we to tell whether it is present? The main clue is an illustrative example discussed in some detail (p. 65).

We may reproduce this in the following simplified form: Suppose an organism has been trained to respond to three signs "F_1," "F_2," "A" in the following way: Presentation of "F_1" or "F_2" in isolation causes food to be sought in places 1 and 2 respectively; "F_1F_2," i.e., the signs presented simultaneously, causes food to be sought in either place indifferently; but the simultaneous presentation of "F_1" and "F_2" with the auxiliary signal "A" attached to "F_1" (which we may represent by "$[AF_1]F_2$") causes food to be sought in place 1 *first;* similarly the sign "$F_1[AF_2]$" causes food to be sought in place 2 first. Then according to Morris, "F_1" and "F_2" signify food at the respective places; "F_1F_2" signifies food at *both* places; and "A" signifies the "preferential status" of the objects designated by the sign to which "A" is attached.

But it is still not clear that the possible denotata of "A" have common "properties." Indeed a dilemma can be set up at this point: Either the dog's preference for goal-objects partially designated by "A" is well founded, because such objects have some distinctive and caninely satisfactory intrinsic properties; *or* the preference is unfounded, and there is no intrinsic difference, either in the corresponding goal-objects or in the comparative agreeableness of the means-end paths leading to them. In the first case, it would seem that the appraisor would signify the intrinsic desirable character of the goal-objects; and the distinction between appraisors and designators would break down. On the other hand, if the preference in question is ungrounded, it is hard to see why the appraisor should, in Morris' system, be called a sign at all. True enough, the presentation of such an appraisor causally influences subsequent behavior, but there is *nothing* in the corresponding goal-objects or in the response-sequences leading up to them which is regularly correlated with the "correct" use of the appraisor. The animal prefers food in place 1 *only* because the presence of food has been announced by a signal to which the dog has been trained to respond favorably; there is no antecedent "preferential status" for the sign to signify. Exactly parallel analysis would apply to Morris' use of *prescriptors* ("signs which signify to their interpreters the required performance of a specific response to some object or situation").

But enough has been said to show why Morris' system has appeared to one reader as vague at critical points in its development and internally incoherent. To summarize: My judgment is that Morris builds upon an excessively narrow basis of "behavioral" primitive terms; that the inadequacy of these terms as building blocks leads him to introduce metaphorical usages which are neither "behavioral," well understood, nor epistemologically primitive; and that the resulting vagueness of his terminology allows him to make, with unjustified confidence, a series of critical decisions on debatable questions which are presented with no better foundation than his own pronouncements.

Having treated Morris' views with the seriousness which their importance deserves, I do not wish to leave a misleading impression of the merits of his work. Let it be said explicitly that his book is one of the most stimulating contributions to the subject to have appeared in many years; that his mistakes are usually more illuminating than other writers' safe glimpses of the obvious; and that all alternative treatments of sign-using behavior, as Morris says, are also "riddled with ambiguities and inconsistencies" (p. 185). But the reader who expects a set of "sharpened arrows" will be disappointed: he is more likely to find a quiver brimful of sling shot.

VIII

Ogden and Richards' Theory of Interpretation

CONTEMPORARY interest in problems of language has stimulated investigation by philosophers of both professional and amateur standing into such questions as the nature of communication and interpretation, the relation of logic to grammar, the part played by conventions in determining the boundaries of intelligible discourse, the number and kinds of distinct functions of language, and the relation of all these questions both to each other and to some of the major problems of philosophy.

Inquiries of this kind have by now advanced, in the opinion of their proponents at least, far beyond the stage of modest faith in the future of a tentatively outlined program. I. A. Richards and C. K. Ogden, for instance, in the course of their book, *The Meaning of Meaning*, with whose doctrines this essay is chiefly concerned, announce a new "science of symbolism," which, by making "the beginnings of a division between what cannot be intelligibly talked about and what can" (p. vii),[1] is in a position "to provide a new basis for Physics" (p. 85), solves the most important problems of the theory of knowledge (pp. 77–86), disposes of "the problem of Truth," and provides a definitive basis for scientific aesthetics (ch. 7).

It is not surprising that a doctrine as pretentious as this should, even without the help of the inviting title of "semantics," be exercising great influence to-day in education, literary criticism, and cognate fields. And if the proposed science of symbolism can show some reasonable promise of achieving even part of its ambitious program, its theoretical basis deserves more serious and more critical attention than it has yet received.

The linguistic transactions which excite most interest in those who hope for immediate practical benefit from an analytic study of symbolism are of a high order of complexity. But the prolonged process of interpretation involved in

[1] All page references in this essay are to C. K. Ogden and I. A. Richards, *The Meaning of Meaning* (3d ed.; London, 1930).

enjoying a poem or understanding a mathematical theory is compounded of numerous minute acts of interpretation, situations in which the apprehended character of an experience leads to an expectation concerning the character of an immediately succeeding experience. And simple acts of interpretation of this kind constantly recur in the daily routine of everyday affairs. It is natural for a study of symbolism to begin by considering these relatively simple though in themselves unexciting acts of interpretation. And this is a practice which Ogden and Richards, in common with most writers on the subject, follow.

In this essay I shall discuss only such acts of interpretation as would commonly be taken to be relatively simple; unless the theory to be examined can provide an acceptable account of *these* situations, its contributions to the understanding of such disputed subjects as aesthetics or the foundations of mathematics are hardly likely to be of much value.

I shall try to describe a class of situations which involve acts of interpretation and are incapable of resolution into parts containing acts of interpretation; let us call situations of this kind *basic* interpretation situations. After outlining the view that Ogden and Richards take of the nature of basic interpretation situations, I shall argue that their position is tantamount to the promulgation of an empirical theory, inadequately supported, however, by empirical evidence, concerning hypothetical features of bodily behavior constituting the factors which causally determine the occurrence of simple acts of interpretation; that in default of the requisite evidence the supposition that some such theory *must* be true is symptomatic of an a priori partiality for certain types of explanation; that the practical applications drawn from the theory are independent of and unsupported by it; and that the procedure involved is characteristic not only of other behavioristic theories of language, but of much pseudoscientific philosophizing.

By a *simple* or *basic* act of interpretation I wish to refer to the conduct of a person who interprets some experience of

[190]

his, or certain features of the experience, as indicating the impending occurrence of another experience having predictable characteristics. When I have the visual and kinesthetic sensations which normally accompany the putting of a lump of sugar into my mouth I expect a certain taste and am startled if the generic quality of sweetness is absent. On hearing a bark of a certain quality I expect to see my dog; having a certain kind of smell leads me to expect to find the toast burning. All such acts of interpretation, unlike the more complex performances involved in reading or aesthetic appreciation, contain no parts which are themselves acts of interpretation.[2] And it should be easy to invent an indefinite number of further illustrations.

It is not necessary that the person involved in such situations (whom we may call the *interpreter*) should use language or formulate an explicit predictive judgment; but it is essential to basic interpretations, as here understood, that they should refer to the *experience* of the interpreter, and be capable of verification *immediately after* the interpretation.

If the description given is sufficient to identify the situations which I have in mind in speaking of basic acts of interpretation, it is to be hoped that my readers will agree with me in the identification of *some* experiences which satisfy the prescription. Without agreement that there *are* relatively simple acts of interpretation, and some agreement as to *which* these acts are, philosophic discussion about language or symbolism is futile. But agreement in identifying instances of interpretation will not preclude reasonable doubt concerning the correct analysis of the features common to all the examples. The determination of such common features, insofar as they exist, and the invention of a suitable vocabulary of criticism for the preservation of the distinctions which emerge in the course of the analysis, are among the most important objects of the philosophy of symbolism.

To basic acts of interpretation Ogden and Richards give

[2] This might be disputed, but the point is of no great importance for the remainder of the argument.

much attention, their account of them forming the basis for their discussion of all other situations of interpretation.

We are invited to consider the situation in which a person, on striking a match, has an experience which leads him to expect the experience of seeing a flame. The interpreter is said to "think of" or "refer to" the flame; it is with analyzing this one relation that the theory is mainly concerned. For a summary version of the answer suggested we may turn to the author's claim to establish "the identification of 'thinking of' with 'being caused by' " (p. 54), a view from which in this form it is agreed that "even the hardiest thinkers" shrink (*ibid.*). To say that when, seeing a match struck, I anticipate a flame is, on this view, to say that previous occasions on which two similar experiences occurred produced in my brain a determinate physical structure which now *causes* me to react in a similar way. And it is to say nothing more.[3]

Let us see if the more detailed version of this view, and the technical language in which it is expressed, can remove the air of paradox from a view which apparently equates interpretation with causation.

In the language of *The Meaning of Meaning*, the complex physical event, striking-of-match-followed-by-production-of-flame, is termed an *external context*. It is convenient to regard

[3] Much of the language used by Ogden and Richards might suggest a doubt whether the structure which is the alleged cause of the act of interpretation is in fact intended to be a physical configuration of the brain. But while such terms as "thoughts," "feelings," "experiences," are freely used as interchangeable with locutions concerning "reactions to stimuli" and "adaptations of the organism"; and while the authors themselves claim that their doctrine is "neutral in regard to psycho-neural parallelism, interaction, or double aspect hypotheses" (p. 83, n. 5), there seems no doubt from the general progress of their argument that a *behavioristic* theory is being presented. This is demonstrated by such a passage as "to be directly apprehended is to cause certain happenings in the *nerves*" (p. 81), which is presented as "the correct answer" (*ibid.*) to questions concerning perception. I shall therefore try to use behavioristic language consistently in reporting the theory.

a complex event of this kind as composed of two partial events, of which the first may be symbolized by "S" and its successor by "R"; and to discriminate between different events having the same generic characteristics by the use of numerical subscripts. (Thus in the example considered here, "S_1" will always denote some striking of a match and "R_1" the production of flame that follows S_1). Now any interpreter who is at this moment "seeing" the match struck, i.e., reacting with eyes and nervous system to the event S_n, has on many previous occasions reacted to a number of similar conjunctions of physical events, or "external contexts," S_1-followed-by-R_1, S_2-followed-by-R_2, etc., the combined effect of a sufficient number of which was to leave in his brain a specific "residual trace" or so-called "engram." It is this engram which now causes in his brain not the simple cerebral event appropriate to S_n alone but a complex event similar to, though not qualitatively identical with, the complex events which were induced by the total external contexts, S_1R_1, S_2R_2, etc. The complex cerebral event evoked by S_n alone in virtue of the effects produced by previous contexts of a certain kind is called a *reference*. If S_n (striking of a match) is in fact followed by R_n (production of a flame) the reference is said to have an object, viz., its *referent*, and S_n is then said to be a *sign* of the referent R_n. To say that an event S_n is a sign of an event R_n for some interpreter is to say, then, that similar conjunctions of events S_iR_i have so modified the interpreter's brain as to cause in the presence of S_n a cerebral event similar to those caused by S_iR_i.

The four technical terms which I have introduced into this summary, viz., *external context, reference, sign,* and *referent,* are central to Ogden and Richards' discussion of all communication and interpretation, of whatever degree of complexity. One example may illustrate this sufficiently: among the "canons of symbolism" which are offered as a substitute for much of traditional logic (pp. 87 ff.) occurs the so-called "Canon of Actuality" (p. 103), a rule which might be rendered as: the referent of a sign (i.e., what it stands for to some interpreter in an act of interpretation) is that event which does actually complement the external stimulus, and not anything that the sign ought to, or is intended to, or should in good usage, refer to.[4] Taken in conjunction with the preceding analysis of basic acts of interpretation, this rule would require us, in case of dispute concerning interpretation (as when we wonder whether a hearer has understood our words) to ask what cerebral events in the past have been *similar* to the cerebral event which occurred in the course of the act of interpretation in question.

This attempt at the solution of a practical difficulty reveals a crucial obstacle to understanding or accepting the theory.

I interpret S_n as a sign of R_n, it is said, if S_n causes in me an event similar to those caused in the past by the S_iR_i. But similar in what way, and to what degree? Certainly if I react to S_n *exactly* as I reacted to S_1 *plus* R_1 I shall not be interpreting S_n but rather mistakenly supposing that R_n is presented simultaneously with S_n. To treat the striking of a match as if it in fact included the production of a flame is to confuse two distinct happenings, as the child does who tries to eat the apple in his picture book. Interpreting S_n, then, involves recognizing that S_n indicates that R_n will probably appear and also recognizing that R_n has *not* yet appeared. If we were permitted to revert to the use of nonbehavioristic language we might simply make the obvious point that *expecting* R_n differs irreducibly from *perceiving* an event qualitatively similar to R_n or remembering such an event. But this, or rather the behaviorist translation of the same

[4] "A symbol refers to what it is actually used to refer to; not necessarily to what it might in good usage, or is intended by the interpreter, or is intended by the user, to refer to" (p. 103). This might be taken as constituting, in conjunction with the other canons, a *definition* of referring, were it not the case that *reference* is a technical term in the theory, with a narrowly circumscribed meaning. A referent is by definition a particular physical event, or possibly a feature of such an event. Thus the "Canon of Actuality" functions as a prohibition against finding the denotation of a symbol in anything other than some specific physical event which would complement, in the manner already described, the event which caused the act of interpretation.

[194]

point, Ogden and Richards refuse to consider; any such description is regarded by them as equivalent to the mystical invocations of language worshippers. For they assume constantly that the *only* alternative to a causal and behavioristic theory of meaning is one which postulates, as they put it, "at least one ultimately and irreducibly mysterious extra entity." (p. 81).[5] But one may hold that expectation is not reducible to causation by memory traces without holding either that expectation is not subject to causal laws, or that expectation itself is indefinable.

Those who favor a behavioristic interpretation of interpretation are unlikely to consider the objection very formidable. No doubt sufficient ingenuity might contrive, within the framework of a behaviorist theory, to concede the differences while clinging to the alleged similarities between interpretations and perception. It might, for instance, be possible to find the ground for the conceded difference in the causal action of the engram (which is present in the interpretation while absent from the earlier perceptions). But it is hard to imagine the heroic embroidery which could succeed in removing the vagueness of the term "similar" which occurs so frequently in the presentation of the theory.

This brings me to a criticism of a more general nature. Let us sympathetically suppose that Ogden and Richards were in a position to specify in fine detail just those conditions of the brain and nervous system which are to be unambiguously indicative of the performance of an act of interpretation. The assertions constituting their analysis of interpretation would then, it is true, become *definite* empirical propositions, capable of experimental verification. But they would even so constitute no more than a sweeping hypothesis based upon as good as no evidence.

For I would suppose that present knowledge of neural structure and available experimental techniques are in too

[5] The comment is made with regard to alternative theories of the interpretation involved in perception but is equally characteristic of their attitude to other attempts than their own to analyze interpretation in general.

[195]

rudimentary a condition to supply the empirical substantiation which any plausible theory of this type would need. Nor do the authors even hint at the existence of such evidence.[6]

Here then we have a theory whose crucial terms are so vague as to be virtually undefined and whose assertions are unsupported by relevant evidence—an excellent example of what William James had in mind when he spoke of psychology as being only the hope of a science. How can we account for the remarkable fact that the theory is apparently used as a ground for specific answers to disputable questions concerning specific complex interpretations, and the still more remarkable fact that the theory itself should to so many people appear not merely plausible but almost certainly true?

An answer to the first part of this question is given by an examination of almost any case of attempted application of the theory. In discussing the definition of "beauty," for instance, we are to reject with impatience and contumely the suggestion that beauty may be indefinable or (as it is expressed in the text) a name for a "simple quality." Anybody who holds such a view "postulates" a quality which is a "mythological referent" and is guilty of relying upon word magic and the survival of "primitive word-superstitions" (pp. 143–144). But no ground is given for all this fury at what has seemed to many thinkers a reasonable hypothesis except the suggestion that an aesthetic character *could not*

[6] It may be added that when the discussion proceeds to the more difficult cases of *false* interpretations and *general* interpretations the use of such terms as "structure" and "place" aggravate the hindrances which beset the search for an evidential basis for the theory. Two quotations selected at random will show that our authors themselves provide good examples of utterance admirably adapted for the application of the denigrating technique which they use freely on other writers: (1) "Every compound reference is composed wholly of simple references united in such a way as will give the required *structure* to the compound reference they compose" (p. 67). (2) The canon of compatibility: "No complex symbol may contain constituent symbols which claim the same '*place*' " (p. 105).

be a referent, and so could not be that with which any interpretative act is concerned. And so we get the following chain of argument: referents are spatiotemporal particulars, interpretation is of referents, the alleged quality of beauty is admittedly not a spatiotemporal particular, therefore no statement can be interpreted as being concerned with a simple quality of beauty. The same line of thought seems to inspire the authors' obvious preference for the view that "beauty" is a word whose function is mainly the emotive, noncognitive one of expressing feelings.

In this way a particular view concerning the analysis of the term "beauty" (which needs specific corroborative evidence in order to be plausible) derives a peculiar kind of support from its connection with the general dogma concerning interpretation. But since the view that "beauty" cannot refer to a simple quality is deduced from the view that all interpretation is of particulars, the first opinion has firmer evidential basis than the second.

Indeed, examination of similar examples (especially those in which the use of abstractions is questioned) will suggest that the *theory* of interpretation is used (as such dogmas often are) as a *substitute* for evidence. The fervor of the semanticist springs from the vision of a state of affairs in which each act of interpretation would be accompanied by an observable bodily condition, as noticeable as a grimace and as unmistakable as a yawn. Such would indeed be a paradise of mutual understanding where the evidence of the senses would immediately settle all disputes concerning meaning. In default of this consummation, the pragmatic function of the apparatus of referents, external contexts, and the like is to delude its manipulator into the belief that he has such evidence, in cases where such evidence is neither furnished nor to be expected, and so to allow him to exercise with less constraint a partiality for explanations conforming to a favorite design.

Why should a theory of the type preferred by Ogden and Richards appear so attractive, especially to philosophers and psychologists of empirical temper? The answer may help to

[197]

explain some of the reasons for the influence which theories of this type have exerted.

There seems to be no doubt that in certain situations in which another person is observed it is possible to know that he is an interpreter and even to know the specific content of his interpretation. When this happens the evidence for the judgment does consist, in part at least, of certain observed features of the other person's behavior. It may even be the case that *some* statements concerning another person's interpretations are wholly translatable into statements about his behavior. This being granted, it has seemed natural to many to take the further step of supposing that *all* acts of interpretation must be accompanied by uniquely indicative bodily characteristics, i.e., to argue that the term "interpretation," regarded in isolation from the various verbal contexts in which it can occur, must be capable of explicit and unique definition by means of terms referring only to observable behavior. It is a matter of indifference whether the characteristics are thought of as belonging to the overt behavior, gestures, and facial expression, or to what might be called the covert behavior of the interior of the interpreter's body. The tendency to make this further assumption is reinforced by the belief that the only alternative to the behaviorist view is some mystical, nonempirical position.

But this is to take a mistaken view of the nature of the definition and use of empirical terms, as any cursory inspection of the experimental sciences would show. The term "mass," for instance, is not definable in isolation apart from the verbal context in which it occurs; and the relation between a statement containing the term "mass" and the empirical consequences of that statement varies according to the range of magnitudes concerned. The operational procedure for determining the observational consequences of statements of the form, "the mass of A, moving with velocity v, in the neighborhood of B, C, D," changes according to the range of values assigned to the variables; the method for deciding the mass of an electron is unlike that for deciding the mass

[198]

of a football. But none of this has any tendency to show that "mass" is not an empirical term. It is sufficient that every statement in which the word "mass" may occur (according to the accepted conventions of the language of physics) should be capable of verification by recognized empirical procedures. And this condition is in fact satisfied in the usage of the term "mass." Nor is it necessary to argue that the variations in the methods used to determine mass prove that a number of different notions are ambiguously symbolized by the one word. The use of the same name for the outcome of the several procedures of verification is justified by the family resemblance of the methods to one another, by their interchangeability over certain ranges, and by the success with which the outcomes of the various methods can be assimilated into the same system of empirical laws.

There is no reason to suppose that the situation is otherwise in respect to the term "interpretation." We determine the performance of acts of interpretation and the contents of the acts by criteria which vary according to the total situation in which the acts are performed. Sometimes, but not always, we rely upon specific bodily conditions; sometimes, but not always, upon the subsequent conduct of the person concerned; sometimes upon his oral testimony; sometimes upon a judgment concerning what we should do in like case. And between these criteria (and the others which could be mentioned) there is a certain continuity or homomorphism. Provided that "interpretation" is used only in statements which can be experimentally verified, the term will be empirical, even though incapable (should it so prove) of unique definition in isolation from the context of usage.

A detailed description of the variant criteria associated with "interpretation," and other terms of importance in the study of symbolism, is certainly a proper concern of the philosopher of language. The natural history of usage which might result would provide us with better defenses against the linguistic confusions which infest all serious discussion in philosophy and the sciences. It is only fair to say here that the school of

[199]

thought which I have been criticizing has provided valuable materials for such a study.[7] But these contributions have been without assistance from the behaviorist theory of meaning and in no way depend for their validity upon its truth. There is not the slightest reason to suppose that a genuinely empirical investigation of the meaning of interpretation would yield a report of behavioristic pattern. That it might, the empiricist is bound to admit; but he is bound also to add that appearances are against any such expectations.

[7] This is notably the case in the writings of I. A. Richards. Much of the specific discussion in *Practical Criticism* (London, 1929) and his more recent book, *Interpretation in Teaching* (London, 1938), is an admirable training for the linguistic method suggested in this paragraph.

IX

Questions about
Emotive Meaning

The separation of prose from poetry, if we may so paraphrase the distinction, is no mere academic activity: There is hardly a problem outside mathematics which is not complicated by its neglect, and hardly any emotional response which is not crippled by irrelevant intrusions. No revolution in human affairs would be greater than that which a wide-spread observance of this distinction would bring about.—I. A. RICHARDS, *Principles of Literary Criticism*, p. 274

1. THE WORK TO BE DONE

THE EXAGGERATION is almost justified by the importance of the topic. The problem of distinguishing between "emotive" and "scientific" or "referential" uses of language is more than a technical puzzle. If we knew the best answer we might make more progress in dealing with the venerable problems of the relations between "Heart and Mind," Religion and Science, Faith and Reason, or the other antitheses that obfuscate philosophical discourse. To have recognized that questions of *meaning* may profitably take precedence over questions of knowledge, evidence, and truth is to have made some progress already. But I am not sure that we have done much more than recognize that scientific discourse is not the sole significant mode of human communication. It is something to be in no danger of confusing Kierkegaard with Clerk Maxwell; but a theory of symbolism might be expected to yield a richer harvest.

To label "nonreferential" uses of language "emotive" gets us no further: the recognition of a difference is insufficient to establish a distinction. We need an analysis of the ground of the dichotomy, carried to a point where it can help in the *practice* of deft and sensitive judgment. The pressing need is not so much for a "new science of semiotic" (too many addled eggs have been laid by the owl of Minerva), as for a "speculative instrument" for improving communication between critics, philosophers, teachers, and all who need to discourse about discourse. The business of such a theory, in Richards' words, "is not to replace practice, or to tell us how to do

[203]

what we cannot do already; but to protect our natural skill from the influences of unnecessarily crude views about it; and, above all, to assist the imparting of that skill . . . from mind to mind."[1]

2. "EMOTIVE" AS A PEJORATIVE TERM

I have suggested that the work remains to be done. But to judge from the immense popularity of the term "emotive language," a clear distinction between the major types of discourse might be supposed to have been firmly established. This is not so. The popular sense of "emotive" is an ingredient in yet another "unnecessarily crude view" about language, which has done more to harm natural skill in interpretation than improve it.

In popular usage, "emotive" is itself a highly emotive term, the literal sense—say *conducive to the expression and arousing of emotions*—being quite subordinate to the pejorative implications. "Emotive" is a debunking term. It is ironical that a champion of the dignity of poetry as indefatigable as Richards should have contributed to the currency of a cant term which incites the depreciation of feeling. Like other terms it was intended to make obsolete, "emotive" is one of those words which "stupefy and bewilder, yet in a way satisfy, the inquiring mind."[2] It satisfies by implying a sharp but untenable opposition between thought and feeling; in the end it bewilders those who ask for a doctrine and are given a word.

It would be unfair to hold Richards responsible for a jejune simplification and distortion of his own more careful doctrine. Yet the lack of a consistent and coherent theory of "emotive meaning," whether in his earlier or his sharply modified later writings, is partly to blame for the confusion. I will rehearse some points of difficulty in both.

3. RICHARDS' EARLY THEORIES

I take the weakest point of the doctrines of *The Meaning of Meaning* and *Principles of Literary Criticism* to have been the

[1] *The Philosophy of Rhetoric* (London, 1936), p. 116.
[2] *The Meaning of Meaning* (3d ed.; London, 1930), p. 231.

[204]

excessively narrow definition of "referent" on which they are based.[3]

The "causal theory of meaning" in these early works was frankly nominalistic; in the exemplary "sign-using situation," the sign must refer to a specific spatiotemporal event. Only the "names" of referents, so stringently conceived, were allowed to count as "symbols proper"; all other elements of discourse, from "universals" to punctuation signs, were to be construed as having the status of mere "symbolic accessories." The fashion in which the auxiliary symbols contributed to the primary task of the indication of particulars was never made clear; and the most sympathetic reader was left wondering whether such last-ditch nominalism was inspired by anything more than a confused reluctance to admit the existence of "universal denizens of a realm of being." But one may be as suspicious of a Platonist ontology as seems judicious and still recognize the inadequacy of a theory of symbolism which takes as a standard case the relation of a "name" to the spatiotemporal particular to which it refers.

A parallel can be found in the attempts of latter-day phenomenalists to regard the apprehension of a sense-datum as the basic exemplar of indubitable knowledge, in terms of which other derivative and less reliable cognitive transactions may be explained. "Direct knowledge" of a "pure" sense-datum, uncontaminated by interpretation and inference, far from being the "simplest case" in terms of which more complex situations can be analyzed, appears, in the light of unprejudiced psychological observations, as the exceptional idealized and artificial case. And the same may be said where analysis is translated from the epistemological to the semantic idiom. The naming of a reputable, well-accredited "referent" is one of the rarest of symbolic acts, achievable only in special laboratory conditions. Utterances which are trivially "simple," in the sense of providing no problems of interpre-

---

[3] See "Ogden and Richards' Theory of Interpretation" (Essay VIII of this book).

tation to a child of five, already display an internal structure requiring subtle theoretical analysis.

The key problem is that of accounting for the *interaction* of *symbols:* we should like to know more clearly how the "meanings" of words are "modified" by their contexts, how word order comes to be significant, what determines the syntactical categories of symbols and the relative subordination of clauses or other symbol groupings within wider symbolic wholes. The failure of philosophical grammarians or language theorists to provide an intelligible account of how a series of symbols comes to have the peculiar type of unity associated with *sentences* (something that is recognized with the utmost ease in particular instances) may remind us of the unsolved problems in this field.

Perhaps the greatest danger in this tangle of difficulties is that of being content with a technical terminology which fosters the illusion that problems have been solved. In despite of all good intentions, I take this to have been the effect of the earlier books to which I have been referring.

Consider the prima facie difference between saying "strawberry" (or some other single word) and "There are ripe strawberries in the garden" (or some other *sentence*). In both cases there is something communicated to a suitable hearer— something understood by means of an act of interpretation. Yet there is obviously an important difference between the two cases. To say "strawberry" is to make no assertion and to sponsor no truth claim. No doubt the utterance of single disconnected words or phrases would seem pointless and so fail to be understood in *another* sense of that term; but we cannot understand a sentence constituting a full assertion unless we *also* understand its component symbols. It would seem necessary therefore to begin by distinguishing *two* senses in which symbols may be understood (though not without hope of establishing some relationship between them). The sense of a word may be said to be *presented;* the sense of a full sentence is both presented and asserted.

The earlier linguistic analyses of Ogden and Richards pay

[206]

no attention to the distinction here suggested. All referential discourse is treated as if it were *assertion*, and so necessarily either true or false. And if some use of language is patently not intended to have such truth claims (as is usually the case in literature), there seems no recourse but to relegate it to the realm of "emotive" or nonreferential utterance.

One might as well argue that in a portrait of Hamlet the paint *cannot be* used in the same way as in a portrait of Stalin. Yet both persons, real or imaginary, are *presented* in a similar way; the difference of response is induced by our knowledge that one of the two is not intended to be taken as really existing. Questions of the "reality" of a painting's subject matter ought to be kept distinct from questions about the mode in which the subject is depicted or presented.

Much the same, I suggest, can be said about the representational aspects of a poem. We can recognize that a poem is not intended to convey *information* (except in the case of didactic or propagandistic verse), without commitment to the paradox that "it tells us, or should tell us, nothing."[4] If to "tell" means to *assert*, the dictum has some truth; and in this sense most paintings, unlike photographs, "tell" nothing. But if "tell" means present, represent, or depict, a poem "tells" a good deal. Insofar as poetry does *not* achieve the condition of music it presents a content amenable to intellectual analysis. Whatever else most poems do, they usually succeed in *presenting* a complex aesthetic object which is the source and origin of the complex act of appreciation.

[4] *The Meaning of Meaning*, p. 158. The whole passage is worth quoting: "A poem—or a religion, though religions have so definitely exploited the confusion of function which we are now considering, and are so dependent upon it, as to be unmistakably pathological growths—has no concern with limited and directed reference. *It tells us, or should tell us, nothing.* It has a different, though an equally important and far more vital function—to use an evocative term in connection with an evocative matter. What it does, or should do, is to induce a fitting attitude to experience." The puzzle is to know how a poem that "tells nothing" can induce a fitting, or valuable, attitude. Does it work like music? Are the representational aspects of a poem so unimportant?

To have said so much is, no doubt, to have said very little, and it would be helpful to be able to say more about the characters of the different types of object which are presented for aesthetic contemplation and enjoyment. But all I want to do here is to urge that there need be no insuperable difficulties in granting the existence of such aesthetic objects.

The purpose of this insistence upon the presented content of a work of art is to emphasize the importance of intellectual *understanding* as a factor in aesthetic appreciation. It is easy enough to fall into the intellectualistic fallacy of confusing discourse about the poem with response *to* it. Taken in context, Richards' emphasis upon nonintellectual factors in aesthetic appreciation and Stevenson's similar approach to questions of ethics are valuable. But they fail to do justice to the cognitive factors in aesthetic or ethical experience.

4. RELATIONS BETWEEN ATTITUDES AND REFERENCES

If we could distinguish sufficiently clearly between the referential and emotive aspects of utterance, we should be better prepared to deal with the puzzling question of the relation between the two. Nothing seems clearer than that the two are related: the "attitudes" aroused, incited, or evoked by an utterance are usually conditioned by its content. (So much is this the case that the only practicable way of identifying an attitude or a feeling is to describe an object by which it is normally aroused.) Yet no part of Ogden and Richards' linguistic and aesthetic theories is less satisfactory than their discussion of this critical issue. On the whole, we are invited to notice the relative *independence* of emotive and referential functions. "It is not necessary to know what things are in order to take up fitting attitudes towards them, and the peculiarity of the attitudes which art can evoke is their extraordinary width."[5] Or another passage for comparison:

For emotive language the widest differences in reference are of no importance if the further effects in attitude and emotion are of the

[5] *Ibid.*, p. 159.

[208]

required kind. . . . . What matters [for emotive purposes] is that the series of attitudes due to the references should have their own proper organization, their own emotional interconnection, and this often has no dependence upon the logical relations of such references as may be concerned in bringing the attitudes into being.[6]

Richards here talks of "references" as "bringing the attitudes into being," so that he is ready to recognize some *causal* though tenuous connection between thought and feeling. But whether the relation between reference and the concomitant attitudes be intimate, specific, and invariable (which Richards was hardly inclined to concede) or external, vague, and fluctuating (which seems to have been his view), the relation is *causal*. Either the reference induces some attitude or it doesn't, and that's the end of it, so far as the literary critic is concerned. We can identify and strive to correct a case of mistaken interpretation of "sense" (or referential content) as failing to correspond to the poet's intention; but we can hardly judge an emotive response to be inaccurate or unfitting.

5. BEHAVIORISM AS A MYTHOLOGY

I know that Richards made heroic efforts to provide naturalistic criteria of evaluation. But as soon as a critic takes up the position that statements about the value of experiences (the major concern of the critic) *belong to psychology*,[7] he has no better recourse than to use some *quantitative* criterion of value. A poem, or any other complex stimulus, is valuable to the extent that it can satisfy one desire (or "appetency") without thwarting others. The highest value is achieved through the satisfaction of the widest system of mutually compatible appetencies: "The

[6] *Principles of Literary Criticism* (London, 1925), p. 268. Similar statements are scattered throughout Richards' early writings.

[7] "We shall endeavor in what follows to show that critical remarks are merely a branch of psychological remarks, and that no ethical or metaphysical ideas need be introduced to explain value" (*Principles of Literary Criticism*, p. 23).

most valuable states of mind then are those which involve the widest and most comprehensive co-ordination of activities and the least curtailment, conflict, starvation and restriction."[8]

I will not digress here to consider whether this axiology of self-expression is adequate as a basis for value theory.[9] My present concern is, rather, to urge that it *fails to provide criteria for practice*. Suppose a literary critic to be sufficiently persuaded by this theory to wish to apply it. After reading a poem, he tries to determine the extent to which his impulses have become well ordered and harmonized. He wants to know how much "more than usual order and coherence has been given to his response."[10] How is he to find out? It is a central part of Richards' early doctrine that the system of impulses which make up the affective-cognitive system largely works at subconscious and unconscious levels; and while a feeling of "freedom, of relief, of increased competence and sanity"[11] that follows a reading may be a *general* sign that "all's right with the nervous system," we are[12] expressly warned against trusting the feeling of *conscious* delight. "There are plenty of ecstatic instants which are valueless; the character of consciousness at any moment is no certain sign of the excellence of the impulses from which it arises."[13] But what else can the critic use as a touchstone, if the felt quality of his *own* best response can so easily mislead? The advice to consider "the readiness for this or that kind of behavior in which we find ourselves after the experience"[14] seems so vague as to be worthless.

[8] *Ibid.*, p. 59.

[9] I find it hard to accept the simple equating of the values of all "impulses" (insofar as their satisfaction is independent of the satisfaction of other impulses). But any "weighting" of independently satisfiable impulses would, of course, call for further value judgments in justification.

[10] *Ibid.*, p. 235.   [11] *Ibid.*   [12] *Ibid.*, p. 246.

[13] *Ibid.*, p. 132. He continues, "It is the most convenient sign that is available, but it is very ambiguous and may be very misleading."

[14] *Ibid.* This criterion is said to be "more reliable but *less accessible*" than the quality of the momentary consciousness. A masterly understatement.

In the light of this general analysis by Richards of the criterion of aesthetic evaluation, it is illuminating to follow in detail his own procedure in the criticism of *specimens* of poetry. It would be a very exceptional reader indeed who failed to profit from these admirable demonstrations;[15] and the judgments of value which emerge from such exemplary acts of interpretation are persuasive and well balanced. Yet one can look in vain for any plausible evidence that the critic himself is using the general criterion of harmonious organization of impulses. If this criterion functions at all, it exercises a control so remote as to make its purpose dubious.

What I am suggesting is that Richards' earlier theory of valuation was not a "speculative instrument" for the improvement of practice, but served a different purpose. I believe its function to have been mainly polemical. On rereading the *Principles of Literary Criticism* in preparation for this essay, I recalled the exhilaration with which I first read it; after the unconvincing bombast and flatulent profundity of more orthodox literary critics, Richards' book was an astringent. This aseptic language of "impulses," "appetencies," "references," and "attitudes" was much more engaging than loose talk about capitalized Absolute Values. It seems to me now, however, that Richards was fighting one mythology by propagating another; and I no longer find the mythology of behaviorism even aesthetically satisfying.

If I am right in my analysis, the weaknesses of Richards' earlier critical theories are connected with overemphasis upon the need for a *science* of criticism.[16] When this was coupled with an excessively nominalistic conception of the nature of scientific discourse, the consequences were disastrous. On the one hand, referential discourse was so narrowly defined that on a strict interpretation almost no utterance

[15] If the reader of this essay has any doubts on this point, let him try to form his own critical judgment of the specimen poems in *Practical Criticism* before he reads Richards' comments upon them.

[16] "We need a spell of purer science and purer poetry before the two can

would qualify for that description; while the remaining field of nonreferential discourse was left so spacious that essential distinctions could hardly be made with any effect. That a theoretical structure having such grave flaws could have proved so acceptable is only to be explained by Richards' engaging refusal to be bound by strict adherence to his enunciated general principles.

After all, therefore, there may be some excuse for those popular "semanticists" who view Richards' early theory of symbolism as an instrument for debunking discourse of such mischievously abstract terms as "beauty" or "value."[17] For the new doctrine seems to have been used, not as a "speculative instrument" to improve critical discrimination and sensibility, but rather as a heretical myth to fortify its believers against the outcries of the orthodox.

---

again be mixed, if indeed this will ever become once more desirable" (*Ibid.*, p. 3). On the same page occurs the statement, "Critics and even theorists in criticism currently assume that their first duty is to be moving, to excite in the mind emotions appropriate to their august subject matter. This endeavor I have declined." Beside this, in the margin of the library copy I happened to consult, some unknown hand has written "Good heavens! The book is full of 'emotive' meaning." I think the comment is justified, though I see no reason why a critic should abstain from "emotive writing." It is a constant source of ironic pleasure, however, to watch Richards using emotive language (in his theoretical writings) when he claims to be most "scientific," and using means primarily cognitive (in his applied criticism) when, in his theory, *feeling* is predominantly important.

[17] There is an excellent illustration of this type of popular misinterpretation of Richards' doctrine in Christopher Isherwood's autobiographical novel, *Lions and Shadows* (London, 1938): After attending Richards' lectures on modern poetry "in a moment, all was changed. Poets, ordered Mr. Richards, were to reflect aspects of the World-Picture. Poetry wasn't a holy flame, a fire-bird from the moon; it was a group of inter-related stimuli acting upon the ocular nerves, the semi-circular canals, the brain, the solar plexus, the digestive and sexual organs. It did you medically demonstrable good, like a dose of strychnine or salts. We became behaviorists, materialists, atheists. *In our conversation, we substituted the word 'emotive' for the word 'beautiful';* we learnt to condemn inferior work as a 'failure in communication,' or more crushing still, as 'a private poem.' We talked excitedly about 'the phantom aesthetic state.' But if Mr. Richards enormously stimulated

Many of the objections raised above have been made obsolete by the later development of Richards' thought. But the earlier writings remain so influential and provide such striking illustration of the pitfalls of "scientism"[18] that it has seemed useful to discuss them in such detail.

6. RICHARDS' LATER VIEWS

In his later writings, Richards has moved very far from his earlier position; this is notably the case in *Coleridge on Imagination* (1935) and *The Philosophy of Rhetoric* (1936). These later books, indeed, show more traces of the influence of Plato and Kant than of behavioristic psychology; the mechanical metaphors of stimulus and response have been displaced by the more organic figures of fancy and imagination suggested by Coleridge.[19]

In the light of Richards' lasting preoccupation with the relations between science and the humanities, it is particularly instructive to see how his pilgrimage towards idealism transforms his conception of the nature of scientific method. Science, in the early days, was literally true;[20] but now science

---

us, he plunged us, also, into the profoundest gloom. *It seemed that everything we had valued would have to be scrapped"* (pp. 121–122, italics added).

[18] This might perhaps be defined as belief in the universality of scientific method, resulting in unwarranted claims to be in possession of exact experimental techniques.

[19] It is symptomatic that Richards seems to make little or no use of the emotive-referential distinction in these later writings. (The term "emotive" does not appear in the index of *Coleridge on Imagination* [New York, 1935].) Compare his statement in *Interpretation in Teaching* (London, 1938): "The difference between these moods [the indicative and the optative] is often no more than an intonation. If so, *the sometimes crude antithesis between Emotive and Scientific utterance would be translatable into happier terms . . .*" (p. 393, italics added). However crude the antithesis, it adumbrates a distinction of linguistic function too important to be neglected. The problem is how to understand the distinction without constructing a misleading scaffolding of unsupported and mythical theory.

[20] "The best test of whether our use of words is essentially symbolic or emotive is the question—'Is this *true or false in the ordinary strict scientific sense?'*

itself has to be recognized as mythical in import: "*All* views of Nature are taken to be projections of the mind, and the religions *as well as science* are included among myths."[21]

Now it seems to me that to characterize science as "myth" is highly misleading, if only on the general ground that a word that is intended to have *universal* application loses all significance. If *all* discourse is "mythical," there remains no standard of literal or *non*mythical utterance for contrast; all that remains is a general and confusing implication that science *no less than* poetry or religion is somehow not to be taken at its face value.

How is the scientific "myth," with its exclusive claim to knowledge, to be held separate from the myth of poetry and religion? It is suggested that the former is to be distinguished as simply the claim to unrestricted, unconditional control over Action. What we know, as science, that we must act upon, under pain of imminent danger to our lives if we do not. . . . We step out of the way of the oncoming motor-bus. But our response to any myth is restricted and conditional. . . . If we try to take more from the myth than has gone into it we violate the order of our lives.[22]

This is very puzzling. Here we are told that all myths require "restricted and conditional" responses, while science, which is *also* a myth, calls for absolute acceptance.[23] And what does it mean to say that the claims of science are "unrestricted and unconditional"? We are not always athletically evading the onslaught of motor buses: but if it is asserted that the laws of dynamics, *as hypothetical generalizations*, are always and everywhere valid, the religious believer might retort with

If this question is relevant then the use is symbolic, if it is clearly irrelevant then we have an emotive utterance" (*The Meaning of Meaning*, p. 150).

[21] *Coleridge on Imagination*, p. 177, italics added. Compare the statement on the next page: "To the man of science who objects to the world, which his science investigates so successfully, being called a myth, it will probably be enough to remark that as he investigates it the picture he frames of it changes, and that it is this changing picture that is the myth" (p. 178).

[22] *Ibid.*, pp. 174–175.

[23] Perhaps the answer is that the theoretical aspects of science are here discriminated from empirical generalizations ("Laws of Nature"), to the

comparable or stronger claims for his own doctrines. A man is not, and need not, always be concerned with his personal salvation; but whenever and wherever he is, the imperatives of religion claim unqualified assent and obedience. Is the striving for redemption and purification not to count as "action" in the sense intended? Is the danger of eternal damnation in the hereafter or misery in the present not to be recognized as "imminent danger to our lives"?

I leave these questions in their rhetorical form, because I see no promise of their being answered. Richards' later doctrines seem to have overcome the doctrinaire rigidity of his earlier nominalistic behaviorism only at the cost of an intrusive and pervasive dissolution of structure. And we seem to be still in as much need as ever of a clarification of the relations between the cognitive and affective functions of symbolism.

7. STEVENSON'S THEORY OF "EMOTIVE MEANING"

There is good reason to expect help in our perplexities from Stevenson's recent discussion of "pragmatic aspects of meaning" in his book *Ethics and Language*.[24] His "causal theory of meaning" is in general harmony with the linguistic theory of Ogden and Richards;[25] yet he has managed, with a considerable degree of success, to remedy the weakness of their doctrine.[26]

---

latter of which alone unqualified acceptance is appropriate (cf. *ibid.*, top of p. 175). I doubt that this distinction can be plausibly defended.

[24] All references to Stevenson's views made in this essay will be to *Ethics and Language* (New Haven, 1944). His illuminating essay on "Persuasive Definitions" (*Mind*, 47 [1938]: 331–350) deserves to be read in this connection.

[25] See the acknowledgment of indebtedness (in spite of some divergences) to Richards' work in *Ethics and Language*, p. 76, n. 30. See also p. 42, n. 2.

[26] I like especially (i) his recognition of the analytic rather than empirical nature of the enterprise: "No empirical contribution to the problem is sought, but only a scheme that will guard against the more gross oversimplifications" (p. 65; a similar statement occurs at the foot of p. 79); (ii) his refusal to use the term "emotive" as "a device for relegating the

[215]

The feature of his analysis which has deservedly attracted
the most favorable notice is the painstaking analysis of the
"pragmatic" meaning of symbols (whether descriptive or
emotive meaning) in terms of *dispositions* to respond.[27] His
view (highly condensed) amounts to this. A sign may be
said to have meaning *for a hearer* when it has a disposition
to cause him to respond in regular fashion to other stimuli,
i.e., when reception of the sign regularly modifies his response to *other* stimuli. It is not necessary in this view that
the "pragmatic meaning" of a sign shall be identified with
any single response of the hearer:[28] So long as reception of
the sign induces a stable pattern of response, varying according to the attendant supplementary circumstances, the sign
will have meaning; and to say that the sign causes a "disposition to respond" is merely a convenient shorthand for
referring to the modified routine of behavior (overt and
covert) of which it is the precipitating cause.[29] When the
correlated responses are cognitive in nature the sign has
"descriptive meaning"; when the responses evoked by the
sign are a "range of emotions,"[30] we have "emotive meaning."
In either case, the sign functions only as a result "of an
elaborate process of conditioning"[31] which is taken to be the
general defining characteristic of meaning.

To illustrate: Both "dog" and "Hurrah!" contribute to the
product of a range of responses in a suitable hearer *as a result*

---

nondescriptive aspects of language to limbo"; (iii) his point that "emotive
meaning" must be shown to be a *species* of meaning in general if the term is
not to be misleading (foot of p. 41); (iv) his comments, in this book and his
earlier essays, on the "inertia" of emotive meaning (p. 40).

[27] *Op. cit.*, pp. 46–62.

[28] Compare the criticism in Essay VIII (pp.167-185) of the similar views
of Charles Morris.

[29] "One who gives the stimulus, response, attendant circumstances, and
basis of a disposition, and who states in detail their correlation, has said
all about the disposition there is to say" (*op. cit.*, p. 51).

[30] *Op. cit.*, p. 59.   [31] *Op. cit.*, p. 57.

of previous training—thus both may be said to have generic meaning in the sense intended. In suitable circumstances (normally requiring the simultaneous utterance of other accompanying words) "dog" causes us to *think of* a dog; "Hurrah," however, with proper assisting circumstances, causes us to *feel* excited, or stimulated (or whatever word we choose to employ from our inadequate vocabulary for the naming of feeling). Thus the first word has the differentiating characteristic of *descriptive* meaning, while the second has that of *emotive* meaning.

I shall content myself with a catalogue of doubts about the correctness of this view.

(i) I have some scruples about applying to correlated ranges of response the generic term "meaning." Certainly Stevenson guards his retreat by insisting that he is talking of "pragmatic meaning,"[32] yet it seems to me quite misleading to suggest (as his choice of language, for all its qualification, is bound to do) that speakers' responses (or the causal laws governing such responses) are co-ordinate with denotation or signification of symbols. If we talk in this way, shall we not have to admit that a sunset or a symphony "has meaning," inasmuch as they induce modifications of response to other stimuli? Ordinary people do talk in this way, but I suppose Stevenson wants a terminology less confused and confusing than ordinary usage can provide in this instance.

(ii) It will hardly do to reply that response to a landscape or a piece of music (or, for that matter, to an article of furniture or any natural object) is not "conditioned" and so outside the province of investigations into "meaning." For if "conditioning" means social or group modification of innate response, we shall need to include much more than interpretation of "words" as falling within Stevenson's definition. Stevenson's restriction of analysis to *verbal* meaning[33] seems to need more justification than he gives; much behavior

[32] *Op. cit.*, p. 38.   [33] *Op. cit.*, p. 39.

that makes no use of words undoubtedly involves the use of signs, and a general linguistic theory should be able to include all signs within its scope.

(iii) The suggested characterization of *descriptive* meaning[34] needs more elucidation. Vagueness of reference to such a term as "cognition"[35] may be unavoidable, in default of a more supple psychological terminology. Stress upon linguistic *rules* as a distinguishing characteristic of descriptive signs[36] seems to me, however, definitely mistaken. Some descriptive signs (say a traffic signal) have only the most tenuous syntactical connection with other signs; while "emotive" signs display considerable syntactical complexity, as may be easily seen by the ease with which we can arrange disparaging epithets on a scale of increasing heat.

(iv) What I miss most in Stevenson's analysis is any mention of the function of signs as representative of or substitutes for that which they "mean" (in the sense of denoting or signifying). However hard it may be to give a satisfactory theoretical account of what is to be understood by "representation" (a word which is no doubt as hard to define as "cognition"), its use, or that of some approximate synonym, seems indispensable to any satisfactory analysis of symbolism. If we are properly so reluctant to say that a sunset "means anything," surely it is because we do not believe that it is indicative of anything outside itself. Whether as a result of previous conditioning (the prompting of nature-loving par-

[34] "The 'descriptive meaning' of a sign is its disposition to affect cognition, provided that the disposition is caused by an elaborate process of conditioning that has attended the sign's use in communication, and provided that the disposition is rendered fixed, at least to a considerable degree, by linguistic rules" (*op. cit.*, p. 70).

[35] Stevenson, with his usual candor, stresses this. See the last paragraph of p. 66 ending with the words, "The key terms that are used in the present work—in the analysis both of meaning in general and of ethical meanings —have only such clarity as is afforded by instances of their usage, together with admonitions not to hypostatize and over-simplify."

[36] "It is by such a procedure—that of referring back to other signs— that we preserve a fixed descriptive meaning" (*op. cit.*, p. 69).

ents, reading Shelley, or what you will) we have *regular* or even stock emotional responses seems beside the point. It seems only by a strained metaphor that we can regard the sunset as meaning anything, *in the absence of anything to be signified*. (As soon as we discover that red skies are followed by warm weather, or believe that God speaks in the rainbow, the situation changes. Immediately, the phenomenon becomes, or is supposed to become, representative, and we may properly refer to it as a "sign.")

(v) If the last point is sound, we shall be inclined to deny the status of signs to things which merely produce "emotive meaning" in Stevenson's sense. Insofar as an utterance, or some aspect of it (interaction, tone, rhythm, or other musical aspects) works *directly* upon our feelings, we might profitably speak of *emotive influences*. Such occasions should be sharply distinguished from those where the "emotive" utterance is *interpreted*, as a *sign* of feelings and attitudes expressed by the speaker or intended to be aroused in the hearer. The second type of case seems to me at least as important as the first, and to be more directly relevant to Stevenson's ethical doctrines.[37]

(vi) In this view, there will be but a *single* type of meaning, and "descriptive" will be distinguishable from "emotive" meaning only as American history from British history, i.e., in terms of differences between the respective *designata*.

(vii) There remains the problem of accounting for the superior "vivacity" and "contagiousness" of "Hurrah!" over "I warmly approve!" This may perhaps be done in the following way: The "neutral description" of the alleged feeling

---

[37] Thus in Stevenson's "first working model" (ch. 2 of his book), "This is good" is analyzed into "I approve of this" (*uttered with warmly expressed approval*, equivalent to saying, "Do so as well"). All that would seem to be *relevant* to the ethical issue (was the speaker right in saying "This is good"?) would seem to be *what we understand* by his utterance. On the analysis offered, the grounds for ethical judgment would seem to be (a) that the speaker approves the object, (b) that he wants us also to approve. And these grounds would seem quite inadequate, however "contagiously" his judgment is expressed. I would go so far as to urge that submission to emotive influence is usually positively immoral.

is *descriptively* less adequate—it is easier to communicate the nature of feeling by giving *deliberate* vent to it than by "talking about it"; the use of aseptic language suggests (informatively!) a lack of sincerity in the alleged feeling;[38] conversely, since emotion seems inseparable from its expression, the use of a symptom of the emotion as a *sign* for that emotion strengthens the presumption of its reality; finally, we must allow some importance (though not as much as Stevenson ascribes) to the direct influence of the more "poetic" sign (and its superior aesthetic appeal). With all this, we need not admit a special category of "emotive meaning" or overlook the amount of varied and compressed *information* conveyed by even the "simplest" ejaculation.

(viii) It may be that my disagreements with Stevenson are largely verbal. I agree warmly with him on the importance of the less obvious, "persuasive" employment of symbols which he has emphasized. But I remember also his wise remark about the prevention of "an inconvenient way of speaking."[39] A way of speaking about "emotive meaning" which focuses attention upon the irrational aspects of ethical communication and leaves ethical issues to be resolved by the interplay of generated emotive influence seems not merely inconvenient but almost mischievous.[40] A reversal of emphasis, made possible by a fuller recognition of the informative aspect of utterances, however charged with feeling, may encourage some, perhaps, to search further for a basis of *rational* agreement on ethical questions.

[38] Cf. the effect of "distance" and clinical objectivity produced by the choice of technical medical language in discussing sexual matters.

[39] *Op. cit.*, foot of p. 44.

[40] I wonder if Stevenson has considered the probable emotive influence of his own doctrine. Would not a widespread acceptance of his analysis tend to destroy the present persuasive character of ethical utterances and so leave his theory without an object?

X

Korzybski's
General Semantics

EVER SINCE men began to reflect critically upon the quality of their thinking, they have been conscious of the imperfections of their language. The ambitious designs of science and philosophy must be executed with no better instruments of expression than the "perfected cries of monkeys and dogs"—to use the vivid phrase of Anatole France. And centuries of effort by distinguished scholars have been devoted to the cause of linguistic improvement.

Yet the results remain disappointing; and never before has so much attention been given to the criticism and reform of symbolism. The popular name for such studies in the science of meaning is *semantics*—a discipline to which Peirce, Mead, Karl Bühler, C. K. Ogden, I. A. Richards, Bertrand Russell, Wittgenstein, and Carnap, among others, have made noteworthy contributions.

None of these writers, however, has had so much popular influence as Count Alfred Korzybski, the remarkable man whose doctrines I wish to examine in this essay. (The label, *"General* Semantics," serves to distinguish his doctrines from those of the other writers who have been mentioned.)

There exists today an Institute of General Semantics, which publishes researches and offers advanced instruction; popularizations by Stuart Chase and Hayakawa have become national best sellers; and the proceedings of the Second American Congress on General Semantics (held at Denver in 1941) contain an impressive array of papers by some seventy contributors on applications of semantics to subjects as varied as marital counseling, child guidance, musical appreciation, stuttering, and the prevention of dental decay.

The popular appeal of general semantics can be traced in part to the personality of the movement's founder. Any reader of Korzybski's major work, *Science and Sanity*, must be impressed by the liveliness, vigor, and freshness of the exposition. Korzybski is no plodding, minute thinker, laboriously adding, in a spirit of academic detachment, a few fragments to the coral reef of knowledge: he is a reformer and evangelist.

[223]

For him, society is riddled with mental disease, induced by linguistic maladjustment—a condition which he is anxious to improve.

One quotation, of many which might be chosen, will serve to establish the tone and temper with which Korzybski approaches the problems of general semantics:

> Our rulers, who rule our symbols, and so rule a symbolic class of life, impose their own infantilism on our institutions, educational methods, and doctrines. This leads to nervous maladjustment of the incoming generations which, being born into, are forced to develop under the un-natural (for man) semantic conditions imposed on them. In turn, they produce leaders afflicted with the old animalistic limitations. The vicious circle is completed; it results in a general state of human un-sanity, reflected again in our institutions.[1]

Insistence upon the "unsanity" of present society is a theme to which Korzybski constantly returns.

Now the man in the street will usually not welcome accusations of "infantilism," "animalism," and pathological "unsanity." But he *will* respond with interest and hope to any promise of a cure for the world's too obvious disorders. This is precisely what Korzybski has to offer—a detailed and practical system for re-education in better mental and linguistic habits, "such as can be grasped and applied by any individual who will spend the time and effort necessary to master this system and acquire the corresponding *s.r.* [semantic reactions]."[2]

The benefits offered are immediate and substantial: "They help any individual to solve his problems by himself, to his own and others' satisfaction. They also build up an *affective* semantic foundation for personal as well as for international agreement and adjustment."[3]

How should these claims be tested? If our concern were mainly practical, we would want to investigate empirically

---

[1] Alfred Korzybski, *Science and Sanity* (2d ed.; International Non-Aristotelian Library Publishing Company, 1941), p. 41. All quotations used are from this book.

[2] P. 45.   [3] Pp. xvii-xviii.

the outcome of the linguistic therapy recommended. Sweeping claims of the beneficial results of semantic treatment have been made; but the data are as yet insufficient for a final evaluation.

There is, however, another and related question which can already be discussed with some profit—the question of the coherence and adequacy of the general principles from which the recommended therapy is derived. Fortunately, Korzybski, for all his urgent concern in practical affairs, is free from that short-sighted "practicalism" which shows itself in contempt for theory. He insists rather, in a most commendable way, upon the necessity of an adequate general theory and ascribes the difficulty of instituting semantic reforms to the previous absence of sound theoretical foundations: "The difficulty was that no methodological general theory based on the new developments of life and science had been formulated until general semantics and a general extensional, teachable and communicable, non-aristotelian system was produced."[4]

On Korzybski's showing, then, the program of general semantics depends upon the validity of its theoretical foundations, to which alone this essay will be devoted.

It is worth noting, in parentheses, that Korzybski's theories have important theoretical consequences for a number of controversial and perplexing problems in the philosophy and methodology of science: Here are some representative items:

In psychiatry it [i.e. the theory of general semantics] indicates on colloidal grounds the solution of the "body-mind" problem. . . . It gives the first definition of "consciousness" in simpler physico-chemical terms. . . . It leads to a general theory of psycho-therapy, including all existing medical schools. . . . In biology it gives a semantic and structural solution of the "organism-as-a-whole" problem. . . . It formulates a new and physiological theory of mathematical types of extreme simplicity and very wide application. . . . It offers a non-aristotelian solution of the problem of mathematical

[4] Pp. xvii-xviii.

[225]

'infinity'. . . . It offers a new non-aristotelian semantic definition of *mathematics* and *number*. . . . In physics, the enquiry explains some fundamental, but as yet disregarded, semantic aspects of physics in general, and of Einstein's and the new quantum theories in particular. . . . It resolves simply the problem of "indeterminism" of the newer quantum mechanics.[5]

To this striking but still incomplete catalogue of achievements Korzybski adds the disarming comment: "I realize that the thoughtful reader may be staggered by such a partial list. I am in full sympathy with him in this. I also was staggered."[6]

Any theory which can accomplish so much deserves a respectful hearing—whatever the verdict on its practical bearings upon individual and social reforms may prove to be.

I shall try to do just two things: First, to make a little more definite the general method used in Korzybski's investigations; and then to explain in more detail two components of his theory which seem to be of crucial importance. The topics I have selected for more intensive discussion are Korzybski's attacks upon Aristotelian logic and his theory of abstraction.

I. KORZYBSKI'S GENERAL APPROACH

A distinctive feature of Korzybski's approach to problems of symbolization and meaning is his intention to make general semantics a *scientific* discipline. Repeatedly he insists that general semantics is as empirical as biology or physics.

The program, therefore, is to solve problems of meaning by just those methods of observation, generalization, and experimentation which have proved outstandingly effective in the empirical sciences. Korzybski uses the results of other sciences extensively and wishes his own theses to be submitted to just the kind of test which would be appropriate to the confirmation of a physical or biological hypothesis.

If semantics is to be an empirical science, some operational definition is needed of the central term "meaning":

[5] Pp. 8–9.   [6] P. 9.

"meaning" must be as accessible to empirical recognition as kinetic energy or electrical charge. The important decision is now made to use physiological criteria of meaning, i.e., to test statements about meanings by observations of what is known or assumed to be happening in the nervous system of a biological organism.

This choice of procedure gives a distinctive slant to Korzybski's investigations, for he is, in his own words, mainly interested in "the neurological attitude toward 'meaning'."[7] It follows that one of the most important and basic notions of general semantics will be that of the nervous response made by an organism to a stimulus consisting of symbols.

We are to understand, accordingly, that the reception by an organism of any spoken word, or other symbol, induces a certain response (and especially so in the nervous system). Such response, determined in part by the nature of the symbol-stimulus, but also in large measure by the previous experiences and present condition of the receiving organism, is called a "*semantic reaction.*" (The term refers to emotive as well as cognitive reactions; a feeling of response of dislike or fear on hearing the word "Hitler" is counted as part of the semantic reaction to that word.) First order responses to symbols can themselves act as stimuli to further semantic reactions; and these in turn to others, induced still more indirectly.

Inasmuch as semantic reactions, whether first-order effects of symbolic stimuli, or responses to other semantic reactions previously induced, are *specific natural events* in the nervous system of the organism, the study of meanings becomes a branch of physiology.

But the study of meanings also falls outside the province of physiology. For general semantics undertakes to examine the *correctness* or adequacy of semantic reactions. This, in turn requires us to determine how far semantic reactions are

[7] P. 22. Cf: "The analysis of such *living reactions* is the sole object of general semantics as a natural *empirical science*" (p. ix).

a faithful reflection of the physical reality outside the organism. There is needed a theory as to what constitutes "physical reality," in the light of which to criticize statements purporting to represent that "reality."

It might be supposed that physics would supply all the information that could be needed about the external environment of the organism in a symbol situation. But a mere *description* of the physical world will not suffice for Korzybski's purposes; he requires criteria for distinguishing the "real" from the unreal or illusory. In the end, this leads him into metaphysics.

Korzybski's reliance upon the empirical sciences is colored by his conception of the character of scientific method. Other thinkers, from Hume to Bertrand Russell, Dewey, and the Logical Positivists, who have hoped to use science as a key to philosophical problems have been anxious to stress the "unity" of the scientific method upon which their hopes were fixed. Just because scientific method is a unified, identifiable system of procedures, one may hope, according to these writers, to apply it to unsolved problems of ethics or other controversial disciplines; conversely, if the character of scientific method varied according to the subject matter of its application, the call to *use* that method in untried fields would be less persuasive.

It is very characteristic of Korzybski's approach, however, to stress the *discontinuity* rather than the uniformity of scientific method. He regards contemporary science as having made a sharp and revolutionary departure from older ways of scientific thought, especially those associated with the names of Aristotle, Euclid, and Newton.

The theories of these three great pioneers, we are told, have by now been discredited. But the breakaway has not been complete; nor have its implications been sufficiently recognized. Einstein freed us from the shackles of the Newtonian cosmology; Lobachevski and the other inventors of non-Euclidean geometries overturned the absolute monarchy of Euclid; but Aristotle, in spite of pioneering modern discoveries in multivalued logics, remains the archenemy of correct thinking and sane behavior.

"Aristotelian" is, accordingly, always a term of reproach for general semanticists; and for parallels to the vigor with which they attack this ancient intellectual idol, we must return to Francis Bacon and his tremendous onslaught against the Aristotelian tradition. Non-Aristotelianism is as integral to general semantics as its neurological approach to meaning and its reliance upon scientific method.

Let us, therefore, begin our more detailed examination of Korzybski's doctrines by determining the basis of his quarrel with Aristotle. What exactly is the ground of complaint?

In part, it seems to be a hostile response (shared by many contemporary logicians) to the restrictive assumptions of Aristotle's theory of the syllogism. It is widely recognized today that the type of proposition discussed by Aristotle and his followers is a very special case; that statements need not be analyzed *only* into the "subject-predicate" form; and that many arguments depend for their validity upon formal properties of relations which cannot be described in the Aristotelian scheme.

It is, therefore, correct to say that Aristotelian logic is inadequate—in exactly the same way as simple arithmetic is inadequate. Arithmetic is a good instrument to use in counting sheep or dollars, but more refined mathematical instruments are needed to determine the time taken for a liquid to cool or a plant to grow. The theory of the syllogism is a good logical instrument to use in the evaluation of certain very simple arguments, but more refined logical theories are needed in order to represent the structure of quantum mechanics or the theory of relativity.

But to denounce syllogistic logic on *this* account would be as absurd as to throw away forks and knives because they cannot cut steel. Korzybski has other and more remarkable reasons for his denunciations of Aristotelian logic.

Aristotle, we are told, inculcated the vicious habit of using the copula, "is," as a sign of *identity*. He it was whose

[229]

influence promoted this "delusional" and "unsane" procedure; and we are warned repeatedly against using "the pernicious 'is' of identity."[8] What Aristotle is alleged to have believed and taught is that such statements as "Water is wet" and "Dewey is a philosopher" mean that water is *identical* with wetness, and Dewey is *identical* with the characteristic of being a philosopher. In other words, anybody who believes such statements, in the sense in which an adherent of Aristotelian logic would interpret them, is supposed to be committed to the belief that water is the very same thing as wetness, and Dewey (the man) is the very same thing as being a philosopher (the abstract characteristic).

It is worth noting that Korzybski gives no quotation from Aristotle to support this charge. And it should be said, as a matter of historical justice, that there is no evidence that Aristotle or his followers believed anything so absurd. One sufficient reason is that the view with which they are charged would be inconsistent with the standard syllogistic doctrine of the impossibility of converting universal propositions. If the "is" in "Water is wet" were the "is" of identity, as alleged, the truth of that proposition would automatically entail the truth of the converse proposition that all wetness is water. Now it is, of course, a central part of the doctrine of Aristotelian logic that the proposition *All A is B* can*not* be automatically replaced by the converse, *All B is A*. Again, if Aristotle believed the absurd doctrine which is ascribed to him, he would have to believe that Plato and Socrates and Aristotle himself were all the same person. For, if all of them were *identical* with being a philosopher, all of them must be identical with one another. Even a stupid man would hardly believe in these absurd consequences; and Aristotle was very far from being stupid.

I think, therefore, that Korzybski is setting up a mere bogey when he tries to scare us away from what he calls Aristotelian logic.

Yet after all, it may be objected, what difference does

[8] P. 408.

it make, except to the historian of ideas, whether Aristotle was responsible for the vice of "identification"? If the mistake is prevalent, might it perhaps be conveniently referred to as "Aristotelianism," no matter who was the error's original parent?

Two replies should be made to this. First, a semanticist should himself live according to the code of accurate thought and clear expression for which he is campaigning. Nothing but confusion can result from inserting into what claims to be a sober scientific account the ghosts of historical traditions that never existed. Semanticists should be the last people to go tilting at fictitious windmills.

A more important comment is this. Korzybski's own lack of understanding of what is asserted in Aristotelian logic leads him into the absurdity of supposing the use of the auxiliary verb "to be" is in itself deplorable. Here is one illustrative quotation: "If we use the 'is' at all, and it is extremely difficult to avoid entirely this auxiliary verb when using languages which, to a large extent, depend on it, we must be particularly careful not to use 'is' as an identity term."[9]

This passage intimates that it would be well to avoid the use of "is" entirely, if it were possible. It would be interesting to know whether the speakers of Chinese and Hebrew, languages which contain no auxiliary verb, are free from the delusional identifications from which the Occidental civilizations suffer.

But Korzybski has a simple device for overcoming "the 'is' of identity." It consists, as the following argument illustrates, in confining oneself to *negative* statements.

The present non-aristotelian system is based on fundamental *negative* premises; namely, the complete denial of "identity," which denial *cannot be denied* without imposing the burden of proof on the person who denies the denial. If we start, for instance, with a statement that "a word is *not* the object spoken about," and some one tries to deny that, he would have to produce an actual physical object which would *be the word*—impossible, even in asylums for the

[9] P. 400.

mentally ill. Hence my security, often "blasphemously cheerful," as one of my friends calls it.[10]

It should be plain that this argument is unsound. If the assertion of negative premises gave "unusual security of conclusion,"[11] to use Korzybski's phrase, it would be easy to disprove his own contention that the meaning of a symbol is the semantic reactions it produces. It would be sufficient to say, "The meaning of a word is *not* the semantic reaction it evokes"; and "the burden of proof" would be on Korzybski, who would be denying a denial! It ought to be obvious that a negative statement is *in general* no more "secure" than its logical contradictory, which of the two is true depending entirely upon the nature of the situation to which the statements refer. Korzybski's preference for *negative* statements can only be accounted for by his supposing that *whenever* the word "is" occurs in a statement it stands for identity. If it does not, there is no need to be more suspicious about the positive than about the negative statement.

Korzybski's "general denial of the 'is' of identity"[12] and his consequent misguided preference for negative statements are details, though important ones in his system. More basic in his procedure are the nature of the grounds invoked for this "denial" of identity and the related denial of the traditional laws of thought.

Very often in attacking an "Aristotelian" principle or concept, Korzybski uses the phrase "false to facts";[13] and he expressly states his objection to the view that logic has no physical content.[14] He believes, in fact, that the correctness of logical principles is established like the correctness of physical principles, by appeal to "the facts." We look at the sky to see if the sun has appeared in the position predicted by astronomers; we look at an electron to see if it is identical with itself, as predicted by logicians.[15]

[10] Pp. 10–11. He is fond of this type of argument. See, e.g., p. 61.

[11] P. 10.   [12] P. 11.   [13] E.g., p. 409.   [14] Foot of p. 73.

[15] " . . . 'identity,' which is empirically non-existent in this actual world . . ." (p. ix).

This position sounds attractively empirical and free from rationalistic nonsense. Yet it seems to me to involve a profoundly mistaken view of the nature and function of logic.

Let us contrast the process of physical verification of an astronomical prediction with the proposed process of verification of the logical law of identity. In order to test a statement about the sun's position in the sky, we must first understand the words used to make the statement; but when such words as "sun," "transit," "meridian," and the others used in the astronomical statements *have* been defined, it remains an open question, to be settled by appropriate observation, whether the prediction is true or not. Contrast this with the case of the logical principle. Here too we must have a well-defined language in which to formulate our statement; but this time the specification of the language *already* determines the logical principles. We have not yet described the language if we have failed to say whether "A is B" is to be understood to mean the same as "B is A"; the so-called "laws of thought" are, therefore, already determined by our choice of a language; and there remains nothing to test.

A simple mathematical analogy will make the point clearer. If we find that one drop of mercury combines with another drop of the same substance to produce a *single* drop of mercury, we do not, if we are wise, say that the equation $1 + 1 = 2$ is wrong and that arithmetic ought to be revised. We say instead drops of mercury "so combined" are not the kinds of things to which the principles of arithmetic apply. If we find that a woman loses weight after studying semantics, we ought similarly to say *not* that identity is an illusion, but rather that the principle "A is A" is not intended to be applicable to that sort of situation. (We may notice, however, that it is perfectly correct to say that the lady in question is still the *same* woman—Korzybski's warnings against identity to the contrary.)

What has here been said about the relation of logic to experience and observation is neither new nor original.

The propositions of logic have long been recognized as being "necessary" and so nonempirical; and this view of the nature of logic is held almost without exception by logicians and philosophers. If Korzybski insists on regarding logic as empirical, he must be willing to dispense with the support of expert authority for this part of his doctrine.

I am not quite clear as to the difference which would be made to Korzybski's theories if he were to abandon his crusade against "Aristotelianism." The moderate and defensible position that syllogistic logic is an instrument of limited application, needing supplementation by other types of formal calculi, would hardly generate the heat of his present invectives against "identification." And abandonment of the principle that logic must be "true to fact" would, I am afraid, play havoc with another plank of the platform of general semantics—the principle that scientific knowledge is restricted to reflection of the *structure* of reality. On the other hand, it seems to me that his theory of abstraction would hardly need to be changed; the critical discussion upon which we are now to embark is therefore independent of what has gone before.

2. KORZYBSKI'S THEORY OF ABSTRACTIONS

The topic of the nature of abstractions is of crucial importance in any systematic semantics. When a person who is philosophically unsophisticated compares a language such as English with the world to which it refers, he is easily impressed by the relative poverty of the language. The world seems full of objects and relationships which cannot be adequately described in words; nor is this merely a deficiency of vocabulary—an absence of enough names to be used. Every name that is already in our possession seems incurably "thin" or "abstract" by contrast with the rich specificity of the real things to which it refers. Such vague and confused feelings of the inadequacy of language provoke the ancient philosophical problem of the reality of abstractions. Inasmuch as semantics sets out to be a critic of ordinary language, it can hardly evade this problem; for whatever decision is made with respect to the reality of abstractions will clearly determine some of the paths which semantic criticism of language will have to follow.

Let us now see what Korzybski has to say about the subject. In view of what I said previously, it will be expected that Korzybski will adopt the neurological standpoint; in the case, therefore, of somebody's perceiving an apple (which is said to be a low-order abstraction) Korzybski is interested in describing the relation between the external physical event and the reactions in the nervous system of the person who perceives that apple. As pointed out earlier, for this description to be complete we need some fairly definite notions about the nature of the physical end of the relation; we must have some notion of what is happening "out there." Korzybski's position on this point is stated forcefully and unequivocally:

If we use a language of adjectives and subject-predicate forms pertaining to "sense" impressions, we are using a language which deals with entities *inside our skin* and characteristics entirely non-existent in the outside world. Thus the events outside our skin are neither cold nor warm, green nor red, sweet or bitter., but these characteristics are manufactured by our nervous system inside our skins, as responses only to different energy manifestations, physico-chemical processes. When we use such terms, we are dealing with characteristics which are absent in the external world, and build up an anthropomorphic and delusional world non-similar in structure to the world around us.[16]

What Korzybski calls the "scientific object," the real apple "outside our skins," is accordingly

a mad dance of "electrons," which is different every instant, which never repeats itself, which is known to consist of extremely complex dynamic processes of very fine structure, acted upon by, and reacting upon, the rest of the universe, inextricably connected with everything else and dependent on everything else.[17]

Especially important is it to notice that the scientific

[16] P. 384.   [17] P. 387.

object, this inextricable knot of subatomic energy processes, has *infinitely many characteristics:*

If we inquire *how many characteristics (m.o.)* we should ascribe to such an event [i.e., to the scientific object] the only possible answer is that we should ascribe to an event infinite numbers of characteristics, as it represents a process which never stops in one form or another; neither, to the best of our knowledge, does it repeat itself.[18]

If the scientific object, the real apple outside our skins, has infinitely many characteristics, we can perceive only a selection from these characteristics. This implication accords well with Korzybski's view that abstraction consists essentially in the *omission of details.* "What we see is structurally only a specific *statistical mass-effect* of happenings on a much finer grained level. We *see* what we see because we *miss* all the finer details."[19] And to illustrate what happens, according to this view, during the process of abstraction, Korzybski has "the familiar example of a rotary fan, which is made up of separate radial blades, but which, when rotating with a certain velocity, gives the impression of a *solid disk.* In this case the 'disk' is not 'reality,' but a nervous integration, or abstraction from the rotating blades."[20]

What Korzybski calls the "ordinary object," the apple which is red, cool to the touch, and slightly acid in taste, is to be understood therefore as having the same relation to the external "sub-microscopic physico-chemical processes" as the apparently solid disk to the really separate blades of the rotating fan.

Since the common-sense or "ordinary" apple is obtained by the omission of fine-grained detail, the common-sense apple, (unlike its scientific correlate in the real world) has only a *finite* number of characteristics:

The object represents in this language [i.e., in the language of everyday affairs] a gross macroscopic abstraction, for our nervous system is not adapted for abstracting directly the infinite numbers of characteristics which the endlessly complex dynamic fine structure of the event represents.[21]

[18] P. 387.   [19] P. 376.   [20] P. 382.   [21] P. 389.

I hope the picture is so far clear. The "scientific" object, the real object outside the skin, is the source of energy radiations which impinge upon the nervous system of the receiving organism. This proceeds to "leave out" details and to "manufacture" the gross macroscopic object, the so-called ordinary object.

So far we have been talking about what Korzybski calls "first abstractions." It is important to notice that when Korzybski uses this term or the equivalent phrase, the "ordinary (non-scientific) object," he intends to refer to something *nonverbal*, something that can be tasted or felt. The apple in my hand is a first abstraction; the *word* "apple" however is something else again: "We see that the object *is not* the event but an abstraction from it, and that the label *is not* the object nor the event, but a still further abstraction."[22]

We therefore have three levels to distinguish: that of the scientific reality outside the skin, where the event E occurs; the first-order abstraction or common-sense object, O; and finally the second-order label, L. But this hierarchy of orders of abstraction can obviously be extended; the label L is used in making statements about the object O; if we find new labels which are in turn used for making statements about L itself we shall have advanced to a higher level of abstraction:

We know very well that Smith can always say something *about* a statement (L), on record. Neurologically considered, this *next* statement (L_1) about a statement (L) would be the nervous response to the former statement (L) which he has seen or heard or even produced by himself inside his skin. So his statement (L_1), *about* the former statement (L) is a *new abstraction* from the former abstraction. In my language, I call it an abstraction of a higher order.[23]

We see, therefore, that the step from using abstractions of one order to abstractions of the next highest order is taken whenever we *talk about* the lower-order abstraction.

[22] P. 389.   [23] P. 392.

But Korzybski also, in a way which puzzles me, considers an increase in order of abstraction to occur whenever we make an *inference:* "Obviously, if we consider a description as of the *n*th order, then an inference from such a description (or others) should be considered as an abstraction of a higher order $(n+1)$."[24]

The next point to emphasize is that the hierarchy of orders of abstraction—from scientific event to common-sense object, from common-sense object to verbal description or label, from description to inference, from inference to inferences regarding inferences, and so on indefinitely—constitutes a series containing increasingly more subjective components. The scientific object has highest value—is "the only possible survival concern of the organism";[25] every other term in the generated series of increasing orders of abstraction "represents only a shadow cast by the scientific object."[26] The various orders of abstraction accordingly constitute a series, as Korzybski puts it, "decreasing in value."[27] We have shadows, and shadows of shadows, and shadows of shadows of shadows, and so on.

This somewhat complicated theoretical analysis has direct and important practical consequences. For ordinary, semantically miseducated people have been systematically encouraged to overlook the difference between the different levels of abstraction. Their thinking, feeling, and behaving is, consequently, vitiated by the tendency to "identification" of the various levels of abstraction. They confuse the "ordinary" or common-sense object (the colored apple) with the infinitely complex scientific object of which it is the mere shadow; they confuse the word apple and its definition with the ordinary object; and they confuse the higher levels of abstraction with one another.

In so doing, the semantically benighted revert to the condition of a child or animal who is unaware of the fact that he *is* abstracting. Such "infantilism" or "animalism" lead

[24] P. 443. [25] P. 402. [26] P. 402. [27] P. 406.

[238]

to the construction of a delusional world in which the subjective products of the nervous system are systematically identified with the scientific reality upon which survival depends. This way lies madness—the peculiar madness of the highly verbalized civilization to which we belong.

The way back to mental health is found by inculcating the "consciousness of abstracting." But careful training is needed: differentiation between levels of abstraction cannot be achieved merely by good intentions—it requires careful and prolonged re-education of the nervous system. Perhaps the most interesting aspect of the retraining procedure described by Korzybski is the introduction of what he calls "silence at the objective level." For one great point to be achieved in fighting delusional identification of levels of abstraction is the conviction that reality is nonverbal: "*The objective level is not words, and cannot be reached by words alone. We must point our finger and be silent, or we shall never reach this level.*"[28]

The central aim is to produce a healthy "delay" in nervous reaction; so that in responding to verbal or nonverbal stimuli, we are aware of what it is that we are doing:

There is no doubt that this "delayed action" has many very beneficial effects upon the whole working of the nervous system. It somehow balances harmful *s.r.* [semantic reactions] and also stimulates the higher nervous centres to more *physiological* control over the lower centres.[29]

At a somewhat more sophisticated level of training, the correction of delusional identification is much assisted by the use of special linguistic devices, notably that of attaching subscripts to any words which are commonly used to refer ambiguously to objects belonging to different levels of abstraction. Many of the central terms of discourse (such as "true," "false," "object," "name," "knowledge," "fact," "reality," etc.) are "multi-ordinal" in this way—ambiguous as to the level of abstraction to which reference is intended.

[28] P. 399.   [29] P. 424.

Clarity of theoretical discourse about language requires such multi-ordinal terms to be handled with full awareness of their systematic ambiguity.

So far I have been trying to give a sympathetic account of Korzybski's central theory of abstraction without injecting any comment of my own. Now I turn to criticism.

We have seen that a central doctrine of general semantics is that of the sole reality of the so-called scientific object, that swarm of infinitely complex submicroscopic processes of which the "ordinary object" and all the higher abstractions are mere shadows. And this is where the difficulties of the philosophic critic begin. For surely the terms used in describing this alleged reality are themselves of a very high order of abstraction. The characteristics ascribed to the scientific object, energy, electric and magnetic charge, and so on, are by no means experienced directly at what Korzybski calls the "unspeakable" level. They are, on the contrary, defined in terms of complicated manipulations of scientific instruments and calculated with the help of theoretical physics of a very high degree of abstractness. Now if we should assert, with Korzybski, that all abstractions are "manufactured by the nervous system" we should be compelled to say also that the "mad dance of electrons" constituting the scientific object is likewise manufactured by the nervous system. Korzybski seems close to admitting this when he says that on his view "science becomes an extra-neural extension of the *human* nervous system."[30]

But this line of reasoning leads into hopeless logical circularity. The reason for giving a superior status to the scientific object—for referring to it as a reality and to the series of abstractions emanating from it as shadows—was its alleged independence of what went on "inside our skins"; the swarm of electrons, unlike the abstractions derived from it, was *not* manufactured by the nervous system. If it be granted, however, that the scientific object, also, is a complex of abstract characteristics, the original basis for differentiation between

[30] P. 376.

reality and subjective abstractions disappears. We shall have to say, if we are to continue to use the language of Korzybski's account, that the common-sense object is manufactured by the nervous system under the influence of stimuli from the scientific object, which itself, as a complex of abstract characteristics, is *also* manufactured by the nervous system. We are naturally left wondering what this highly productive and creative nervous system is able to use as the raw material for its amazing construction.

And we shall have to go a stage further. For the "nervous system" itself is a physical (or physicochemical) object of a complex sort, whose characteristics are known to us not directly, but rather by complicated inferences from observation and physiological theory. To be consistent, therefore, we shall have to say also that the nervous system itself is manufactured *by* the nervous system. Or, as Adam said in William Blake's poem, "It is all a vain delusion of the all-creative imagination."

Some of Korzybski's popularizers have by-passed these difficulties by supposing that Korzybski was condemning *all* abstraction as such. As we should expect, they themselves made plentiful use of abstractions in their own strictures against abstractions. For a pledge *never* to use abstractions would be tantamount to a vow of silence. The success of language as an instrument of communication depends upon the possibility of using symbols to refer to recognizable and recurring aspects of experience, that is to say, of *abstract* characteristics of experience. As Korzybski himself says, "All speaking is using abstraction of a very high order."[31]

Now Korzybski, unlike some of his popularizers, is aware of this central importance of the use of abstractions and is free from the absurd desire to ban their use in discourse. In many a passage he refers approvingly to the use of abstractions as when he says that "higher abstractions are extremely expedient devices,"[32] or again "Happy, structurally high abstractions really have a strong creative character."[33] And

[31] P. 136. [32] P. 377. [33] P. 468.

in at least one important passage he explicitly makes the point here stressed, viz., that the scientific object itself must be regarded as characterized by high-order abstractions: "If we enquire: What do the characteristics of the event represent? We find that they are given only by science and represent at each date the highest, most verified, most reliable abstractions. . . ."[34]

This brings us back again to the logical circle. Once it is admitted that the characteristics of the scientific object, which was to have been the touchstone of reality, are themselves abstractions, there is no longer any basis for the sharp distinction between the alleged external reality and the supposed subjectively manufactured abstractions.

Korzybski's reference, in the quotation used a little while ago, to the scientific object as being characterized by "the most verified and reliable abstractions" does suggest another and, it seems to me, more hopeful way of criticizing the use of abstractions. Since abstractions are used to make verifiable predictions, their validity can reasonably be tested by the success of the predictions in which they occur. If any abstraction is an indispensable component of a system of statements whose truth is confirmed by observation and experiment, we can regard it as valid. On the other hand, if the introduction of a term leads to the making of false or meaningless predictions, we may regard that term as improperly used. (If a man claims that electrons are inhabited by devils, we can properly ask him to specify the verifiable consequences which flow from his claim; and we may eventually conclude that he was misusing the terms which occurred in his statement.) But such a pragmatic approach to problems of meaning would certainly provide no grounds for the sweeping assertion that terms such as "red," "warm," and "sweet" refer only to events occurring inside the skin. Or that the objects to which we refer in everyday contexts are "manufactured" by the nervous system. On the contrary, such investigation would very soon show that the central

[34] P. 307.

terms of the statements in which Korzybski's theory is presented (such terms as "reality" and" manufactured") are themselves instances of semantic confusion. My conclusion is that Korzybski's epistemological doctrines, on which so much else in his system depends, are confused. And I do not see how this part of his theories can be salvaged.

Another major respect in which Korzybski's account of abstraction needs improvement is his description of what goes on during the *process* of abstraction.

We have seen already that Korzybski holds the view that abstraction consists in "leaving out details." He thinks of the nervous system as a kind of coarse-grained sieve or filter; infinitely complex waves of physical energy distributions strike the filter, lose much of their individual detail in passing through it, and eventually produce the abstraction. The nervous system of the receiving organism has to play a part in this process—for have we not been told that the nervous system "manufactures" the abstraction?—yet its role is passive, like that of a camera, radio, or other mechanical device for recording energy.

This account of the function of the nervous system in abstraction is dangerously oversimplified. Consider a very simple case of abstraction—say that in which a man perceives that a group of geometrical figures are all alike in being isosceles triangles. Not even this simple process could well be described as consisting in mere omission of details. Certainly the man who sees that a number of geometrical figures are all isosceles triangles is deliberately neglecting all kinds of details in which the several figures differ from each other—their size, specific shape, orientation, relative positions to one another, and so on. But he might continue indefinitely neglecting one item after the other, without ever arriving at the positive perception of the general respect in which all the figures are similar. The process of abstraction, as this simple case illustrates, has a positive as well as a negative side. If we abstract a general character from a group

[243]

of specimens, we must allow ourselves to overlook certain respects in which the specimens differ among themselves; but we must also, on pain of failing to perform a genuine act of abstraction, see clearly the elements of resemblance on which our selection of the particular abstraction is founded.

Korzybski tells us:

> We can now define "consciousness of abstracting" as "*awareness* that in our process of abstracting we have *left out* characteristics." Or, consciousness of abstracting can be defined as "*remembering* the '*is not*' " and that some characteristics have been left out.[35]

If I were using this kind of language to describe my point of difference, I should have to say that more useful "consciousness of abstracting" would require awareness that we have left characteristics *in* as well as awareness that we have left characteristics *out;* and the self-critical employment of abstractions would require us to remember *what it is* that we have "left in" as well as *what it is* that we have left out. In other words, criticism of the employment of abstraction should induce lively awareness of the specific processes used in arriving at the particular abstraction in question. And this awareness should include attention to both the positive and negative aspects of the abstractive process.

One reason for regarding this point as important is the fact that the term "abstraction" is highly ambiguous, being used to refer to a number of different processes which sometimes have very little in common with one another. Only detailed attention to what is meant by "abstraction" in the specific context in which the term is used will guard us against the mistakes which might otherwise result.

It is ironical that Korzybski himself, for all his warnings against imputing unwarranted identity to the objects denoted by any general term, should himself have used the central term, "abstraction," so misleadingly. For consider some of the different ways in which he uses that word:

(i) Energy waves strike the organism which then sees something which it recognizes as a red apple. The apple

---

[35] P. 416.

(not its name) is said to be an abstraction from the swarm of electronic processes from which the energy waves radiated.

(ii) Smith *calls* the apple which he sees (the "ordinary" or "commonsense" object) by the name "apple." The name "apple" is said by Korzybski to be an abstraction from the apple.

(iii) Smith talks about the word "apple," as, for instance, when he says " 'apple' is a noun." Each word he now uses, e.g., the word "noun," is said to be an abstraction from the word "apple." We need not proceed to the higher levels of abstraction in Korzybski's scheme.

In these three cases we have three *different* kinds of relations: (i) the relation between a common-sense object and the scientific object which is alleged to generate it; (ii) the relation between an object and the word which is a label for it; (iii) the relation between a word and some other word which can be used in a description of that first word.

The strange thing is that in none of these three cases do we have an instance of what is *commonly* understood by abstraction. For we commonly mean a process in which we notice resemblances and common elements in a group of presented individuals. But nobody *first* perceives the colorless and odorless scientific object and *then* abstracts color from it. (Still more absurd is it to suppose that this unconscious perceiving involves leaving out details and so arriving at a residue of sensible qualities, color, shape, etc., which were not even present in that from which the details were omitted.)

I hope it is sufficiently obvious that the process of naming the apple and that of describing the name of an apple are equally remote from what we have in mind when we commonly talk about "abstraction." Nor can either of *these* processes be regarded as processes of neglecting details. We do not get the *name* "apple" by neglecting to notice the ways in which one apple differs from another; we do not get the word "noun" by omitting details of the word "apple."

It seems to me, in short, that the first three steps in Korzybski's hierarchy of orders of abstraction are based on different relations, and that neither the second or third of the steps could be regarded as involving "abstraction," either on Korzybski's view of that process or on any other which is generally accepted today.

If one takes these difficulties seriously, very little remains of Korzybski's theory of abstractions except some hypothetical neurology fortified with dogmatic metaphysics.

I say "dogmatic metaphysics" advisedly, because I have been unable to find any better ground for the principle of the superior unshadowy reality of the so-called "scientific object." It should be added that Korzybski is an unabashed metaphysician, though he flaunts his metaphysics too seldom for this to be noticed by a casual reader. His system, he explains, "involves full-fledged structural metaphysics. . ."[36] and again, "The real problem before mankind presents itself in the selection of a structural metaphysics."[37] It is a weakness of Korzybski's presentation that his own metaphysics is presented without any explicit considerations in its favor. Repeated invocations of the supposed support of scientific findings is no substitute for reasoning, even in metaphysics.

Enough has been said to make it clear that I regard the theoretical foundations of general semantics as logically incoherent and in need of thoroughgoing revision. This does not necessarily imply a finally adverse judgment on the merits of general semantics; the history of science has provided a number of examples of confused theoretical systems, which were able to produce useful and interesting results. But we must not make the mistake of supposing that lack of clarity and self-consistency is a positive merit in a theoretical system. The little girl who asked her mother whether it was necessary to be married in order to have a baby was told that marriage was a help. It would be a help to logicians, philosophers, and other champions of clarity of thought, if the foundations of general semantics received some house cleaning. And it is in the hope of encouraging such logical renovation that this essay was prepared.

[36] P. 44.   [37] P. 483.

Additional Notes
and References

I. LINGUISTIC METHOD IN PHILOSOPHY

An address at Cornell University, February, 1945. Published in *Philosophy and Phenomenological Research*, 8: 635–649.

II. VAGUENESS: AN EXERCISE IN LOGICAL ANALYSIS

1. Originally published in *Philosophy of Science*, 4 (1937): 427–455. It was ably discussed by Carl G. Hempel in his paper "Vagueness and Logic" in *Philosophy of Science*, 6 (1939): 163–180. See also the paper by Irving M. Copilowish, "Border-Line Cases, Vagueness, and Ambiguity," *ibid.*, pp. 181–195.

2. Hempel is in general agreement with my results—with one or two exceptions to be noted later. He regards both descriptive and logical terms as subject to vagueness, concludes that "no term of any interpreted language is definitely free from vagueness" (*op. cit.*, p. 170), and accepts my proposals for symbolizing vagueness (*ibid.*, p. 165). He supplements my mathematical definition of vagueness by obviating tacit assumption of a metrical order in the objects to which the vague term is applicable (*ibid.*, pp. 165–166, small type). I can accept this willingly since my account was in any case intended as a sketch of what *might* be done in more detail—not as a complete theory.

The chief new contribution that Hempel makes to the discussion is to analyze vagueness in terms of Charles Morris' old distinction between "syntax," "semantics," and "pragmatics." He concludes (i) that "vagueness" is a term whose "determination requires reference to the symbols, its users, and their designata" (*ibid.*, p. 166), and (ii) that there can be no parallel semantical concept. I agree with the first point (though I should have less confidence than Hempel shows in making the distinctions which divide all semiotic into three parts). But I do not see that he has made his second point convincing. The argument seems to be that a semantic concept of vagueness would involve a "graduated" relation of designation (which I am prepared to grant); and that a language containing such a gradable relation of designation would not be translatable into English (*ibid.*, p. 176). But he simply asserts the latter, without proof. If sentences would need to be qualified, as he suggests, by a numerical index showing "the degree to which they designate" the corresponding state of affairs, perhaps the rule of translation might be that all sentences qualified with a sufficiently high index of degree of designation should be translated into the corresponding English sentence without index. Such a "rule" might well allow some sentences of the new terminology to resist translation into English; and it would certainly obliterate some differences in symbolization in the course of the translation. But would this be so serious? If "English" is to mean the language *as we can teach ourselves to speak it*, I see no reason yet to suppose that a more precise terminology for vagueness cannot be introduced into English. Nor is there, for all I can yet see, any necessary obstacle to the treatment of vagueness as a "semantical" notion.

With regard to Hempel's argument that the introduction of explicit terminology for vagueness "does not involve any modification of the principles of logic" (*ibid.*, p. 178), I would agree, perhaps, that it *need not*, i.e., that we can try to maintain the traditional logical principles while modifying the definition of the concrete terms we use. But I think we can also accept more generalized principles of inference in relation to which our present logical principles will appear to be special cases. I don't find Hempel's comment that "the question of logical principles arises, strictly speaking, only on the abstract level where language is dealt with as a theoretical semantico-syntactical system" (*ibid.*, p. 174) very helpful. The question is how *much* we need to abstract from the actual linguistic habits of the speakers of the interpreted languages; and whether the traditional principles of logic are not, in some ways, excessively abstract.

On the other hand, Hempel's remarks on the desirability of using such methods to reduce vagueness as involve no reference to the behavior of observers (*ibid.*, pp. 177–178) have much to recommend them.

3. More work remains to be done on this subject. I agree with Peirce that "logicians have too much neglected the study of vagueness" (*Collected Papers*, 5.505). It is tantalizing that his remark, "I have worked out the logic of vagueness with something like completeness," (*ibid.*, 5.506) leads only to an editorial footnote "Where?" (on the same page). Where indeed is such a logic to be found—if "logic" is the right word for it?

III. THE JUSTIFICATION OF INDUCTION

1. Based upon an address delivered at the Tenth Interna-

tional Congress of Philosophy, Amsterdam, August, 1948. The abstract appeared in the *Proceedings* of the Congress (Amsterdam, 1949), pp. 791–793.

2. For arguments from a similar standpoint see Frederick L. Will, "Will the Future Be Like the Past?" (*Mind*, 56 [1947]: 332–347).

IV. THE SEMANTIC DEFINITION OF TRUTH

1. Originally published in *Analysis*, 8 (1948): 49–63. Reviewed by Andrzej Mostowski in *Journal of Symbolic Logic*, 13 (1948): 150–151.

2. In an article entitled "Designation and Truth," which appeared in the same volume of *Analysis* (pp. 93–96), P. T. Geach has pointed out that the suggested formulation of a definition of truth in section 3 of my paper is incorrect. The sentence, *For all x and y, if x is a sentence and y uniquely designates x, then y is true $\equiv$ x,* is in fact not well formed and therefore cannot belong to a meta-meta-language, as I suggested. However, as Alonzo Church has suggested (*Journal of Symbolic Logic*, 13: 151) it could be replaced by the sentence: *For all x and y, if x is a sentence and y uniquely designates x, then the result of substituting y for 'z' and x for 'p' in 'z' is true $\equiv$ 'p' is true.*

3. See also J. F. Thomson, "A Note on Truth," *Analysis* 9 (1949): 67–72, and P. F. Strawson, "Truth," *ibib.*, 83–97.

V. RUSSELL'S PHILOSOPHY OF LANGUAGE

1. Originally published in *The Philosophy of Bertrand Russell* (Library of Living Philosophers, vol. 5; ed. P. A. Schilpp; Northwestern University, 1944).

2. In Russell's reply (*op. cit.*, pp. 691–695) he finds himself in partial agreement with my criticisms but not "on the points that are most important."

We agree that the theory of types has to be construed as concerned with words, not things, if self-contradiction in the enunciation of the theory is to be avoided.

Russell denies that in his "ideal language there would be only proper names" and thinks that I must be (wrongly) supposing him to hold we cannot be acquainted with relations. In the essay I hedged on this, since I was not clear whether Russell would allow that universals might have logically proper names; in any case, as I said, "it would still be necessary that the names of particulars should be private"; and this still seems to me sufficient to disqualify Russell's "ideal language."

Russell finds the charge that he requires a "perfect" language to be isomorphic with the world it symbolizes an "amazingly crude travesty." I still think the charge is fairly leveled against some of Russell's earlier doctrines; if it cannot be brought against his present position, so much the better.

On the theory of descriptions the differences between us are too great to be easily bridged. When Russell says, "To say that we can understand without acquaintance seems to me equivalent to saying that we can acquire a habit without ever being in situations such as would give rise to it" (*ibid.*, p. 695), I believe he is missing the point of my discussion. If *this* were what "acquaintance" meant, to say that the meaning of a sign was known by acquaintance would be to say *only* that we had at some time learned to use it by applying it to instances. But I cannot see that there are any important philosophical uses of *this* sense of "acquaintance."

3. The paper was reviewed by Ernest Nagel in *Journal of Symbolic Logic*, 9 (1944): 78–79.

4. (Section 2, p. 117.) I referred to *three* entities, K, L, and M, in order to preserve strict parallelism with the passage from Russell cited earlier in the essay; *two* entities would, of course, have sufficed.

5. (Section 2, p. 119.) The phrase "the *words* 'K' and 'L' are syntactically similar" is, strictly speaking, nonsensical. For "K" and "L" are capital letters, not words at all. I hope the reader will have understood that "K" and "L" are supposed to be replaced by suitable words.

6. (Section 2, p. 119.) With regard to the need for an infinite hierarchy of senses of "syntactically similar" I assume the following: That some propositional functions taking words as arguments cannot sensibly take names of words as arguments; that some taking names of words as arguments cannot sensibly take names of names or words as arguments; and so on. If these plausible assumptions can be rejected, perhaps *two* syntactical levels would suffice.

7. Mr. Yehoshua Bar-Hillel has called my attention to the interesting discussion of what I have called "syntactical types" in Carnap's *Der Logische Aufbau der Welt* (Berlin, 1928). Sections 29 to

31 of that book contain a clear exposition of the need to make the kind of distinction I was defending in the essay.

8. On the difficulties of formulating the theory of types see Paul Weiss's paper, "The Theory of Types," in *Mind*, 37 (1928): 338–348.

VI. WITTGENSTEIN'S *TRACTATUS*

Originally published as "Some Problems Connected with Language" in the *Aristotelian Society Proceedings*, 39 (1938–1939): 43–68. See also L. Wittgenstein, "Some Remarks on Logical Form," *Aristotelian Society Proceedings*, Suppl. vol. 9 (1930): 162–171.

VII. THE SEMIOTIC OF CHARLES MORRIS

1. Originally published under the title "The Limitations of a Behavioristic Semiotic" in *Philosophical Review*, 56 (May, 1947): 258–272.

2. Morris' reply to his critics, "Signs about Signs about Signs," appeared in *Philosophy and Phenomenological Research*, 9 (1948): 115–133. The remarks addressed to me (see "Reply to Mr. Black," *ibid.*, pp. 119–121) show disarming good humor and moderation.

In general, Morris suggests that his critics (including myself) "have measured the book by claims which it did not profess" (*ibid.*, p. 116). His latest statement of intention is not explicit; he wants, it seems, to deny that he was "creating a science" and to stress rather the *preparatory* nature of his study. The book, he repeats, "sketches a program more than it records an achievement" (*Signs, Language, and Behavior*, p. 246); and the program is that of reducing the vagueness and ambiguity of current discourse about signs.

This is sufficiently modest, to be sure; and so long as Morris claims only to have effected some improvement in the vocabulary of semiotic it would be ungracious to persist in objection. But I have still to be convinced that Morris' vocabulary and the distinctions on which it is based really constitute an improvement.

3. I am glad that Morris agrees ("Signs about Signs about Signs," p. 118) with my criticisms about the lack of connection between a sign such as "black" and any goal-object. He says now that "the term 'response-sequence' needs modification by dropping out the reference to goal objects . . ." (*ibid.*, p. 119).

4. Morris disposes of my strictures on the vagueness of the

[253]

term "influence" by reference to "the simple fact" that "the phrase 'influences a response to some other stimulus' is a part of the definition of 'preparatory-stimulus' and *not* in itself a definition of 'sign' " (*ibid.*, p. 119). How sad it is that facts are seldom as simple as this: The term "preparatory-stimulus" is *part* of the definition of "sign" and any objectionable vagueness in defining *it* will inevitably infect the definition of "sign." Of course Morris did not *want* the action of a drug on an organism to count as a preparatory stimulus (and said so on page 7 of his book); my point remains that his definitions of "preparatory-stimulus" and "sign" do not exclude such a case and are therefore incorrect in their present form.

5. One crucial point in my essay which deserves more investigation is the suggestion that the use in semiotic of terms like "condition" or "significata" may involve reference to a meta-language. (If this were right, semiotic or the criticism of signs could hardly be a descriptive science.) Morris replies that we can use "condition" without needing to analyze its signification. I don't share his confidence in the reliability of this admittedly crucial term.

VIII. OGDEN AND RICHARDS' THEORY OF INTERPRETATION

First published in *Journal of Philosophy*, 39 (1942): 281–290.

IX. QUESTIONS ABOUT EMOTIVE MEANING

1. This was published in *Philosophical Review*, 57 (March, 1948): 111–126) as the opening paper of "A Symposium on Emotive Meaning." It was followed in the Symposium by replies from Stevenson ("Meaning: Descriptive and Emotive," pp. 127–144) and Richards ("Emotive Meaning Again," pp. 145–157).

2. Richards' article—if I may praise it without impertinence —seems to me a most effective statement of the underlying purposes of his concern with language. It comes close to being that eloquent sermon on education he finds unlikely to be forthcoming in our present condition of semiotic confusion. As I reread it, I feel we are divided by little more than a difference of emphasis—a strife between allies for which an agreed division of labor might be an eirenicon. Richards stresses the urgency of *practice* in interpretation (see especially his excellent description in the first paragraph of p. 154 of his article); while I am more concerned to clarify the

terminology of critical discourse. He sees the advantages of "the study of metaphor, *through metaphor*" and a theory that "would not be a prose account of poetry so much as a poetic account of prose" (*ibid.*, p. 146): I would suppose that we are still far from exhausting the resources of *referential* discourse about language and its functions. Why shouldn't *both* be tried?

3. Let me record some of the points on which we agree. We both say that the bandying about of "emotive" has done more harm than good (*ibid.*, p. 145), that scientism (as I defined it in the article) is as unjustified as it is widespread, that science has no monopoly of "understanding" (whatever that question-begging term is taken to mean), and that "to distinguish, relate, and mediate between the modes of language, or the species of meaning, we need no more than, and no less than, Philosophy" (*ibid.*, p. 153).

4. Enough divergence of judgment remains to prevent this harmony on all major issues from becoming insipid. Richards on rereading the *Principles of Literary Criticism* is "more impressed by its anticipations of my later views than by the occurrence of anything to retract" (*ibid.*, p. 156, n. 15), and he draws my attention (*ibid.*, pp. 147, n. 4; 149, n. 8) to passages in this book and *The Meaning of Meaning* which conflict with my interpretations of these works. I think the fact is that these earlier writings embodied incompatible tendencies, the conflict between which has been to some extent resolved in Richards' later work. That the early works "have been read as supporting scientism" he admits (*ibid.*, p. 151, n. 11); I do not think he can hold the readers solely responsible.

5. Stevenson's replies to my criticisms of his doctrine are candid and admirably undisputatious in tone. I share with him the conviction of the importance of cultivating "a certain linguistic tolerance—a habit of mind that prevents divergent languages, so frequent in philosophy, from being a source of misunderstanding" (*op. cit.*, p. 139) and I shall try, in what follows, to distinguish *verbal* from more substantial points at issue between us.

6. The question whether the affective consequences of ethical assertions shall be described by the phrase "emotive *meaning*" or, as I prefer, by the phrase "emotive *influence*" may seem to be a trivial question of choice of labels. I consider it to be more than this. If the minutiae of Stevenson's definition of "emotive meaning" could at all times be held clearly in mind, the phrase might serve as a harmless abbreviation. The definition is too complex for such

total recall, however; and even the vigilant reader will slide into assuming that "emotive meaning" refers to a species of *what is commonly understood by* "meaning." However accommodating this notoriously ambiguous word may be, it maintains a nucleus of steady connotation: in the senses both Stevenson and myself have primarily in mind, it is never proper to say *x* "has meaning" (or "is a sign") unless *x* refers to (designates, denotes, indicates, points to) *something other than itself*. This was the point I numbered (4) in my article in the Symposium (section 8). Stevenson's reply does not satisfy me: I think he is *wrong* to call a sound a *sign* or to ascribe to it *meaning* when, and insofar as, it causes an affective disposition.

Stevenson wants to *extend* the usual meanings of "meaning," because he is impressed by the importance of certain analogies between hearers' cognitive and affective reactions to words. The points of resemblance are the following: (1) Whether one says "Hurrah!" or "I am enthusiastic," the utterance consists of conventional sounds (words) whose use has to be learned; (2) Each utterance *causes* a disposition to respond (either by thoughts or by feelings) in a suitably qualified hearer. These resemblances incline Stevenson to say that both utterances have meaning, distinguished as emotive and referential, respectively. (This is not quite accurate, since "Hurrah!" may also be said to have some nonemotive meaning, but I hope it will be clear what the point is.) The chief point of unlikeness is: (3) The *cognitive* disposition evoked by "I am enthusiastic" is actualized by thoughts *about* the speaker's feelings; the *affective* disposition evoked by "Hurrah!" is actualized by feelings *of* enthusiasm. Or to put it briefly: the declarative sentence communicates to the hearer a thought, the ejaculation infects him with an attitude. This unlikeness between the two cases inclines *me* to deny any *significance* to a word or sign, *qua* inciter, promoter, or promulgator of affective attitudes.

The case is common enough in philosophical controversy: one man, impressed by a hitherto neglected relation of similarity, wants to modify his vocabulary to emphasize the similarity, while his conservative opponent holds out for the good old ways of talking. What harm can it do to grant Stevenson and those who agree with him their metaphor of "emotive *meaning*"—provided they remember that it *is* a metaphor?

Well, for one thing, it tends to bring into undue and mistaken prominence what are, in my judgment, the wrong factors to emphasize in situations of ethical agreement or disagreement. So far as concerns the analysis of the cognitive factors in response to ethical assertions, there is really less disagreement between Stevenson and myself than might at first seem to be the case. When a man says "Hurrah!" I take him to be conveying information about his feelings. Stevenson agrees (*op. cit.*, p. 139), with the reservation that the information is "*suggested*" rather than stated. This amounts to saying that "the interjection is not syntactically related . . . to other terms" (*op. cit.*, p. 140). I grant the distinction (though I have my doubts about this notion of *syntactically related*); it would certainly be odd to say that "Hurrah!" *names* or *designates* the speaker's enthusiasm. The point to stress is that Stevenson agrees with me (and other critics of his position) about *some* of the information conveyed (in a wide sense of the term) by evaluative utterance. Stevenson regards the autobiographical information conveyed (e.g., that a man who says "x is good" approves of x) as trivial (*op. cit.*, pp. 140, 141) and so do I; but unless I have quite misunderstood him he wants to regard attitudes *induced* in the hearer (the tendency to approve caused by hearing it said that x is good) as being far from trivial. I regard such induced attitudes as *irrelevant* to sound ethical judgment. To count at all, the approval must be *ethical* approval (not the kind of approval I feel for a "good" stroke at tennis or a juicy beefsteak), and I do not see how Stevenson's account provides for discriminating *this* kind of "approval" from others. I should have supposed the important question for the conscientious man was not "Do I have a tendency to favor x" but rather "Are my feelings relevant and justified—*ought* I to feel the way I do?" It may not be as hard as Stevenson suggests (*op. cit.*, p. 143) to give an account of how "practical reason" works in such situations.

X. KORZYBSKI'S GENERAL SEMANTICS

A public lecture delivered at the State University of Iowa, April, 1946. Not previously published.

Index

INDEX

Fringe: bounded by another fringe, 37; location of, 34–39; replacement of the notion of, 29; use of the term, 28

Geach, P. T., 251

Geometrie und Erfahrung (Einstein), 26n

Gesammelte Aufsätze (Schlick), 142, 163

"Goal-object," 172

Gödel's Theorem, 98n

Greek Philosophy (Burnet), 38n

Ground of Induction, The (Williams), 65

Hahn, H., 151n

Hempel, C. G., 249–250

Hume, D., 4, 21, 61, 65, 79n, 228

Ideal language, 113, 134–138: consequence of abandoning the pursuit of, 138

Illusion, special form of argument from, 12

Induction: end of, in common with deduction, 84; question of its inferiority to deduction, 80

Inductive argument: defined, 66; probability interpretation of, 68

Inquiry into Meaning and Truth, An (Russell), 111n, 112, 134n

"Interpretant," 178, 182

Interpretation, 199

Interpretation in Teaching (Richards), 200n, 213n

Introduction to Semantics (Carnap), 105n

Intuitionism, 36, 37

"Is Existence a Predicate?" (Moore), 126n

Isherwood, Christopher, 212n

James, Henry, 25

James, William, 111, 196

Johnson, S., trying to refute Berkeley, 11

Justification: inductive, not final, 87; inductive, of inductive methods, 86–88; meaning of, 61, 63; need of a standard of, 64; no deductive one possible for induction, 66–68; standard employed by critics of induction, 65–66

Kant, 213

Keats, John, 83

Keynes, J. M., 48n, 71n, 72n

Kierkegaard, S., 203

Kokoszynká, M., 94n

Korzybski, Count Alfred, 223–246: a reformer, 223; advocates delayed nervous reaction, 239; approves of abstractions, 241; his metaphysics, 246; on abstractions, 234f; on "ordinary object," 236; on "scientific object," 235; stresses general principles, 225; tries to be silent, 239

Language: analysis of, 143; definition of, 43; "philosophical" investigation of, 163; use of the word, 165; users of, defined, 49

Language (Bloomfield), 49, 153n

Language and Reality (Urban), 112n

Language, Truth and Logic (Ayer), 142

Laplace, 72n

Lewis, C. I., 3–7, 19

Limiting sense, 14–18

Linguistic proposals, 78

Lions and Shadows (Isherwood), 212n

Lobachevski, 228

"Locata," 180, 183

Logic: alleged to have physical content, 232; aristotelian, 229–230; nonempirical, 233–234

"Logical Atomism" (Russell), 111

Logical constructions, 127, 128, 129

Logical form, 157–160

Logical paradoxes, 115n

Logical Positivism, 141

Logical Syntax of Language, The (Carnap), 141n, 150n

Logical types, 117, 118

Logically proper names, 135, 251–252

Logique, Mathématiques et Connaissance de la Réalité (Hahn), 151n

Logische Aufbau der Welt, Der (Carnap), 254

Lukasiewicz, J., 92n

Macaulay, 171

MacIver, A. M., 145n

Malcolm, N., 78n

Manual of Psychology (Stout), 33n

Mathematical Logic (Quine), 127n

Maxwell, Clerk, 203

Mead, G. H., 223

Meaning: ambiguity of the term, 21; causal theory of, 205; evidence for, 22; physiological criteria for, 227

Meaning of Meaning, The (Ogden and Richards), 189–200, 204, 207, 208, 214n, 255

Meinong, A. R. v., 124n

INDEX

INDEX

Sceptical arguments, linguistic analysis of, 12f
Sceptical paradox, an illustrative, 3f
Schlick, M., 142, 163, 164
Science and Sanity (Korzybski), 223–247
Scientific method, 228
"Scientism," 213, 255
"Semantic Conception of Truth, The" (Tarski), 91n
Semantic definition of truth, 91–107
"Semantic reaction," 227, 239
Semantical types, need for, 91–92
Semantics, General, 223–246: attacks "is" as sign of identity, 229–231; attack on Aristotle, 229; attitude toward meaning, 227; Institute of, 223; needs theory of reality, 228; practical consequences, 224; prefers negative statements, 231–232; scientific in intention, 226; Second American Congress of, 223
Semiotic, 169, 203
Sense-datum, "direct knowledge" of, 205
Sentence, defined, 95
Sign, 193: definition of, 171–177
"Significatum," 179–183
Signs, Language and Behavior (Morris), 169–185, 253
Solipsism, 8, 12, 21
Spinoza, B., 11
Stebbing, L. S., 123n, 125n, 128n, 129n, 144, 145, 158
Stevenson, C. L., 208, 215–220, 254: reply to his criticism, 255–257
Stimuli: direct, 172; preparatory, 172, 176
Stout, G. F., 33n
Strawson, P. F., 251
Structure, 157f
Subjective: features of an utterance, 40; meaning of, 39
Syllogism, theory of, 229
"Syntactic similarity," 119–121, 252
Syntactic types, 119–121

Tarski, A., 91, 93, 98, 99, 105, 106n, 107
Théorie Physique, La (Duhem), 25n
Theory of descriptions, 122–129
Theory of Types and ordinary language, 114f

Thomson, J. F., 251
"Token, Type and Meaning" (MacIver), 145n
Tractatus Logico-Philosophicus (Wittgenstein), 141–165
Treatise on Probability, A (Keynes), 71n

Ultimate constituents, 113, 122, 128, 136
Unambiguity, definition of, 46
Universals: and proper names, 252; as "symbolic accessories," 205
"Unsanity," 224
Untersuchungen zur Gegenstandtheorie (Meinong), 124n
Urban, W. M., 112n

Vacuous terms, 18–21
Vague symbols, logical relations between, 54–58
Vagueness, 25–58: an experiment in, 52–54; analysis of, from the formalist standpoint, 55; and ambiguity, 42n; and variety of application, 31; as a defect of language, 27; described, 30f; distinguished from generality, 31; featured in scientific discourse, 28; Hempel's views on, 249–250; illustration of features of, 35; objective, 42; of propositions, 30n; Peirce on need for its study, 250; shown in ordinary language, 42n; subjective, 29; summary of arguments pertaining to, 28–30
"Valuata," 180, 183
Vienna Circle, 111n
Von Frisch, 181

Wahrscheinlickheitslehre (Reichenbach), 48n
Weinberg, J., 142n
Weiss, P., 253
Wells, H. G., 31n
Whitehead, A. N., 106n
Will, F. L., 251
Williams, D., 65n
Wisdom, John, 136n, 142
Wittgenstein, L., 111n, 141–163, 223, 253

Zeno, 38

[264]